The Active World

Industry, Agriculture and Services

Peter Jones
and
Bob Pike

Acknowledgements

The author and publisher would like to thank the following:
The staff and pupils of Benfield School, Newcastle; Barclays Bank plc,
International Services Branch; De Beers Corporation; Department of
Agriculture and Water Supply, South Africa; Department of Geography,
University of Wittersrand, South Africa; Indian Tourist Board; Japan
Information Centre, London; Mr C. B. McDonald; Mars Confections Ltd.;
Nissan Car Plant, Sunderland; Northern Territory Tourist Commission; South
Australia House, London; the University of Stellenbosch, South Africa.

Design by Peter Smith and Barrie Richardson.
Illustrated by Angie Deering, Ray Mutimer, and Asset Art and Design/Steve
Staindale.

Cover photography by the Hutchison Library.

Photographs by courtesy of The Associated Press Ltd (60); Promotion
Australia, London (73, 78br); Barnaby's Picture Library (13c, 43, 46br, 62,
80tl, 80cl); Compix (36b, 68); Douglas Dickins (23t); Robert Harding (94c);
Hutchison Library (15tl, 35, 39, 64c, 94tr); John and Penny Hubley (21, 47);
High Commission of India (18c, 44, 46bl, 82, 87); Japan Information Centre,
London (23b, 31, 51, 59); Felicity Kendall (76); Nissan (94br); Northern
Territory, Australia (78br, 78cl, 79); Christine Osborne (28cl); OXFAM/Peter
Wiles (18t); OXFAM/Jeremy Hartley (28cr, 32c, 32b); OXFAM/Keith Mason
(80tr); OXFAM/R. J. Sewell (32t); OXFAM/K. Warren (77); OXFAM/John Ogle
(92); OXFAM (94bl); Howard Phillips (13b, 36t); Planning and Economic
Development Department, Northumberland County Council (53); Elizabeth
Pearson (80cr): Satour (16t); South African Tourist Board (16b, 36c, 41, 64t);
Susan Picton (15tr); Mike Spencer (94tl); Tropix (64b).

General sources of information: United Nations Statistical Yearbooks;
UNESCO Statistical Yearbooks; the Food and Agricultural Organisation
Yearbooks; the International Labour Organisation Yearbooks; the World
Development Reports (the World Bank).

The publishers have made every effort to trace all the copyright holders, but
if they have inadvertently overlooked any, they will be pleased to make the
necessary arrangements at the first opportunity.

Arnold-Wheaton
A Division of E J Arnold & Son Limited
Parkside Lane, Leeds LS11 5TD

A member of the Pergamon Group
Headington Hill Hall, Oxford OX3 0BW

ISBN 0 560-26521-2

Copyright © Peter Jones and Bob Pike 1987

First published 1987
Printed in Great Britain by A. Wheaton & Co. Ltd.,
Hennock Road, Exeter.

Contents

Enterprise Earth

An everyday thing like a bar of chocolate is usually bought and eaten without a moment's thought. The story behind the chocolate bar and how it came to be in the shop is, however, highly involved. Many different people, doing many different jobs from all over the world, have contributed to making it.

The making of a chocolate bar starts with a variety of different products which we call **raw materials.** These come from all over the place (see fig 1), and may even be items that have already been manufactured by other industries (such as the printed wrappers). The process of **manufacturing** transforms the raw materials into a new product for sale.

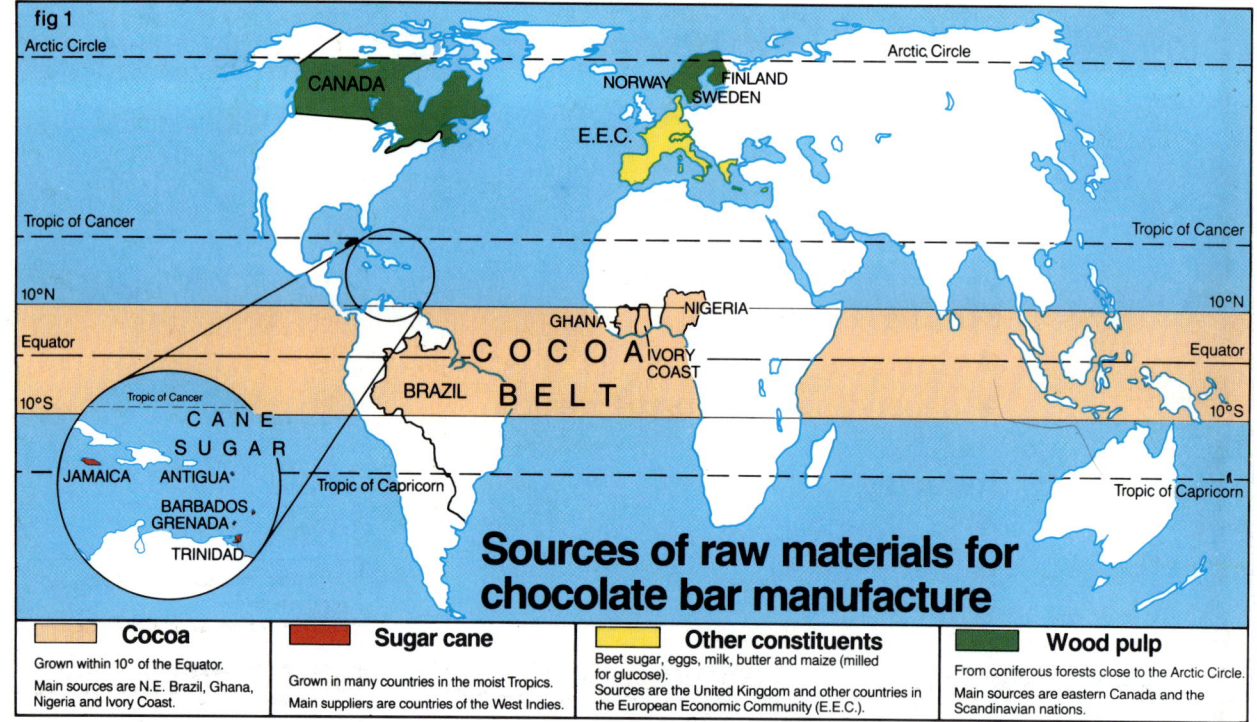

fig 1

Sources of raw materials for chocolate bar manufacture

Cocoa	Sugar cane	Other constituents	Wood pulp
Grown within 10° of the Equator. Main sources are N.E. Brazil, Ghana, Nigeria and Ivory Coast.	Grown in many countries in the moist Tropics. Main suppliers are countries of the West Indies.	Beet sugar, eggs, milk, butter and maize (milled for glucose). Sources are the United Kingdom and other countries in the European Economic Community (E.E.C.).	From coniferous forests close to the Arctic Circle. Main sources are eastern Canada and the Scandinavian nations.

The activities involved in the production of the chocolate bar are divided into three different categories (see fig 2). This is true for every manufactured product. There are

- **primary (or extractive) activities:** the natural products are obtained from the environment by occupations such as farming, forestry, fishing and mining
- **secondary (or manufacturing) activities:** the form of the product is altered and made into something different
- **tertiary activities:** these support primary and secondary activities, but nothing is actually made. Examples include services such as transport, retailing and advertising

Activity A

Look at fig 1 and fig 2.

1 Fill in a simple chart like the one below to show the type of raw materials used to make a chocolate bar.

Natural products	Processed natural products	Manufactured raw materials

2 With the help of an atlas draw up a second chart to show the origins of these raw materials.

Raw material	Country	Continent

3 Answer these two questions in two brief sentences.
a what are tropical regions?
b which of the raw materials come from the tropical regions?
4 Start keeping a 'Dictionary of Geography'. In it write down the meanings of all the special words you come across in geography lessons, these words are shown in **bold** type. Your first entry could read

primary activities: extractive activities which obtain natural materials from farming, fishing or forestry, or from mining and quarrying.
Now add your own definitions of **secondary** and **tertiary activities.**

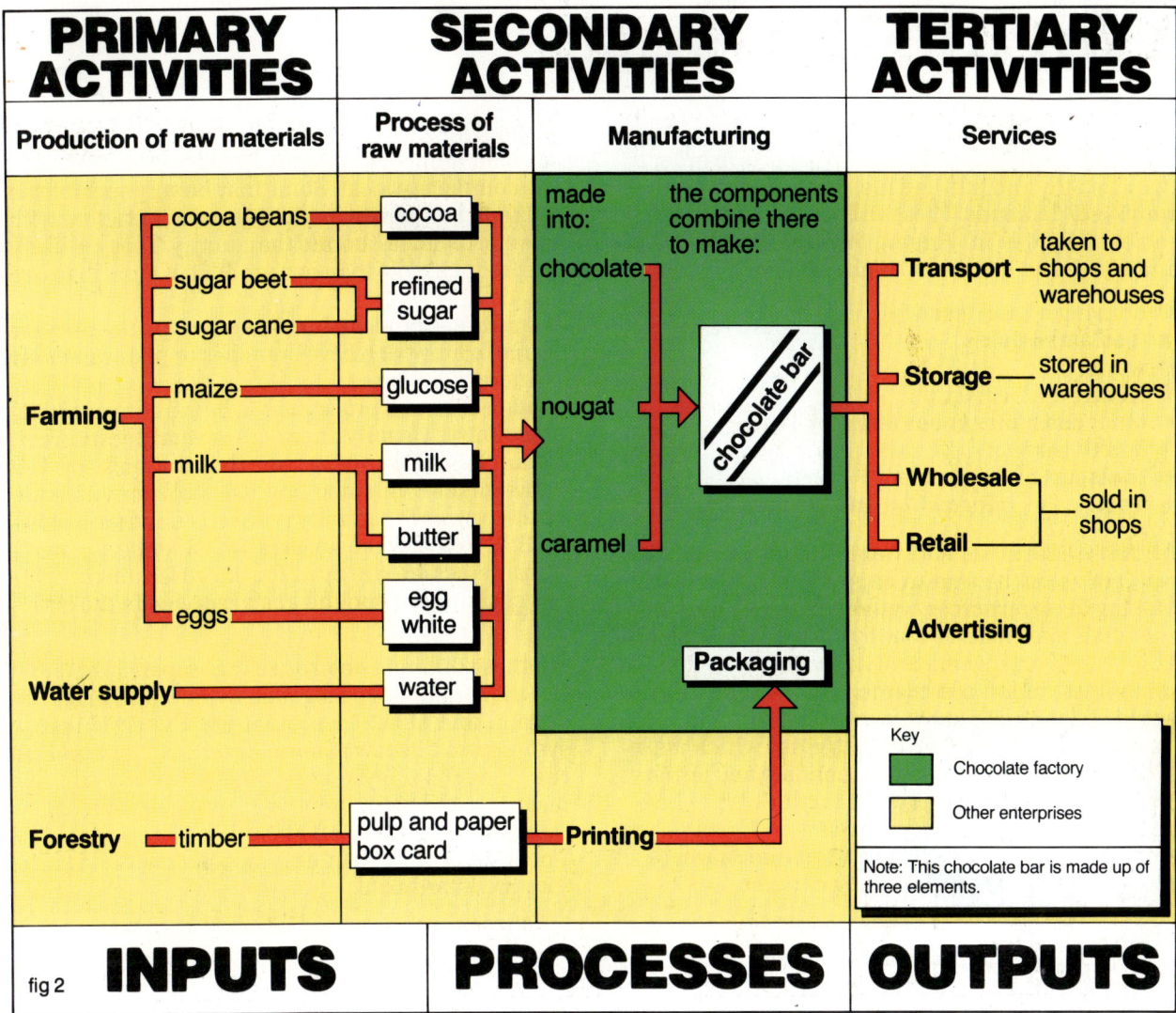

PRIMARY ACTIVITIES	SECONDARY ACTIVITIES		TERTIARY ACTIVITIES
Production of raw materials	Process of raw materials	Manufacturing	Services

fig 2

INPUTS   PROCESSES   OUTPUTS

Fig 2 shows all the stages by which a chocolate bar is made. Manufacturing industry is an example of a **business system** or **enterprise**.

Like all systems it has

- **inputs:** these are things that are needed from outside, such as raw materials, workers, land, buildings, machinery and money
- **components:** these are the **technical processes** in the factory that use all the inputs
- **flows of material:** raw materials go through the technical processes and gradually change into the finished article. For this to happen a **flow of energy** is needed
- **outputs:** these are the final products or finished articles, as well as wages, profits, by-products and waste

Activity B

1 Draw three columns in your notebook. Put the heading 'Primary Activities' on top of the first column, 'Secondary Activities' on top of the second and 'Tertiary Activities' on the third.
a list in the correct column the activities shown in fig 2.
b add in the correct column these activities or occupations:
teaching, nursing, hairdressing, ship building, sweet making, newspaper printing, fishing, lemonade manufacture, coal mining, electricity generating, road haulage, fruit canning, making computers, tax inspectors, brick making, quarrying, car making.
2 Complete the following paragraph by filling in the missing words. All the missing words are key words found on these two pages.
'Manufacturing is a system which has i _ _ _ _ _ such as raw materials, workers and power. The components are the t _ _ _ _ _ _ _ _ _ processes which are applied to the raw materials. The finished articles are one of the o _ _ _ _ _ _ of the system. The manufacturing system can only operate successfully because it is interlinked with many other e _ _ _ _ _ _ _ _ _ _.'
3 Add all the words printed in bold type to your dictionary of geography.

World Systems

People need certain **basic essentials** to exist like food, water and shelter. Beyond mere existence, in order to live a healthy and fulfilled life, they have many other **wants and demands.** These will vary according to the society they live in. Among these basic essentials, and wants and demands, might well be:

- housing or **residence**
- **food** and **drink**
- **work**
- **leisure** and recreation
- other **consumer goods** and **services**
- **health care**
- **transport** and movement
- knowledge, **information and ideas** and values

All these essentials and wants are in the end the result of using the **resources** provided by the Earth. Making these resources available to satisfy the basic essentials and wants is done by the **business system.** This overall arrangement of economic activities is sometimes called **commerce.** The features of the world of commerce are shown in fig 3.

As we have seen (page 4), the activities which make up commerce are of primary, secondary and tertiary types. Any business in any of these three types is set up to provide a commodity or service and is called an **enterprise.** An enterprise may vary from a farm or a shop to a huge factory or mining complex.

- **small businesses** are usually run by one person, or a small number of people, in one place. They may be completely local. Some may be very specialised
- **larger businesses** may have one main factory with several branches around the country. They are likely to produce more than one product in more than one place
- **multi-national businesses** or companies are very large firms which have branches or plants in many different countries
- **state-run enterprises** are run by the government of a country. Usually there are several locations or branches depending on the policies of the government. In some countries all activities are state-run, as in centrally planned countries like the USSR and Czechoslovakia. In others only some businesses are run by or for the government, such as coal mining and the postal service in the UK

All these different enterprises are separate systems. But they are all linked together in the world business system, and affect each other e.g. the agricultural systems provide raw materials and feed the workers, the industrial systems supply processed raw materials and equipment, and service systems give transport, education and health facilities.

These enterprises can only be successful because they are interlinked.

fig 3

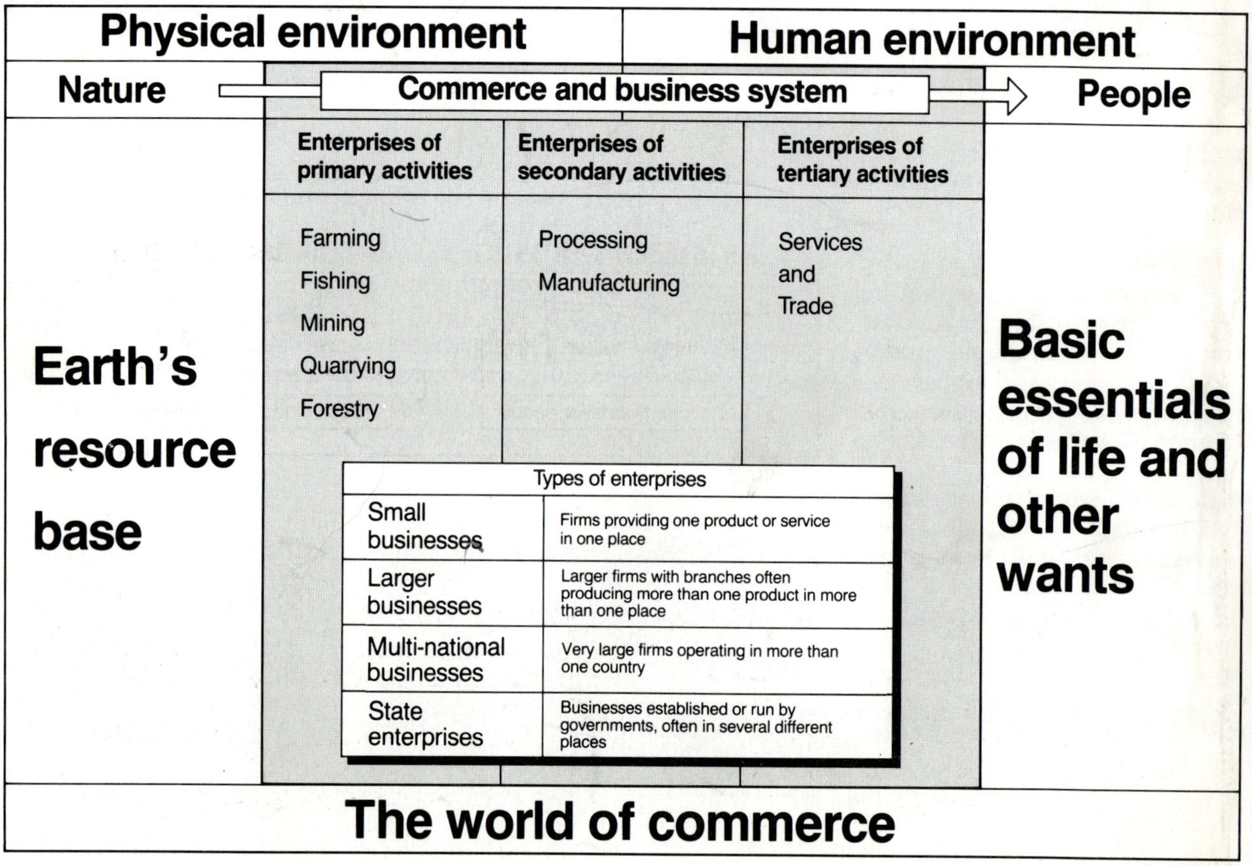

Physical environment				Human environment
Nature	Commerce and business system			People
	Enterprises of primary activities	Enterprises of secondary activities	Enterprises of tertiary activities	
Earth's resource base	Farming Fishing Mining Quarrying Forestry	Processing Manufacturing	Services and Trade	**Basic essentials of life and other wants**

Types of enterprises	
Small businesses	Firms providing one product or service in one place
Larger businesses	Larger firms with branches often producing more than one product in more than one place
Multi-national businesses	Very large firms operating in more than one country
State enterprises	Businesses established or run by governments, often in several different places

The world of commerce

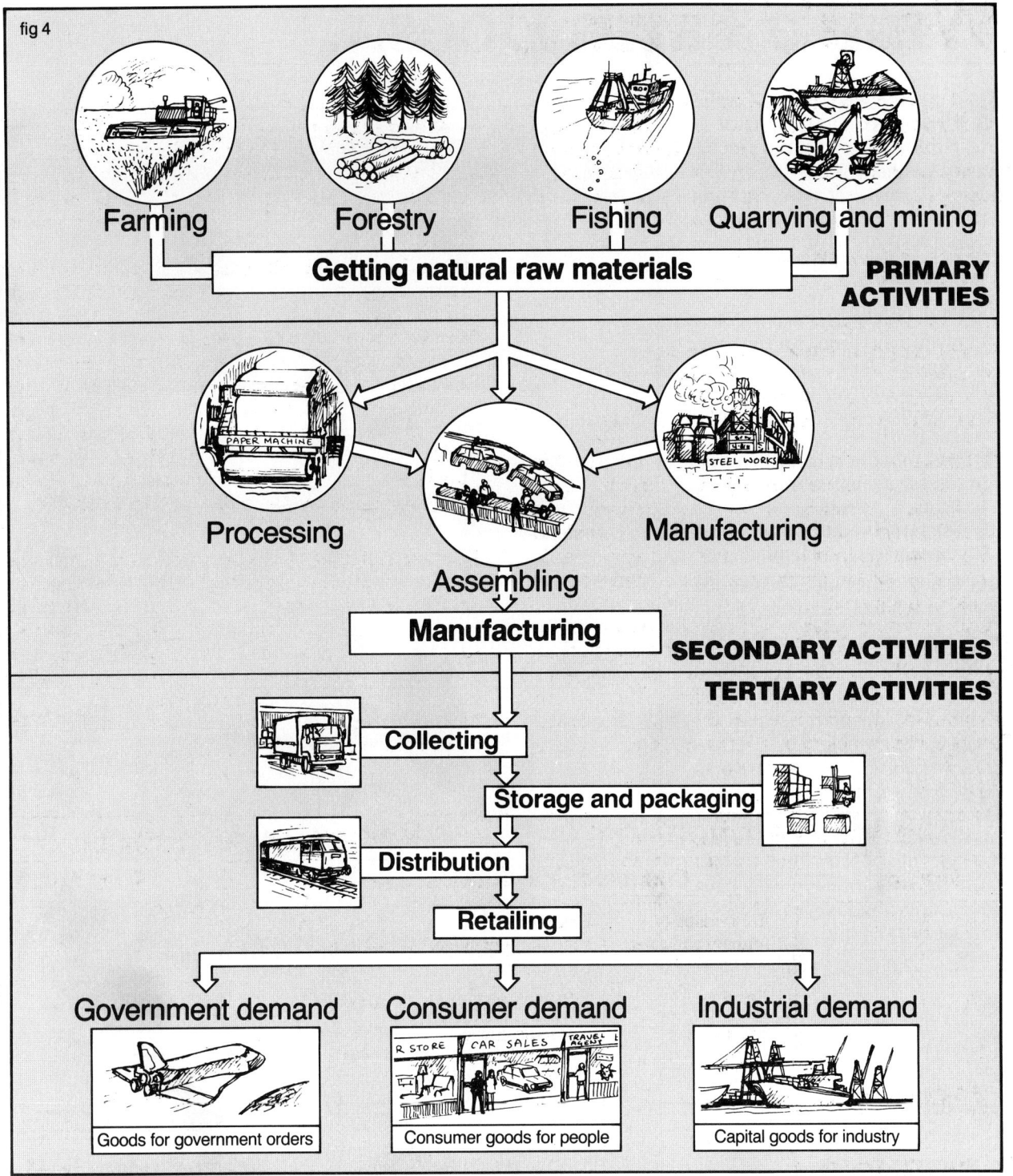

fig 4

Farming **Forestry** **Fishing** **Quarrying and mining**

Getting natural raw materials

PRIMARY ACTIVITIES

Processing **Manufacturing**

Assembling

Manufacturing

SECONDARY ACTIVITIES

TERTIARY ACTIVITIES

Collecting

Storage and packaging

Distribution

Retailing

Government demand **Consumer demand** **Industrial demand**

Goods for government orders | Consumer goods for people | Capital goods for industry

Activity

1 What is the difference between people's basic essentials of existence and their wants?
2 What does the word 'demands' mean?
3 What types of demands are shown?
4 Use fig 4 to describe, in about 100 words, how the products of a farm or forest are made available for people to buy in a shop.

Research project

Find out and list all the enterprises that are found within a half-mile radius of your school or home.
Classify them in two ways: in 'types of activity', and in 'types of enterprise'.
Draw up your results as two graphs for display.

What a Farm Does...

Many people who are not part of the farming community tend to forget that a farm is just as much a business enterprise as a factory, or a large department store. Farming is a **primary** activity, and part of a wider system which includes secondary and tertiary activites.

As fig 5 shows you, a farm is a business which:

- produces food and/or raw materials from the natural environment
- provides employment and wages for its workers
- can provide a place to live for farming families and their workers
- manages the appearance and conservation of the landscape

But a farm does more than this. It affects what other people do:

- many people work in the activities which provide all the farm needs
- many people work in activities which use the output of farms

The way in which a farm works may vary according to its type. Different farms will have different patterns of inputs, components, and outputs. Nevertheless, all farms of whatever type do have some contact with other activities and services.

Activity A

Look at fig 5.

1 List all the needs of a farm.

2 List all the work that a farm provides for other workers under the headings 'Work Produced by a Farm's Needs' and 'Work Produced by a Farm's Products'.

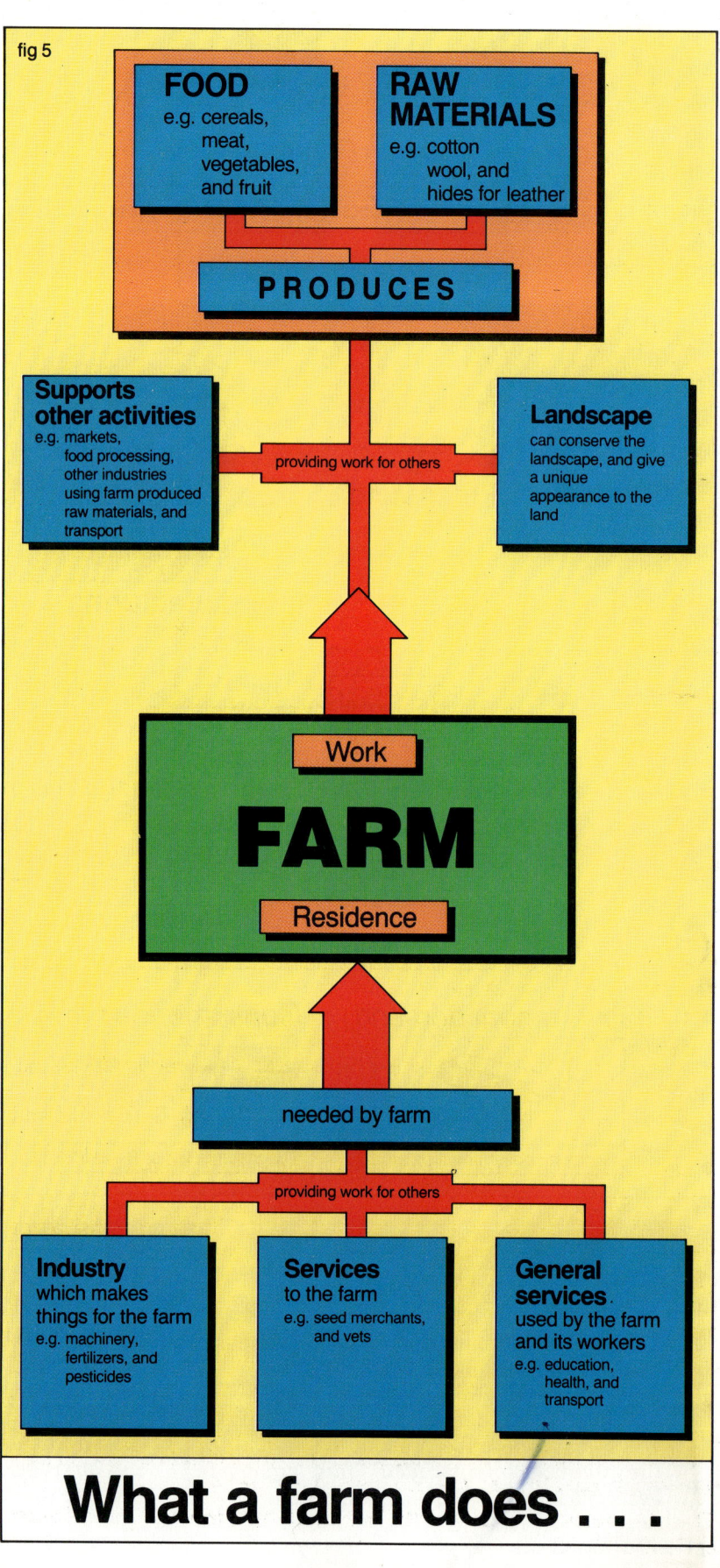

fig 5

FOOD e.g. cereals, meat, vegetables, and fruit

RAW MATERIALS e.g. cotton wool, and hides for leather

PRODUCES

Supports other activities e.g. markets, food processing, other industries using farm produced raw materials, and transport

providing work for others

Landscape can conserve the landscape, and give a unique appearance to the land

Work

FARM

Residence

needed by farm

providing work for others

Industry which makes things for the farm e.g. machinery, fertilizers, and pesticides

Services to the farm e.g. seed merchants, and vets

General services used by the farm and its workers e.g. education, health, and transport

What a farm does . . .

fig 6	Main land use	Main function	Main scale of use	Some examples
A G R I C U L T U R A L S Y S T E M S	**Arable**	subsistence	intensive	Peasant farms, e.g. Indian rice farms
			extensive	Shifting cultivation, bush fallowing
		commercial	intensive	Market gardening, horticulture, polder farms, bush fallowing
			extensive	Commercial cereal and Prairie farms, plantations
	Mixed	subsistence	intensive	Crofting types, some tropical peasant farms
			extensive	Nomadic pastoralists using rented grazings, e.g. Fulani. Settled tropical cultivators, e.g. Dayaks
		commercial	intensive	Temperate mixed farms of Europe, USA corn belt farms
			extensive	Cereal/livestock farms of Pampas type grasslands. Collective farms of the Russian Steppes
	Pastoral	subsistence	intensive	Sedentary pastoralists of East Africa
			extensive	Nomadic pastoralists
		commercial	intensive	Grassland dairy farms
			extensive	Ranching, hill sheep farms
	Special	mainly commercial	arable	Glasshouse cultivation, floriculture, hop farming
			pastoral	Factory livestock units, poultry farms, urban farms

Fig 6 is a classification of the **agricultural** systems to which all individual farms belong. There are four main categories.
- **arable** farms whose main activity or source of income is from growing crops
- **pastoral** farms whose main activity or source of income is from animal products
- **mixed** farms whose activity and incomes include both crops and animal products
- **special** farms of a highly specialised and unusual nature

Within each of these categories a farm may produce food and raw materials only for the people who work on it. These are **subsistence** farms. Those that depend entirely or mainly on the income from the sale of their products are **commercial** farms.

Commercial farms can in turn be divided into two, depending on the way they use the land.
- **intensive** farms are often small but the output per worker, and the output per area (called the **yield**), are both high
- **extensive** farms are usually larger. The farm may produce a larger amount in total, but the yield per hectare is usually smaller. These farms are often highly mechanised and so the output per worker may be even higher than that of the intensive farm

The chart shows how many of the world's types of farms fit into different agricultural systems.

Activity B

1 Make a large copy of the Agricultural Systems chart.

2 Give an example of each of the following:
a an extensive, commercial pastoral system.
b an intensive, commercial mixed system.
c an extensive, subsistence pastoral system.
d a commercial, arable special system.

3 Add to your dictionary of geography all the technical words used to describe agricultural systems appearing on these pages.

Inputs and Outputs

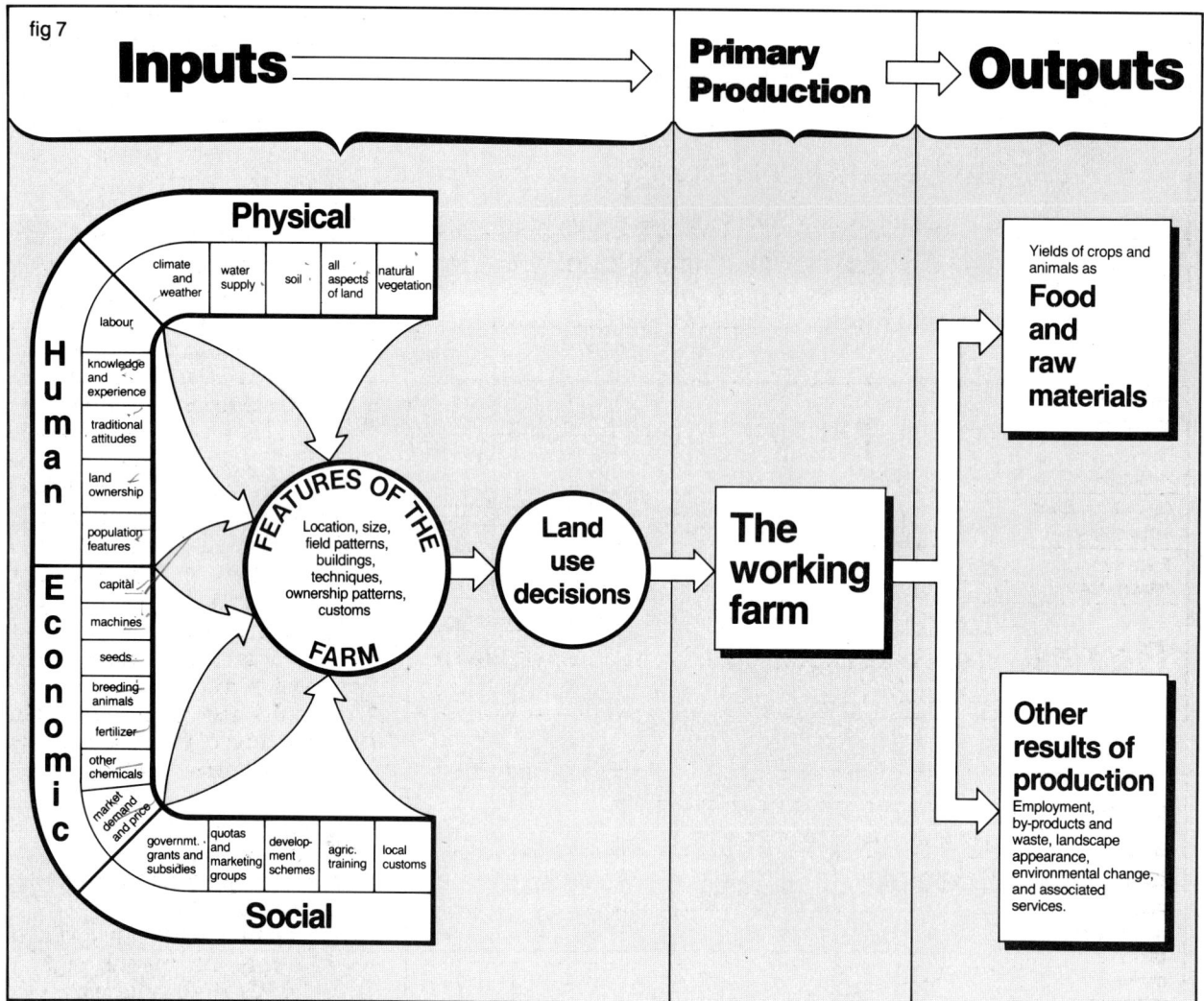

fig 7

Inputs ➡ **Primary Production** ➡ **Outputs**

Physical

| climate and weather | water supply | soil | all aspects of land | natural vegetation |

Human
- labour
- knowledge and experience
- traditional attitudes
- land ownership
- population features

Economic
- capital
- machines
- seeds
- breeding animals
- fertilizer
- other chemicals
- market demand and price

FEATURES OF THE FARM
Location, size, field patterns, buildings, techniques, ownership patterns, customs

Social

| governmt. grants and subsidies | quotas and marketing groups | development schemes | agric. training | local customs |

Land use decisions

The working farm

Yields of crops and animals as **Food and raw materials**

Other results of production
Employment, by-products and waste, landscape appearance, environmental change, and associated services.

All farms have a particular pattern of land use, fields and methods; these result from decisions made by whoever runs the farm. In some cases there is a lot of choice, especially where advanced technology is available; in other cases there is only a limited choice as to what they can do.

Many things affect the decisions that can be made. These influences are the **inputs.** The diagram shows that they fall into four groups.

- **physical:** the factors of nature which affect the possibilities for different crops and animals
- **human:** the numbers, skills and attitudes of available workers
- **economic:** the money involved, either the cost of investing in buildings, equipment, machinery and so on; or the market, transport and selling price of the products
- **social:** the effect of Governments in influencing agricultural methods, production and prices; although they do include cultural and social factors

The work of the farm is the result of all these influences on the farmer, and on what the farmer

decides is the most suitable pattern of crops and animals in the situation. The result of what the farmer does is the **output.**

The overall picture of any farm is the result of all these features of **input, components** and **output.**

Farms are different because their location affects how each of the inputs and outputs works.

Activity A

Look at fig 7.

1 List all the physical features which affect a farm as shown on the diagram.
2 Can you think of any other natural features not shown here which would affect farming?
3 What type of inputs to a farm are the following: government grants and subsidies, seeds, and land ownership.
4 What are the features of a farm?
5 How are the human inputs different from the economic inputs?
6 List seven outputs from a farm.

fig 8 The effect of distance on crop growing

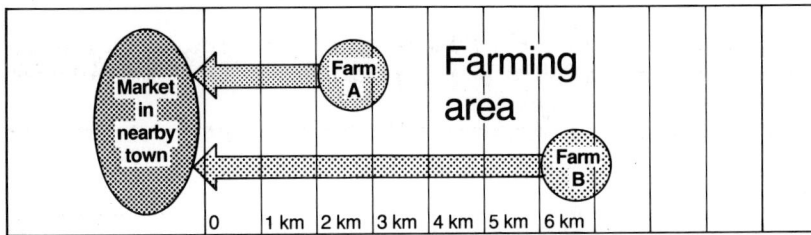

Map Two farms A and B are near a town. A is 2 km away and B is 6 km away

Price per tonne at market	X	£10									
	Y	£20									
Distance from market in km		1	2	3	4	5	6	7	8	9	10
Cost of transport in £ per tonne	X	1	2	3	4	5	6	7	8	9	10
	Y	5	10	15	20	25	30	35	40	45	50
Price minus transport cost	X	9	8	7	6	5	4	3	2	1	0
	Y	15	10	5	0	−5	−10	−15	−20	−25	−30

Figures Both farms can grow crops X and Y. But crop Y is easily damaged and so costs much more to transport.

Profit and loss

Price received by farmer at market minus cost of transport.

In £s per tonne

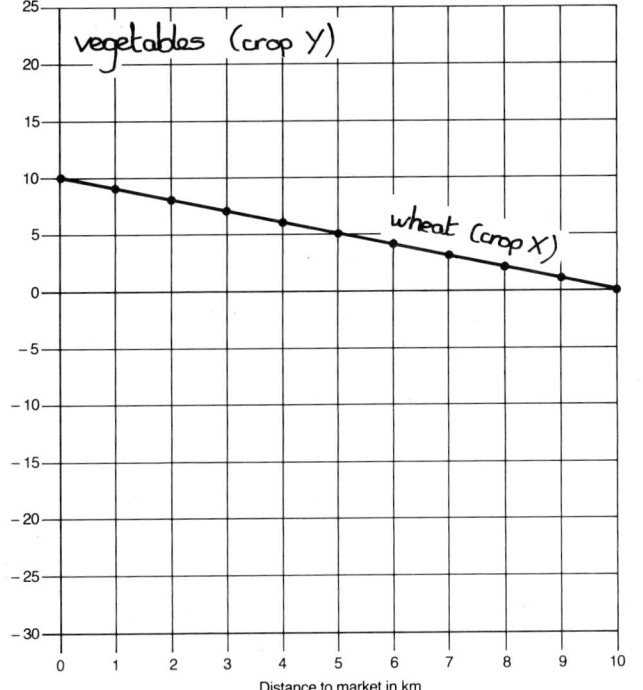

Graph The profit made from each crop depends on how far away from the market town the farm is.

E.g. at 1 km it is £9 per tonne for crop X, but only £4 per tonne if the farm is 6 km away.

A farmer's decision about land use can depend upon how near the farm is to the market where the farm's goods are sold. This is because **profit** results from:
total sales − [cost of production + transport costs]
Therefore, the further the farm is from the market the lower the profit the farmer makes as the transport costs are greater.
Fig 8 shows two imaginary farmers whose farms are at 2 km and 6 km from a market in a nearby town. The two farmers can grow either cereal or vegetables but each farmer must consider two things:
● vegetables have a high selling price per tonne at the market, but
● vegetables are more expensive to transport because they can be easily damaged and will lose freshness and quality quickly
The sums for these costs at each kilometre from the market have been worked out for you. If you complete the graph you can find out which crop each farmer will find most profitable to grow.
The results from your graph will show you one of the reasons why land use patterns develop.

Activity B

1 Make an accurate copy of the graph in fig 8.
2 Use the table of numbers to draw a profit line for vegetables like the one for wheat.
3 From your graph work out the following distances:
a where wheat is no longer profitable to grow.
b where vegetables are no longer profitable to grow.
c where wheat is more profitable than vegetables.
4 Which crop will farm A grow and which farm B?
5 Explain in sentences the reasons for your answer.
Research project
Can you describe a pattern of market gardens, nurseries and garden centres around your local town or city? Plot them on a local road map. Draw circles around your town at three kilometre intervals. Does the pattern show any effect of distance from the centre?

Africa

Africa is a continent full of strange and exciting things. This is where, it is thought, mankind evolved. It is a continent of dark ancient forests, of vast arid deserts, of long mysterious rivers. There was a university in West Africa before there was one in London; a steam engine was used here two thousand years ago; and there is a long history of metal working.

Today, Africa is a continent of great contrasts between different ways of life; a continent of conflict between the races, between tribes and nations. By the year 2000 it is projected to hold 15% of the world's population.

We will be studying examples of enterprises from two countries in Africa: Nigeria and South Africa.

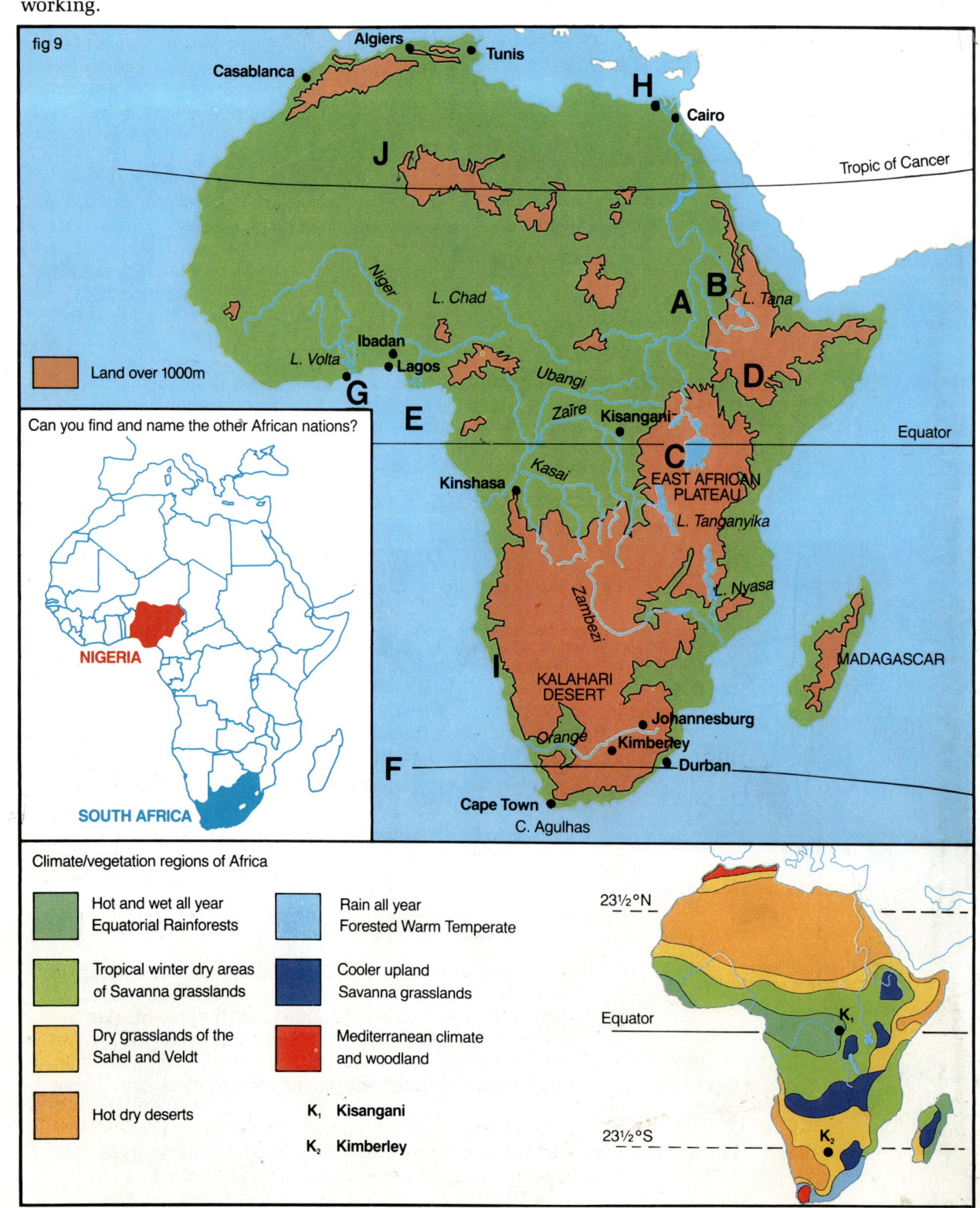

fig 9

Land over 1000m

Can you find and name the other African nations?

NIGERIA

SOUTH AFRICA

Climate/vegetation regions of Africa

Hot and wet all year Equatorial Rainforests

Rain all year Forested Warm Temperate

Tropical winter dry areas of Savanna grasslands

Cooler upland Savanna grasslands

Dry grasslands of the Sahel and Veldt

Mediterranean climate and woodland

Hot dry deserts

K_1 Kisangani

K_2 Kimberley

Climate Graphs: how to describe them

fig 10

This is an example of a **climate graph**. It has been drawn from these monthly temperature and rainfall figures of Kimberley, a town on the Veldt of South Africa.

	Jan	Feb	Mar	Apr	May	Jun	Jul	Aug	Sep	Oct	Nov	Dec
Temp. °C	24	23	21	17	13	9	9	12	16	19	22	24
Rain mm	71	79	76	33	23	8	10	10	18	25	43	61

Notice:
- a **line graph** shows the temperature. This is always at the top
- a series of twelve small **bars** show rainfall at the bottom

Look for the following things:
- find the three months of **highest temperature**. This will tell you which hemisphere it is in (June, July, August = Northern Hemisphere; December, January, February = Southern Hemisphere)
- find the **highest monthly temperature** *24°C in January & December*
- find the **lowest monthly temperature** *9°C in June & July*
- find the **annual range of temperature** (take the lowest temperature from the highest) *24 – 9 = 15°C*
- find the **amount of rain in the wettest month** *79 mm*
- find the **amount of rain in the driest month** *8mm*
- notice if there are periods of **low rainfall** (dry season) *April – Nov.* or **high rainfall** (wet season) *Dec – March*
- add the amount of rain shown by all 12 bars to give **total annual rainfall** *457 mm*

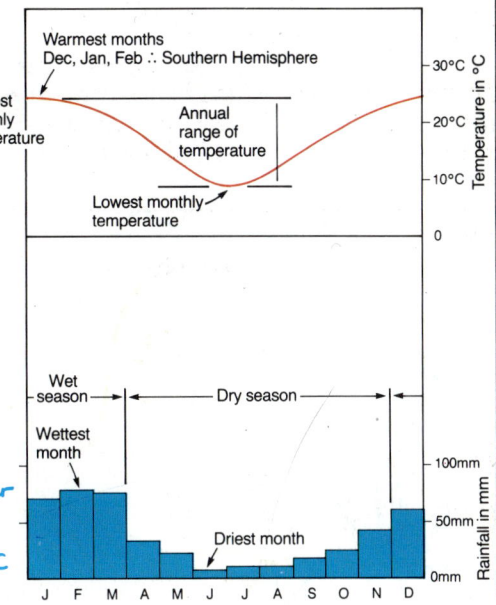

Kimberley, South Africa

photo 1

photo 2

Activity A

1 Make your own copy of the map of Africa. Use your atlas to find and label the features A to J.

2 Use your atlas to find the latitude of Kinshasa and Tunis. Now write about 100 words describing what physical features you would see, and what climate and vegetation regions you would pass through, travelling from Kinshasa to Tunis.

Activity B

1 Use these figures to draw a climate graph for Kisangani:

	Jan	Feb	Mar	Apr	May	Jun	Jul	Aug	Sep	Oct	Nov	Dec
Temp. °C	26	26	26	26	26	25	24	24	24	25	24	25
Rain mm	54	84	178	157	137	107	132	165	183	218	198	85

2 Use the method outlined in fig 10 to describe the features of the climate shown by the graphs.

3 Use your atlas and fig 9 to find the answer to these questions:
a what are the latitude and longitude of Kimberley and Kisangani?
b what countries are the two places in?
c in what climate and vegetation regions are these two towns found?

4 Look at photos 1 and 2. Which of the two climates (like Kimberley or Kisangani) produces the vegetation shown on each photo? In two sentences, give reasons for your answer.

Nigeria

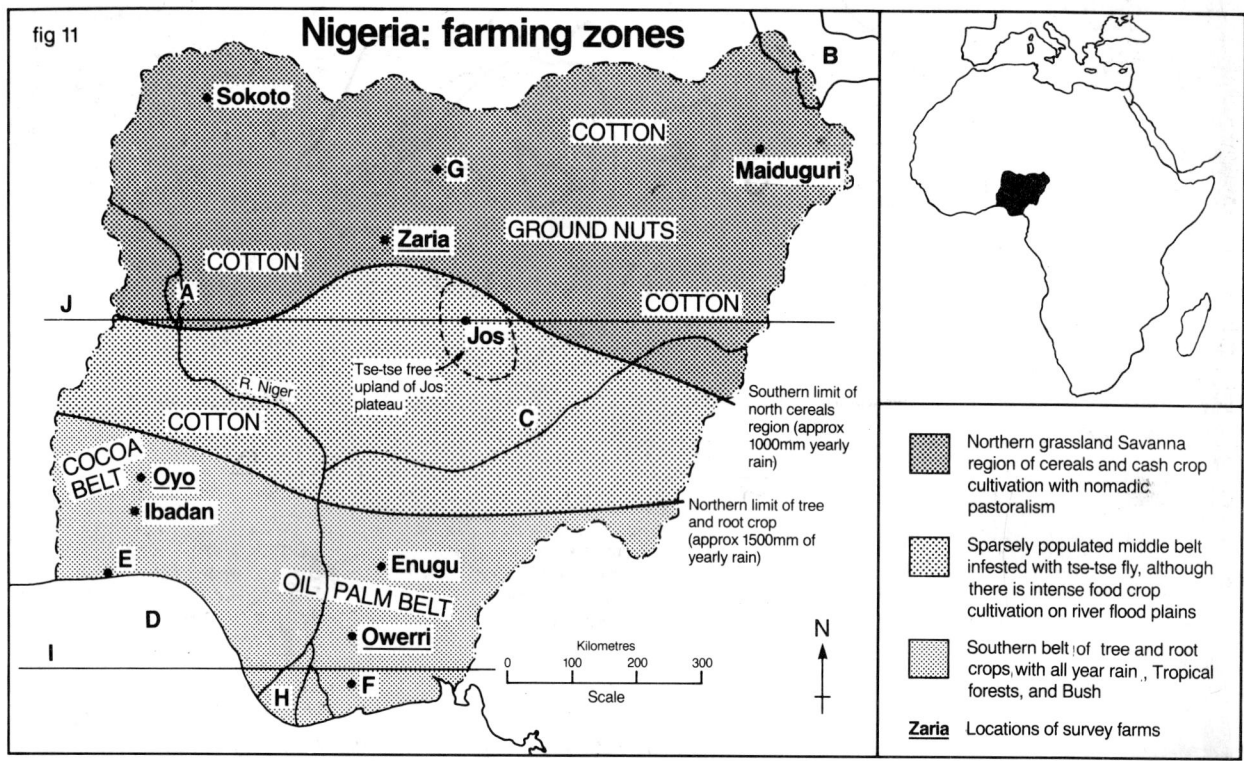

fig 11

Nigeria: farming zones

Sokoto

COTTON

Maiduguri

G

GROUND NUTS

Zaria

COTTON

COTTON

J

A

COTTON

Jos

Tse-tse free upland of Jos plateau

R. Niger

C

Southern limit of north cereals region (approx 1000mm yearly rain)

COCOA BELT • Oyo

• Ibadan

Northern limit of tree and root crop (approx 1500mm of yearly rain)

E

OIL PALM BELT

• Enugu

D

I

• Owerri

Kilometres

0   100   200   300

Scale

H   • F

N

B

Northern grassland Savanna region of cereals and cash crop cultivation with nomadic pastoralism

Sparsely populated middle belt infested with tse-tse fly, although there is intense food crop cultivation on river flood plains

Southern belt of tree and root crops, with all year rain, Tropical forests, and Bush

Zaria Locations of survey farms

Nigeria is a tropical country in West Africa. It has three main natural regions (see fig 11).

● a southern wet, forested belt: mainly concerned with tree and root crops, with little livestock farming

● a seasonally wet middle belt of savanna bush and including the damp, humid valleys of the Niger and Benue rivers: the spread of the disease-carrying tse-tse fly limits settlement and population

● a northern savanna grassland region with a tropical climate of wet summers and dry winters: containing cereal and cash crop cultivation, and nomadic cattle-keeping in the drier areas

The farm surveys opposite show some of the main features of Nigeria's agriculture. Despite different climates and crops they are surprisingly similar.

● many farms are small, they use traditional hand methods and family labour

● a form of **shifting cultivation** is usually practised: a plot of land is farmed very heavily for a few years and then left to rest, the farmers then move on to another area. The natural vegetation re-grows on the used plot, this replaces plant foods back into the soil. The plot can be farmed again after a few years

● food is mainly grown for subsistence: this means food is grown to feed the family, only the surplus is sold

● where farms do concentrate on a **cash crop** (which is grown for the market), it is usually sold to foreign-owned companies and exported abroad

● cattle are not kept in large numbers, except in the drier north, because of the disease spread by the tse-tse fly

Activity A

1 Look at fig 11. Use your atlas to help you name features A to J.

2 Copy this chart and complete it from the details on this page:

	Natural vegetation	Climate	Main crops
Northern belt			
Middle belt			
Southern belt			

3 Add these words to your dictionary of geography: cash crop, and shifting cultivation.

Activity B

1 Imagine you are a visitor to one of the farms. Write a letter home describing your impressions of the farm. Use the appropriate photograph to help you.

2 Choose one of the farms from Nigeria. Look back to fig 5 page 8, and draw your own large diagram for this farm filling in its particular details.

photo 3: Small holding, Nigeria

photo 4: Oil palm plantation, Nigeria

Nigeria farm survey

fig 12

Farm	Cocoa smallholding (Southwestern Nigeria)	Bush fallowing (Southeastern Nigeria)	Peasant farm (Northern Nigeria)
Location	Akinlalu village in main cocoa belt of Oyo state.	Near town of Owerri.	Hanwa village near city of Zaria.
Size	1.7 hectares	1.4 hectares	3 hectares
Classification (see p. 9)	Intensive commercial arable	Intensive commercial arable	Intensive subsistence arable
Environment of area where farm is sited	Rainfall 1,500mm/year. Lowest monthly temp. 18°C. Tropical climate, rain all year – most in March and Sept. On edge of Yorubaland plateau over 300m high. Northern edge of Tropical rain forest in Ogunu river valley.	Rainfall 2,300mm/year. Lowest monthly temp. 18°C. Tropical climate, rain all year (Equatorial). Edge of Niger Delta at 100m high. Tropical rain forest.	Rainfall 118mm/year. Lowest monthly temp. 18°C. Tropical, summer rain, winter drought climate (Savanna). High plains of Hausaland over 500m high. Savanna grassland. Only a few trees.
No. and size of fields/plots	Area of cultivation 1.1 ha made up of { 0.7 ha cocoa, 0.4 ha food crops } Area of fallow 0.6 ha	Area of cultivation 0.7 ha made up of { 0.2 ha tree crops, 0.1 ha homestead field, 0.4 ha distant field } Area of fallow 0.7 ha	Area of cultivation 2.9 ha Area of fallow 0.1 ha (Upland 2.8 ha, lowland 0.2 ha)
Crops and livestock	**Crops** Cocoa trees, Oil palms, Plantains (banana-like fruit), Cassava } for family use, Maize }, Maize for sale, Peppers and vegetables but only a few **Animals** 7 chickens, 2 goats. No cattle as in area of tse-tse fly.	**Crops** Tree crop plot: Oil palms, Bananas, Coconut palm, Palm bush under planted with yams, cassava, maize and vegetables Homestead plot: cassava } for, maize } family, yams } use Distant plot: cassava under planted with groundnuts and maize **Animals** No cattle, 6 goats, 24 chickens	**Crops** Millets, Sorghums } 83%, Groundnuts } of area Cowpeas (lentils), Yams } 15%, Sugar cane } of, Rest is fallow } area **Animals** 10 cattle, 6 goats, 5 chickens
Labour force	Family household of seven. Work shared: 75% adult males, 15% women and children, 10% hired in. 75% of work is weeding	Family household of nine. (Work shared, but holding has enough work for the equivalent of two males.)	Family household of six. (9/10ths of work done by adult males.)
Farming methods	Traditional hand methods in partly cleared forests. Plots once cleared used for 4 – 5 years then left fallow to recover. Cocoa trees in a small grove take 5 years to fruit and give a good yield for 15 years. Spraying against disease.	Root crops and maize grown under cover of oil palms. Root crops grown in mounds. Simple hand tools. Fallow period allows soil to recover.	Traditional cultivation with simple hand tools. Work highly seasonal, most in May, June and July.
Use of products	Root crops used for families. Maize to sell in local markets. Cocoa sold after drying to Nigerian Government Cocoa Marketing Board.	Tree products for sale to large multinationals. Root crops and maize for family use. Any surplus food sold in Owerri.	For family consumption. Any surplus sells in local market in Zaria.

South Africa

Farming regions of South Africa

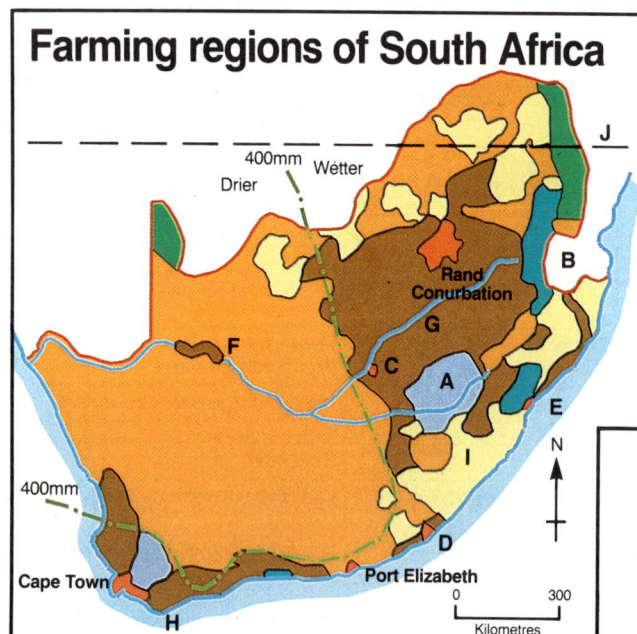

400mm Wetter
Drier

Rand Conurbation

Cape Town

Port Elizabeth

0   300
Kilometres

Legend:
- Main city/industrial regions
- Commercial farming of crops and cattle
- Commercial animal rearing mostly of cattle in areas above 400mm rain, and sheep in drier areas
- Vineyards and orchards of Cape Province
- Subsistence farming of the Black Homelands
- Forestry
- Largely unused

— South Africa border
—·— 400mm yearly rainfall line

fig 13

Use your atlas to find and name
Countries **A, B**
Cities **C, D, E**
Rivers **F, G**
Cape **H**
Black Homeland **I**
Line of latitude **J**

Unlike Nigeria, South Africa is outside the Tropical zone. This means that the climate is different, in fact there is a great range of rainfall conditions in the country which affects the distribution of farming types.

- central South Africa is covered by a high flat grassy plateau called the High Veldt, here the rain is mainly in summer: crops grown are cereals and tobacco, with dairy and beef cattle production. Towards the drier western areas the land becomes semi-desert, ranching occurs here, this is the commercial rearing of beef cattle and sheep
- in the southern and eastern areas on the coast there is rain all year round: crops grown are sugar cane and tea, these are cash crops
- in the southwest the rain is mainly in winter, droughts are common in summer: crops grown are citrus fruits and vines, with dairy cattle production. **Irrigation,** the artificial addition of water to the soil, is needed in some areas during the dry summer

The farming zones shown on the map also include large areas of subsistence agriculture. These are mainly in the areas of the so-called Black Homelands. The Homelands are areas which have been allocated to the black community under the South African Government policy of separate development for blacks and whites. Before this the land was already occupied mainly by blacks practising traditional agriculture.

It is difficult for the blacks to improve farming in the Homelands because:

- the environment is less favourable to farming than much of the country
- there is little wealth in the black community to pay for the improvements
- the amount of land is not enough to support the population concentrated there

photo 5: Cutting sugar cane, South Africa

photo 6: Vineyard, South Africa

The photographs and farm surveys show the contrasts between different farming areas and types.

Activity A

1 Look at fig 13. Make your own copy naming features A-J from your atlas.

2 Briefly describe the location, climate and farming of the zones shown on the map.

3 Choose two of the factors described on page 10 that affect farming. In what ways have these influenced farming in
a Nigeria   b South Africa?
Use your atlas and other books from your library to help you further.

4 Put the following words in your dictionary of geography: High Veldt, irrigation, ranching.

fig 14

South Africa farm survey

Farm	Schoongezicht fruit and mixed estate (Southwestern S. Africa)	Specialised veldt livestock farm (Central S. Africa)	Homelands farm in Bophuthatswana (Northern S. Africa)
Location	East of Capetown, near Stellen Bosch	30km west of Kroonstad in Orange Free State	North of Zeerust in Bophuthatswana, Northern Transvaal
Size	About 1100 hectares	About 870 hectares	4 hectares
Classification (see p.9)	Intensive commercial mixed	Extensive commercial mixed	Intensive subsistence arable
Environment of area where farm is sited	Rainfall 914mm/year. Temp. Jan 21°C July 12°C. A Mediterranean type climate. In the Simonsberg Hills on south facing slopes and valley floor of the Krommer river.	Rainfall: 750mm/year. Temp: Jan 20°C July 10°C. A summer wet, winter dry Interior Continental climate. On part of the great African plateau grasslands known as the Veldt at 1500m above sea level.	Rainfall: 495mm/year. Temp: Jan 24°C July 11°C. A semi-arid summer, wet winter, dry Interior Continental climate. On the low lying part of the Transvaal Plateau at 1200m above sea level.
No. and size of fields/plots	Pine plantation (timber) 160 ha Dry vines 82 ha Pasture 52 ha Fruit 50 ha The rest is natural vegetation.	Open Veldt grassland 480 ha Arable land for cereals 334 ha Sown grasslands 32 ha Food crops 24 ha	One field plot for food growing.
Crops and livestock	**Crops** Grapes (vines) Citrus fruit and plums Pine trees for timber Specially planted Cape Fybos pasture **Animals** 200 pedigree Jersey dairy cattle ± 250 young cattle sold annually	**Crops** Maize Wheat Oats Sown rotational grasses Potatoes **Animals** 400 mainly Merino breed of sheep, with some cross breeds for mutton. 200 cattle	**Crops** Sorghums Millet Maize **Animals** 2 goats
Labour force	50 full time males 120 part time, fruit harvest workers	Family farm with 18 full time workers and shepherds.	Worked by women and old people. Men work in the mines of the Rand.
Farming methods	Highly mechanised farm with modern dairy equipment and viticulture. Large use of chemicals for fertilizer and pest control. Pasture irrigated.	Mechanised cereal production. Open range sheep and cattle grazing. Two small dams to store water and wind pumps to bring up underground water in dry winter season.	Traditional hoe cultivation. No machinery. New Government schemes to replan farming settlement underway.
Use of products	Grape – use to make wine (sold locally and throughout South Africa). Fruit – exported via a co-operative to Europe. Dairy – local market for milk; nationwide for cheese.	Sheep – fine Merino wool for export, cross-breeds give mutton. Cattle – mainly dairy for milk for nearby cities, half used to make butter and cheese in local town. Crops – mainly for fodder for the animals, wheat marketed.	For own consumption, but not self sufficient, rely on man's income to supply extra food.

Activity B

1 Look at the farm surveys. Which of the farms:
a is largest?
b has irrigation?
c keeps cattle?
d is mainly subsistence?
2 Which of the three farms is most like the Nigerian farms?

3 Choose one of the photographs and describe what it shows. You could draw a simple labelled sketch of it.
4 Which of the farms is it most like?
5 Write a brief description of this farm.
6 Look back to page 10. Draw a large poster size version of fig 7, but leave the boxes empty. In those boxes show the details of one of the South African farms.

Changing Agriculture

Farming systems change in the course of time. This is true of all types of farms.

What goes on in any working farm results from the inputs and outputs of the farm (see page 10). If any of these inputs or outputs change this alters the farming practices. For example, increasing the water supply by irrigation is an **input change;** this can lead to improved yields and the growth of new crops. Similarly, a fall in the market price of one crop is an **output change;** this can cause a farmer to change the crop pattern.

Changes can happen in a number of ways:
- individual farmers can do things to improve their farms and production
- groups of farmers may join together to do things they would be unable to do alone e.g. setting up a **cooperative,** where expensive fertilizers and equipment can be bought and shared, and farm products processed and sold
- governments may encourage and pay for large scale changes in farming required by the needs of the country e.g. building large dams, giving grants to farmers or improving agricultural education

These types of change might include many different things. Some will involve changes in the sizes and patterns of fields and farms. Some will improve crops and animals. Some change the way that farmers work the land. New land may be **reclaimed** (or rescued) from forest, hill, marsh, desert, or even from the sea-bed. Land which has been lost or damaged by misuse in the past may be given a new lease of life if it is carefully restored.

The photos above show some of the changes brought about in India by the **Green Revolution.** This began about forty years ago with experiments by agricultural scientists to improve the yields of basic cereal crops. The growing world food shortage made it necessary to increase production.

New **high-yielding varieties** of wheat were first tried in Mexico. Many such varieties of wheat and rice were soon introduced to many developing countries, like India and Nigeria.

photo 7: New wells

photo 8: Mechanisation

Other new farming methods were encouraged at the same time. Some of these were the direct result of using the new **miracle** seeds. For example, they needed large amounts of fertilizers and new growing methods.

fig 15	**Project work**	Make a large copy of this drawing. Try to find out the different ways in which farming is changing, or developing. Write them in the empty boxes. Give as many different examples as you can.

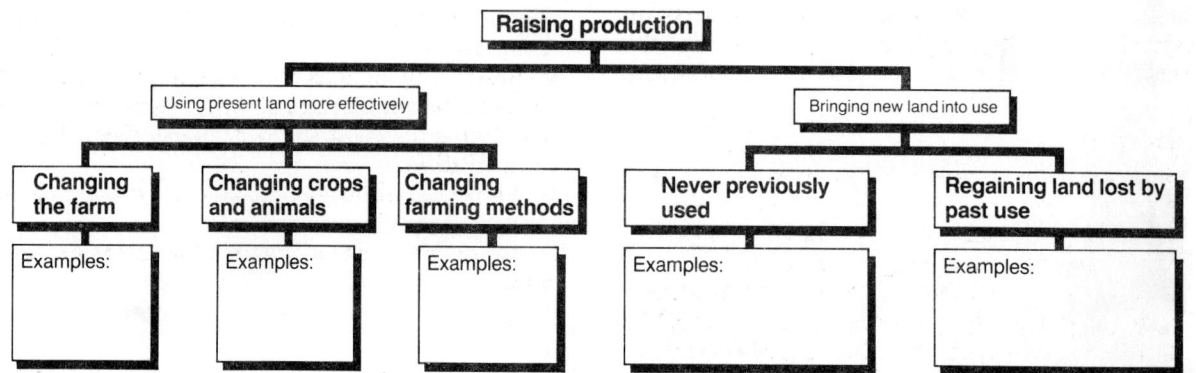

fig 16   **Some changes in farming from around the world**

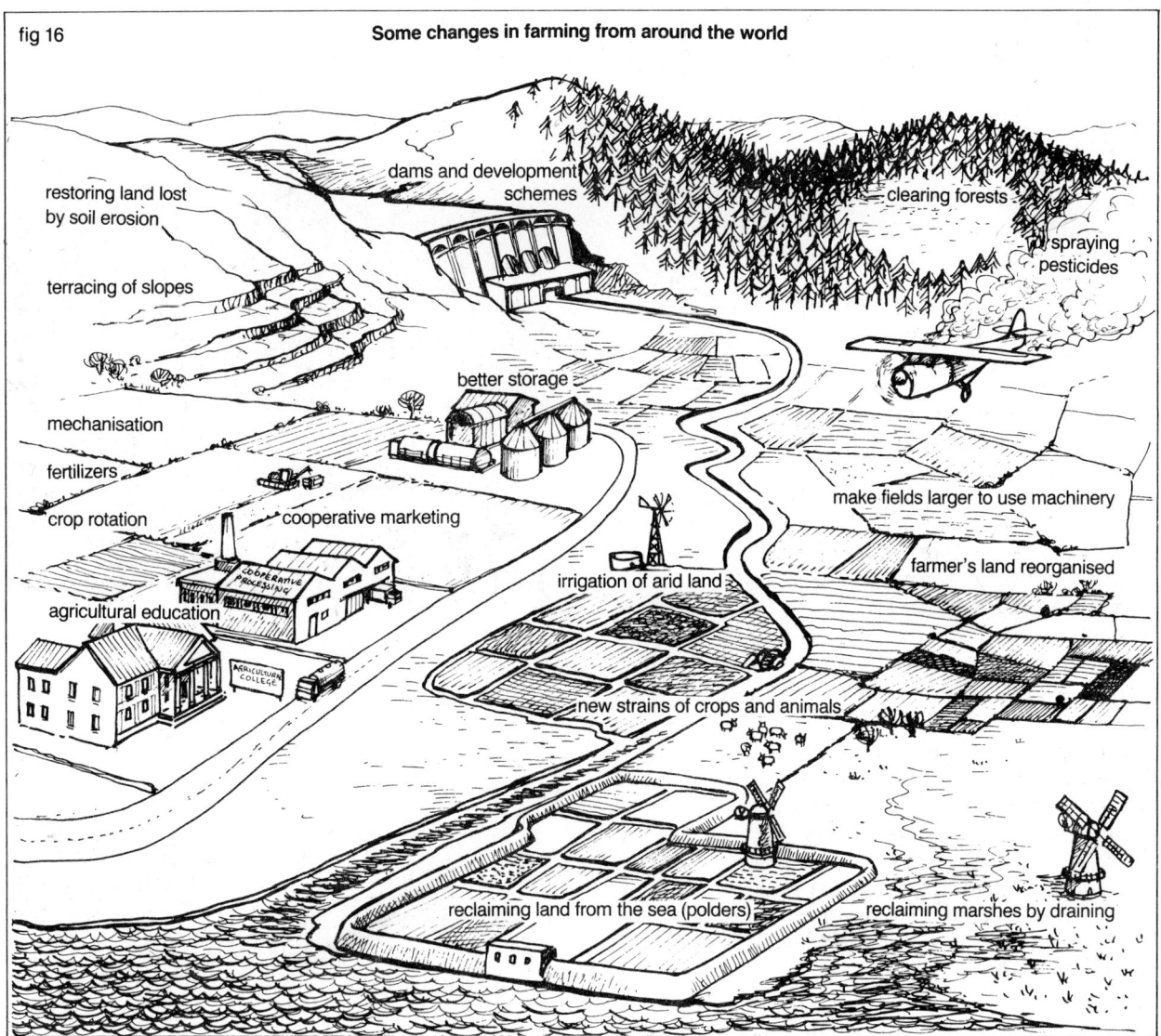

restoring land lost by soil erosion

dams and development schemes

clearing forests

spraying pesticides

terracing of slopes

mechanisation

fertilizers

better storage

crop rotation

cooperative marketing

make fields larger to use machinery

agricultural education

irrigation of arid land

farmer's land reorganised

new strains of crops and animals

reclaiming land from the sea (polders)

reclaiming marshes by draining

Growing these high-yielding cereals needs careful attention:

- the seeds must be sown much more carefully
- weeds must be controlled
- the fertilizers have to be applied in the correct amounts, at the right times, and in the right way
- they suffer more from pests and plant diseases, and should be sprayed, which will protect them
- their water needs must be properly worked out and controlled .

The farmers have to learn and understand so many new things. For this reason, the results of the Green Revolution so far have not always been successful. Even when they are, many farming families think the taste of the grain from the new varieties is not so good.

Activity

1 What sorts of agricultural change can be done by:
a individual farmers, **b** groups of farmers working together, and **c** governments?
2 What do you think are the advantages of using the new high-yielding 'miracle' seeds?
3 List any four problems of using these seeds.

Fig 16 shows some of the ways in which farming can change: some take place in developed countries, some take place in developing countries, and some happen in both.

Not all the changes made in farming bring the intended results:

- clearing forests can let the rain wash away the newly exposed soil
- chemicals to fertilize the soil, and kill pests and plant diseases, may contaminate the soil and water supplies
- irrigation in **arid** (or dry) lands may leave salty deposits in the topsoil when some of the water evaporates
- destroying hedges to make larger fields may change the appearance of the scenery, and remove the living environment of some species of plants and wildlife
- the weight of heavy machinery can damage the soil

These are just a few examples, but there are many more.

Asia

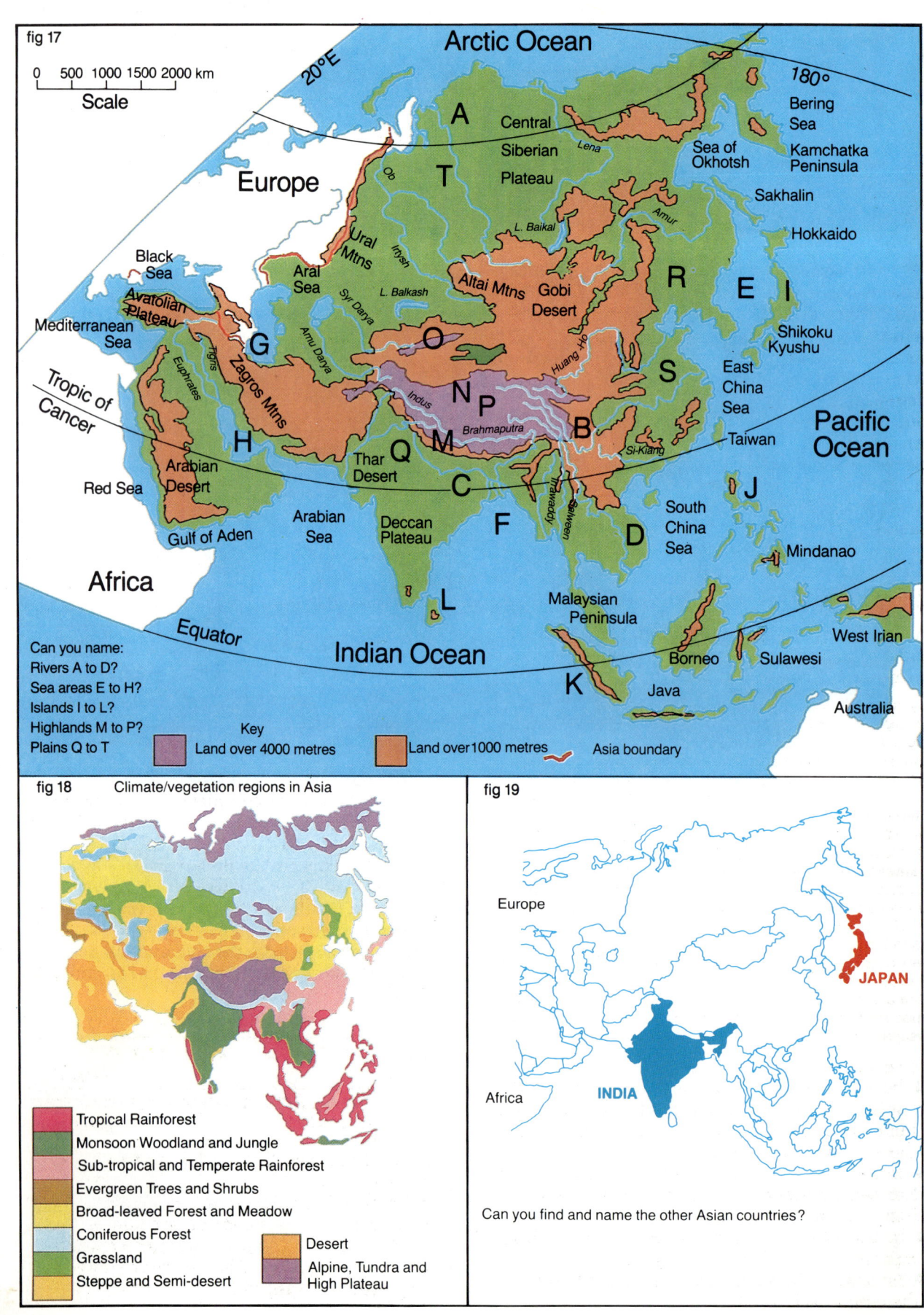

fig 17

Scale
0 500 1000 1500 2000 km

Arctic Ocean

20°E

180°

Europe

Central Siberian Plateau

Lena

Sea of Okhotsk

Bering Sea

Kamchatka Peninsula

Sakhalin

Hokkaido

Ob

Ural Mtns

Irtysh

Black Sea

Aral Sea

L. Baikal

Altai Mtns

Gobi Desert

Amur

Anatolian Plateau

Mediterranean Sea

Syr Darya

L. Balkash

Huang Ho

Shikoku
Kyushu

Tropic of Cancer

Amu Darya

Zagros Mtns

Euphrates

Tigris

Indus

Brahmaputra

Si-Kiang

East China Sea

Taiwan

Pacific Ocean

Red Sea

Arabian Desert

Thar Desert

Deccan Plateau

Irrawaddy

Salween

South China Sea

Africa

Arabian Sea

Malaysian Peninsula

Mindanao

West Irian

Equator

Indian Ocean

Borneo

Sulawesi

Java

Australia

Can you name:
Rivers A to D?
Sea areas E to H?
Islands I to L?
Highlands M to P?
Plains Q to T

Key
Land over 4000 metres
Land over 1000 metres
Asia boundary

fig 18   Climate/vegetation regions in Asia

- Tropical Rainforest
- Monsoon Woodland and Jungle
- Sub-tropical and Temperate Rainforest
- Evergreen Trees and Shrubs
- Broad-leaved Forest and Meadow
- Coniferous Forest
- Grassland
- Steppe and Semi-desert
- Desert
- Alpine, Tundra and High Plateau

fig 19

Europe

JAPAN

INDIA

Africa

Can you find and name the other Asian countries?

photo 9:

photo 10:

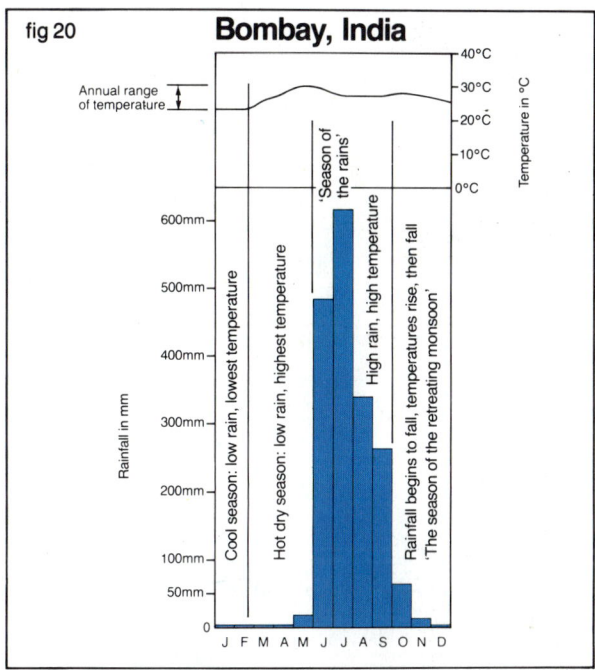
fig 20 **Bombay, India**

Asia is a large continent spreading over a wide variety of different economic and physical situations. We will be studying enterprises from two countries in Asia: Japan, a highly advanced developed country where most people work in industry; and India, a fast developing country where the majority of the population are still farmers.

An important influence on farming in many countries in Asia is the **monsoon** climate.

A monsoon climate has a very sharp change in weather conditions from one season to another, caused by a reversal in the wind direction. The winds bring different patterns of rainfall and temperature at different times of the year. India and Japan have different monsoon climates.

The onset of the summer monsoon is described by A.C. Newcombe below; he worked in the Punjab in India at the turn of the century. Compare his account with the climate graph of Bombay, in fig 20.

By the middle of April, the weather becomes unpleasantly hot. During the hottest time the temperatures are 52° to 54°C and the night temperature is seldom below 38°C.

The advent of the monsoon wind which blows from May to September from the southwest, is eagerly looked for as the heavy rains it brings cool the air and **soak the parched country.** The cooling of the air is at first delightful. It is not only the strong wind that does this but there is an actual fall in temperature.

On the arrival of the Southwest monsoon, it is pretty to see **the gathering of the rolling clouds** of all shapes and sizes and variations of colour from different shades of grey to deep black. During the first fall there is **a seething, hissing noise** as the raindrops reach the ground and are quickly absorbed in the hot earth. Steam rises at first, but after a few days **the air becomes very humid.** During my first rainy season, one rain gauge in the Punjab recorded 22 inches in 10 hours.

By the middle of September, the rains become lighter, the sun appears more often and not so hot and the clouds gradually disappear.

You can see the pattern of the monsoon:
● from May/June the summer is dominated by the Southwest monsoon; the winds bring hot, wet air from the equatorial oceans to the south, which causes heavy summer rains
● from October the wind direction changes; the Northeast monsoon winds bring cooler, drier air from the land to the north
● by the end of February the temperatures climb rapidly; there is a season of dry, hot weather
● the onset of the Southwest monsoon in May starts the whole cycle again

Activity

1 Using your atlas complete the keys to the maps of Asia.

2 Look at photos 9 and 10. Describe in three sentences what each one shows.

3 Look at fig 20. In which season do you think each photograph was taken?

4 Describe the climate of Bombay using the method on page 13.

5 Use the following statistics to draw a climate graph for Tokyo, Japan:

	J	F	M	A	M	J	J	A	S	O	N	D
Temp. °C	3	4	8	13	17	21	24	26	22	16	11	5
												Range 23
Rain mm	56	71	112	124	145	165	135	145	221	188	107	53
												Total 1522

6 Label your graph to show the seasons you recognise.

7 Describe Tokyo's climate.

8 Look at A.C. Newcombe's account of the monsoon in India. Explain in your own words what you think is meant by the five phrases that have been emphasised.

Alter Inputs: Change System

fig 21

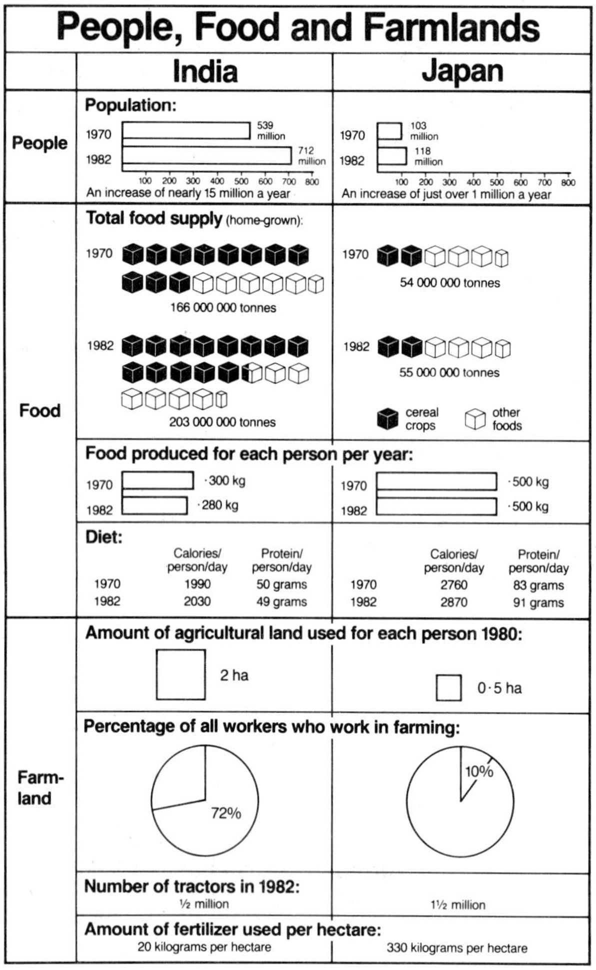

People, Food and Farmlands

		India	Japan
People	Population:	1970 — 539 million 1982 — 712 million An increase of nearly 15 million a year (scale 100 200 300 400 500 600 700 800)	1970 — 103 million 1982 — 118 million An increase of just over 1 million a year (scale 100 200 300 400 500 600 700 800)
Food	Total food supply (home-grown):	1970 — 166 000 000 tonnes 1982 — 203 000 000 tonnes	1970 — 54 000 000 tonnes 1982 — 55 000 000 tonnes ■ cereal crops □ other foods
	Food produced for each person per year:	1970 — ·300 kg 1982 — ·280 kg	1970 — ·500 kg 1982 — ·500 kg
	Diet:	1970 — Calories/person/day 1990, Protein/person/day 50 grams 1982 — Calories/person/day 2030, Protein/person/day 49 grams	1970 — Calories/person/day 2760, Protein/person/day 83 grams 1982 — Calories/person/day 2870, Protein/person/day 91 grams
Farm-land	Amount of agricultural land used for each person 1980:	2 ha	0·5 ha
	Percentage of all workers who work in farming:	72%	10%
	Number of tractors in 1982:	½ million	1½ million
	Amount of fertilizer used per hectare:	20 kilograms per hectare	330 kilograms per hectare

Fig 21 shows some of the differences between the people, food and farmlands of India and Japan.

- India's population is over six times that of Japan, and growing at a much faster rate
- India's total production of food has risen between 1970 and 1982 by about a quarter. Japan's has hardly increased at all
- the fast growing Indian population means that the food produced per head of population actually fell a little
- Japan produced more food for each person and the actual rise in food supply matched the population growth
- Japanese people have a better diet. In India it has hardly changed from 1970 to 1982 and both the average calories and protein levels are lower than recommended by the United Nations World Health Organisation for healthy living
- Japan's farmlands are much more mechanised and fertilized than India's. Despite only a quarter as much farmland per person and a much lower percentage of farmworkers, it produces nearly twice as much food per person

India is a very large country with many differences in its natural conditions. There is a wide range of crops and farm patterns. Most people still work on the land, and peasant farmers throughout the country still follow a **subsistence** way of life; farming in India is similar to that of many developing countries.

The first task for farmers in India is to produce enough to feed the family. Any surplus may be sold to pay for the items that the farmers cannot produce themselves.

Farms are still very small, under two hectares, often with scattered fields, and farmed in traditional ways. Farmers often have to borrow money for seeds and fertilizers: their success still depends on the weather, and so in some years they cannot produce enough. It is difficult to repay the debts. Most rural families live near the poverty line and worry about food shortages. However, things are changing.

Farming in Japan is quite different from many developed countries. Farming is centred around vegetables, fruit and, of course, paddy field rice growing. Only 10 per cent of the working population are involved in agriculture. One third of these people work as full-time farmers, most have another job as well.

Farming is very modern and highly mechanised, and the land is used very **intensively.** Unlike many of India's farms, Japanese farms are mainly **commercial enterprises,** selling their output to the large populations of the many cities.

There is a limited area of land for farming and the average size of farm is under one hectare. To provide enough food for all the people of Japan the country must import food supplies from abroad.

Activity A

1 What do the following words mean: subsistence, intensively, commercial enterprises, population pressure?
2 Write a brief summary of 50 words each, for: Indian farming; and Japanese farming.
3 Look at fig 21. Write down any differences you notice in India between 1970 and 1982.
4 Write down six differences between food and farmlands in India and Japan.
a draw graphs to show differences in their diets.
b describe the differences your graphs show.

In both countries farming has been changing, but for different reasons. India has to produce more to feed its rapidly growing population. Japan has very limited amounts of farmland and so must import a lot of its food. In their different ways, they are both examples of countries where there is **population pressure** upon the available agricultural resources.

fig 22

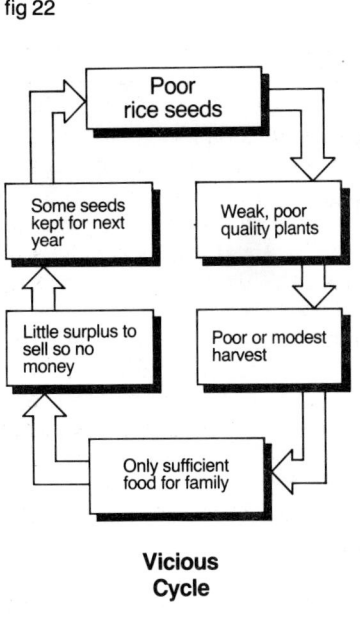

Vicious Cycle

photo 11: Rice farming, India

fig 23

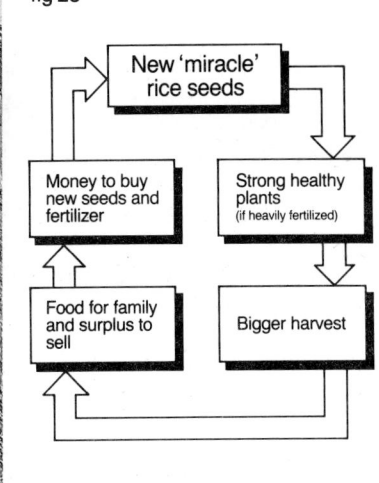

Green Revolution

Fig 23 shows one change on some of India's farms. This is part of the Green Revolution (see page 18). The many new methods have produced an increase in India's total food production shown in fig 21.

Farming in Japan was based on many full-time workers but it is now mainly a part-time, highly mechanised activity.

Activity B

1 What are the changes which result from using new 'miracle' rice.

2 Describe the features of traditional Japanese farming from photo 12 .

3 Try to draw a circle diagram like the ones for India to show the effects of mechanised farming in Japan shown in fig 23.

photo 12: Tea picking, Japan

photo 13: Mechanised tea picking, Japan

A Village of Change

Palanpur is a village in the western part of the Indian state of Uttar Pradesh, and is like many villages in this part of the Ganges Plain. It is beside the railway joining the country town of Chandausi to the large city of Moradabad, 31 kilometres to the north. About 200 kilometres west lies Delhi, the capital of India.

The main monsoon rains come in July and August, but there are a few light rains in December and January. The total yearly rainfall varies quite a lot: in 1970 it was only 439 millimetres, while in 1971 it was 1,039.

In 1975 there were 112 farming households, with a total of 762 people. Nearly half the farms are only 6 to 12 hectares in size, and there are none larger than 30 hectares. Different crops are grown in different seasons. The main ones are shown in this table:

	Dry Season (Rabi)	Wet Season (Kharif)
Time sown	Oct/Nov	June/July
Harvested	April/May	Sept/Oct
	wheat (42%) peas, beans and lentils (16%) barley (4%)	millet (26%) maize (9%) padi rice (5%) groundnuts (5%)

One or two crops are grown through the year because they take ten months to grow fully. The main one is sugar cane, grown to sell to the nearby government sugar mill. As a result of this pattern, most land is double-cropped, usually involving some kind of irrigation. Most of the livestock kept by the 112 households are used as draught animals to pull ploughs and carts and to work the more traditional waterwheels for irrigation. Altogether in 1975 there were 157 bullocks and he-buffaloes and 105 cows and she-buffaloes.

The farmers in Palanpur saw their crop yields rise during the years from the 1950s to the 1970s. Wheat yields went up over 4 times, millet by nearly 3 and rice by nearly 40 times. But not all the farmers benefited in the same way.....

fig 24

HE HAD A DIESEL PUMP SO THAT HE COULD WATER THE LAND WITH THE RIGHT AMOUNT AT THE RIGHT TIME.

TWO SCIENTISTS ARRIVE IN THE VILLAGE TO INVESTIGATE 'THE GREEN REVOLUTION.'

....BUT NOT EVERY FARMER WAS AS SUCCESSFUL.

HERE IS PART OF THEIR REPORT.

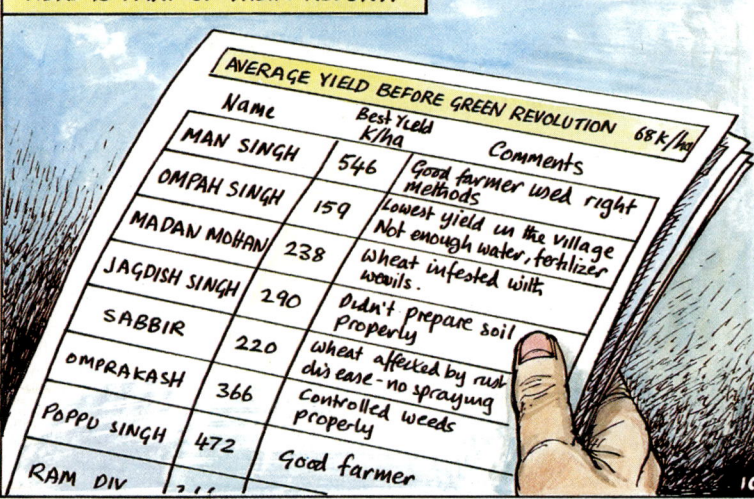

AVERAGE YIELD BEFORE GREEN REVOLUTION 68 k/ha		
Name	Best Yield k/ha	Comments
MAN SINGH	546	Good farmer used right methods
OMPAH SINGH	159	Lowest yield in the village
MADAN MOHAN	238	Not enough water, fertilizer
JAGDISH SINGH	290	Wheat infested with weevils.
SABBIR	220	Didn't prepare soil properly
OMPRAKASH	366	Wheat affected by rust disease - no spraying
POPPU SINGH	472	Controlled weeds properly
RAM DIV		Good farmer

MORE WHEAT CAN BE SOLD SO INCOMES RISE.

EVERYONE HAS INCREASED THEIR YIELD.

THE WAY FORWARD?

An attempt to start a co-operative for processing and marketing was prevented by social divisions in the village, people also feared being cheated by officials; however this could be one way of developing further.

Either: Write a short play, with your class, about the changes that might result from a village meeting to talk about the cooperative.

Or: Write down what advice you think Ompah Singh would get about his farming from Man Singh, Jagadesh Singh, Sabbir and Omprakash.

Feed the Nation

One factor affecting farming which has become more and more important in recent years is **government policy.** It is not only important in the developed world countries, but even more so in the poorer nations of the developing world, like Nigeria.

Since its independence in 1960, Nigeria developed serious problems connected with food production in agriculture. This is surprising because during this period Nigeria's earnings from the export of crude oil have been very large, but it seems that not enough of this money was invested in improving agriculture.

Fig 25 shows Nigeria's problems during the 1970s. The stages in describing these problems are as follows:

- a very fast growth in the number of people
- a much slower growth in the production of food at home
- the average diet stayed at about the same level
- large food imports were therefore needed to make up the gap between the needs of the population and what was produced at home
- the value of food imports went up by 20 times: food imports used up valuable money needed for investment in other activities

The problem of growing more food has been made more difficult by the migration of energetic young adults from the rural areas into the towns and cities, to look for a better lifestyle: much of the work on farms has been left to the older people staying behind. In rural areas people are still cultivating small, unimproved plots of land using traditional methods; during the years 1971 to 1982, there has been an actual decrease in the tonnage of export crops produced. Those most likely to change the situation and raise farm production are the younger adults.

The features of Nigerian society have made development particularly hard. There are problems resulting from colonial rule under the British and the large number of different tribal groups, with a lack of cooperation between the different groups and regions. There was a civil war from 1967 to 1970, when the South-East region tried to become independent of the rest of the country.

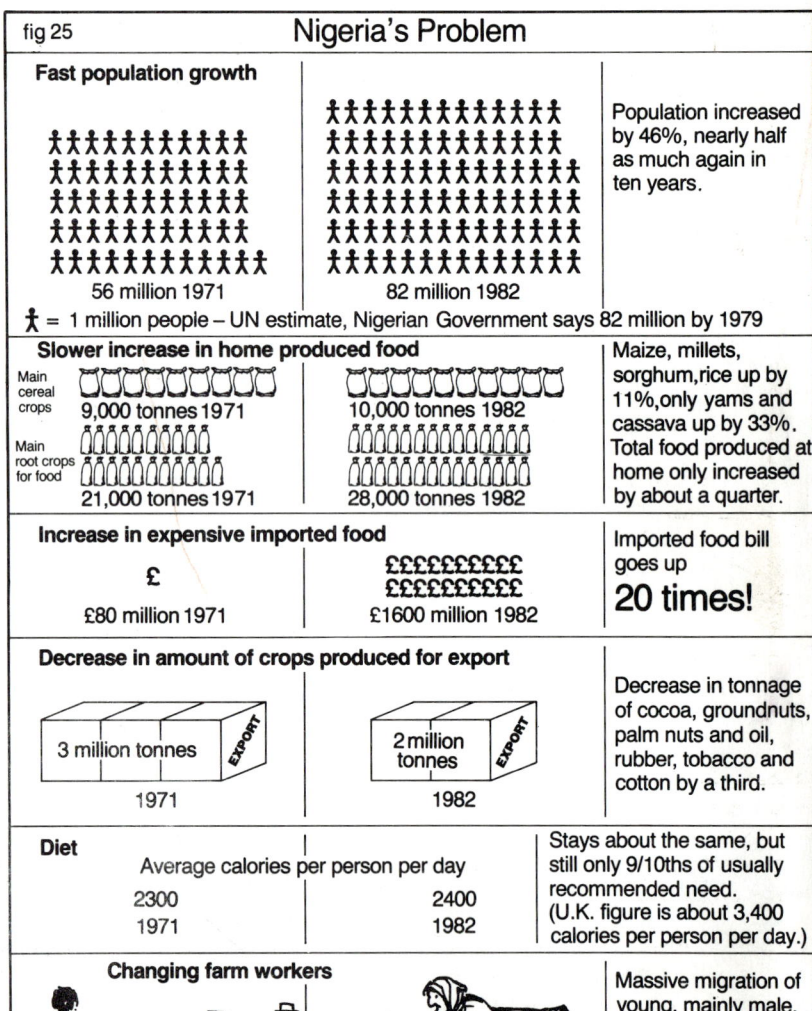

fig 25 — Nigeria's Problem

Fast population growth

56 million 1971 — 82 million 1982

Population increased by 46%, nearly half as much again in ten years.

= 1 million people – UN estimate, Nigerian Government says 82 million by 1979

Slower increase in home produced food

Main cereal crops: 9,000 tonnes 1971 — 10,000 tonnes 1982

Main root crops for food: 21,000 tonnes 1971 — 28,000 tonnes 1982

Maize, millets, sorghum, rice up by 11%, only yams and cassava up by 33%. Total food produced at home only increased by about a quarter.

Increase in expensive imported food

£80 million 1971 — £1600 million 1982

Imported food bill goes up **20 times!**

Decrease in amount of crops produced for export

3 million tonnes 1971 — 2 million tonnes 1982

Decrease in tonnage of cocoa, groundnuts, palm nuts and oil, rubber, tobacco and cotton by a third.

Diet — Average calories per person per day

| | 2300 (1971) | 2400 (1982) |

Stays about the same, but still only 9/10ths of usually recommended need. (U.K. figure is about 3,400 calories per person per day.)

Changing farm workers

Massive migration of young, mainly male, adults to towns and cities. Farming left largely to middle age and elderly men and women.

Activity A

1 Look at fig 25 and then write out the following sentences about Nigeria's food problem, choosing the correct alternatives:

Between 1971 and 1982, Nigeria's population grew (slowly/quickly). It grew by (46%/10%). There was a (faster/slower) increase in home grown food. The production of the main food grains went up by (11%/33%) while production of root crops for food rose by (11%/33%). The tonnage of all (imported/home produced) food rose by about a quarter in total.
The average diet (stayed the same/improved). It was (more than/less than) the usual recommended need for healthy living. To make up the gap between its supply and its needs, Nigeria had to (export/import) food. Crops grown for export during this time actually (rose/fell) in total tonnage.

2 List the stages of the food problem.
3 Why are many farms in Nigeria still unimproved traditional plots?

For a country with a fast growing population, improving agriculture under all these circumstances is very difficult and needs strong government action.

To solve the problem of agricultural production, the Nigerian Government has set up a number of plans over the last few years.

The aims of the Government in doing this are:
● to produce more food and raw materials for a fast growing population
● to increase production of livestock and fish to meet home needs
● to increase production and processing of export crops
● to reduce the dependence on oil for foreign earnings
● to expand job opportunities in rural and urban areas
● to employ the increasing workforce

To solve the problems completely, it will need a rate of growth in agriculture which is six times what it is now. This is most unlikely. There are not enough earnings from oil sales to pay for it all; even if there were, the levels of administration, trained workers and rural services are not sufficient.

The main purpose of the present national plans in farming is to help the small farms, which produce 90 per cent of the country's food. Special areas of help have been set up, called Agricultural Development Projects (ADPs); these vary in size from 4,000 to over 16,000 square kilometres.

Within an ADP, farmers are encouraged to work together in self-help groups called **cooperatives.** The cooperatives are run with the help, advice and support of the state governments. They offer the loans, subsidies, services and trained experts needed by the farmers. The kind of assistance given by the Government through the ADPs is shown on fig 26.

The effect of Government action is being seen now in improving production in the ADP areas, but there is still a long way to go. For example, in 1984 there was still only one fieldworker for every 2,500 farms, compared with India's figure of one for every 200 farms.

The ADPs are not the only help the Government gives.
There is:
● agricultural education
● the bringing in of foreign experts and the training of agricultural fieldworkers
● the setting up of model farms
● encouragement of large scale farms partly by foreign investment
● spending on large projects like irrigation, drainage schemes, and new rural roads

Government action effects farm decisions very strongly. It also produces agricultural change.

Activity B

1 How fast will agriculture need to grow if Nigeria is to solve its food problem in the next five years?

2 Why is this rate of growth unlikely?

3 What is an ADP?

4 How does an ADP help improve farms?

5 What are the other two main tasks of an ADP?

Practical work. Design a poster which could be used to encourage traditional farmers to think about how to improve their production. Remember that many of them may not be able to read.

fig 26 One solution of the Nigerian Government

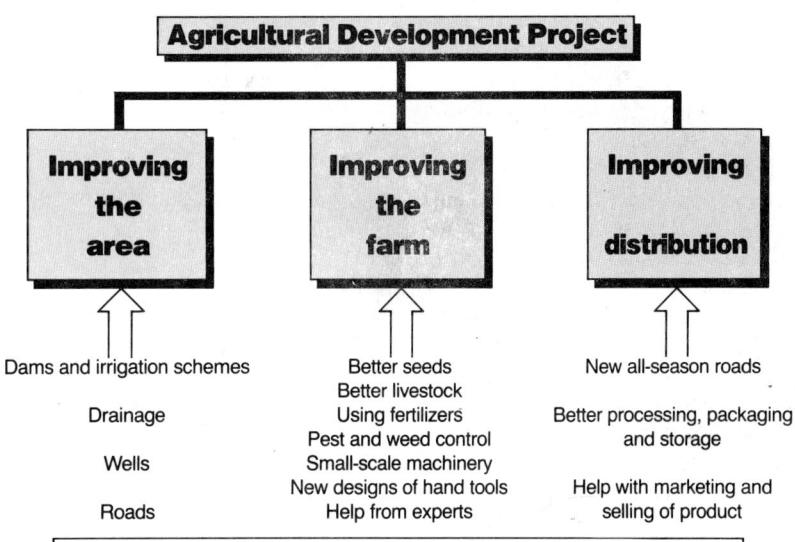

Effects of one ADP in Kaduna State on crop yields

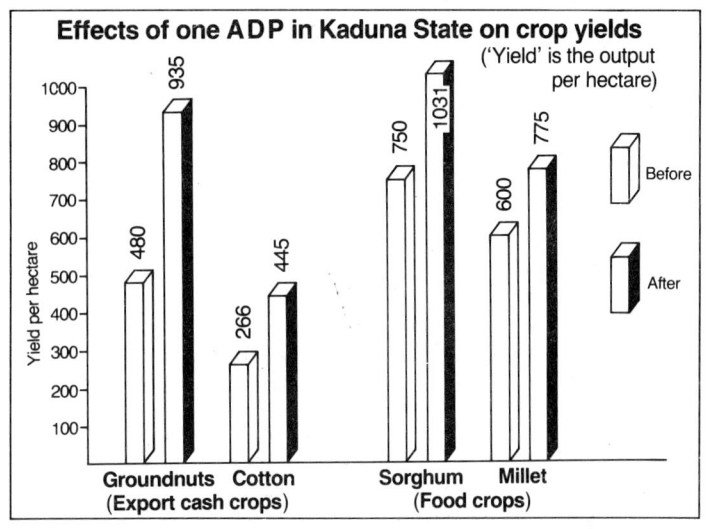

Unforeseen Impacts

Primary activities like farming, forestry and fishing affect the environment in many ways; any change in them has an impact on the environment. Some **environmental impacts** are intended and some are unforeseen. For instance:

- new fishing boats and nets in Minakuppam, India, increased production, but reduced local fish stocks (page 30)
- the Bakolori Dam in north Nigeria helped increase the amount of irrigated land near the dam, but led to losses for farmers further downstream (page 34)
- clearing forests to make new farmland can increase food production, but it sometimes leads to soil erosion (page 32)

Such impacts affect the use people can make of the land today and in the future. As the world population continues to grow it is important that the land is used carefully. It needs to be **conserved** for future generations.

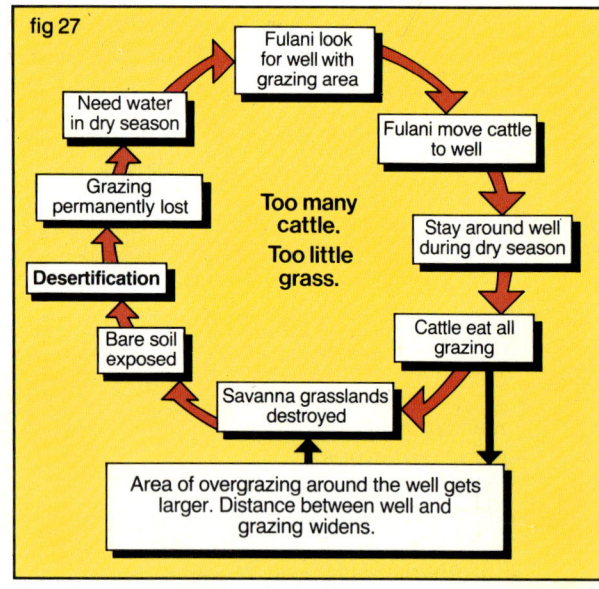

fig 27

Fulani look for well with grazing area → Fulani move cattle to well → Stay around well during dry season → Cattle eat all grazing → Savanna grasslands destroyed → Area of overgrazing around the well gets larger. Distance between well and grazing widens. → Bare soil exposed → Desertification → Grazing permanently lost → Need water in dry season → (back to start)

Too many cattle. Too little grass.

The Fulani nomads in northern Nigeria graze their cattle on the edge of desert land. Where too many cattle are kept overgrazing may destroy the grassland. The bare soil suffers soil erosion. This can turn the land into desert: this is called **desertification** (see fig 27).

photo 14: Salination

photo 15: Desertification

In northwest India farmers **irrigate** the land: they add water to it because there is so little rain. The hot sun draws up water from the soil. When the water evaporates it leaves behind dissolved materials from the soil; these form a salty layer. This salty layer makes the soil useless: this is called **salination**. It can only be prevented if the farmers ensure that the soil is kept continually damp and drain it carefully.

Activity A

1 Look at fig 27 and describe the impact that it shows.

2 Look at photo 14 and try to draw a circle diagram to show this different environmental impact.

3 Add the words environmental impact, conserved, desertification, and salination to your dictionary.

fig 28

Some impacts of farming, forestry and fishing on the environment

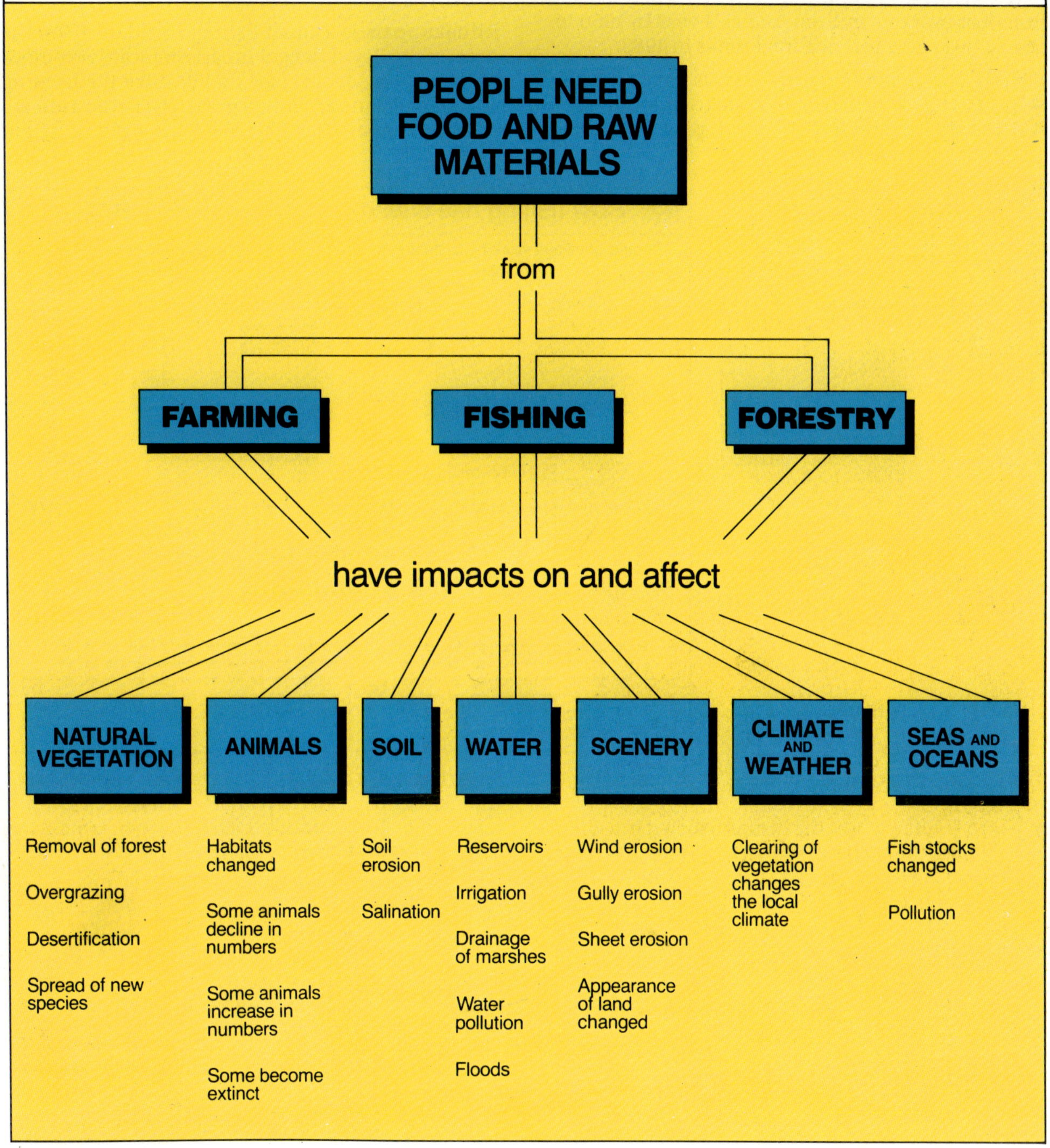

PEOPLE NEED FOOD AND RAW MATERIALS

from

FARMING   **FISHING**   **FORESTRY**

have impacts on and affect

NATURAL VEGETATION	ANIMALS	SOIL	WATER	SCENERY	CLIMATE AND WEATHER	SEAS AND OCEANS
Removal of forest	Habitats changed	Soil erosion	Reservoirs	Wind erosion	Clearing of vegetation changes the local climate	Fish stocks changed
Overgrazing	Some animals decline in numbers	Salination	Irrigation	Gully erosion		Pollution
Desertification	Some animals increase in numbers		Drainage of marshes	Sheet erosion		
Spread of new species	Some become extinct		Water pollution	Appearance of land changed		
			Floods			

There are many more environmental impacts of farming, forestry and fishing than the ones we have just seen. These impacts affect a variety of different areas, fig 28 shows some of them: they can occur in any part of the world and in any country, no matter what its stage of development.

Activity B

1 Make a detailed careful copy of fig 28.
2 Add to it any other examples of environmental impacts you have come across in your work so far.

Fishing and Change

Fishing gives an extra source of food for many people living in villages around the coast of India.

Although much of the fishing is still done in the traditional village ways, the amount caught has risen from just over one million tonnes a year in 1960 to nearly two and a half million tonnes in 1982.

Fishing is like farming in some ways, they both are

- **primary** activities collecting natural products
- **subsistence** activities in developing countries, supporting local villages

- showing large increases in production
- undergoing **change** as traditional methods are slowly being replaced by modern ones
- becoming much more **commercial**

Minakuppam is a small fishing community on the coast of the Bay of Bengal in eastern India, very close to the city of Madras (see fig 29). Like the farming village of Palanpur, (see page 24), the fishing village of Minakuppam has had many changes in recent years.

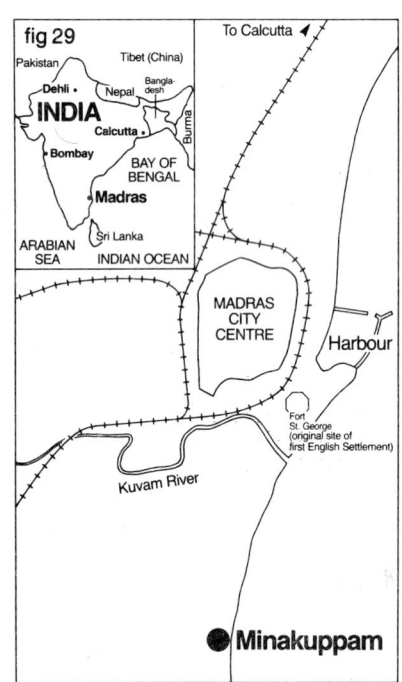

fig 29

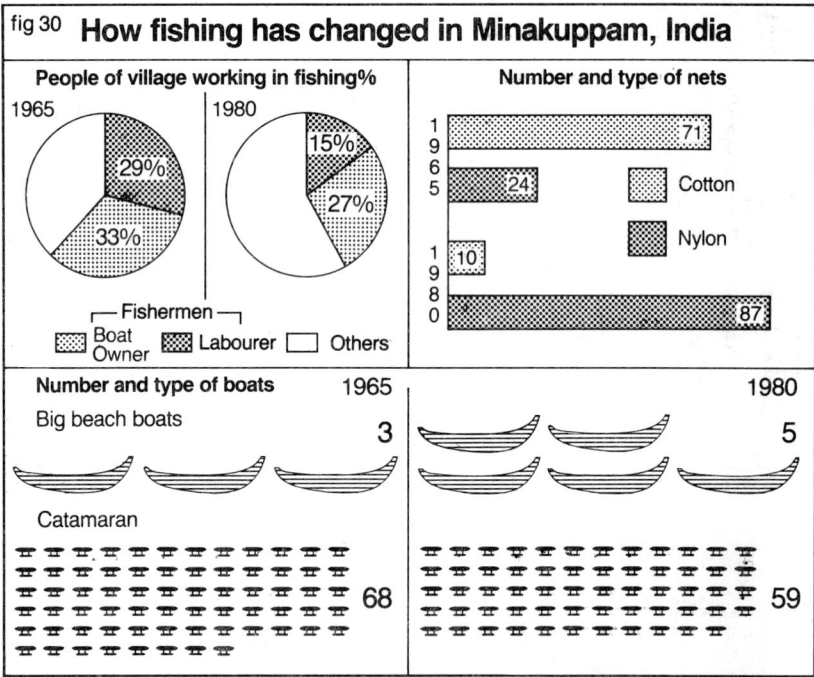

fig 30 **How fishing has changed in Minakuppam, India**

Fishing in Minakuppam is done in different ways (see fig 31):

- **beach seining** where the nets are carried in a wide circle from the beach in a large open boat paddled by up to 15 people. The net is hauled in by up to 15 more people on the shore. It is done for about six months when the sea is very calm
- **purse seining** used to be done by four or five fishermen on two log catamarans. One catamaran is paddled in a wide circle back to the other so the net forms a trap or 'purse' for the fish when it is pulled in to the boats
- **gill netting** needs only one catamaran and two fishermen. The net is cast from the catamaran and hauled in after the fish have swum into it and been trapped by their gills

Recent changes have affected fishing in Minakuppam greatly. The first is the type of boats. Modern small trawlers with diesel engines and winches (to pull in the nets) can cover much wider areas and catch a lot more.

However, these boats cannot be kept on the open beach at Minakuppam, and need the sheltered harbour on the north side of Madras. Some village fishermen now work on these boats and get a fixed

wage instead of a share of the catch. However, most of the fishing trips are still short, although a few are overnight. They mainly catch prawns which are processed and frozen in Madras for export.

The other main change is the use of nylon nets replacing cotton ones. They are stronger, last longer, and make fishing easier so that it needs fewer workers.

There are fewer job opportunities for those fishermen who do not own their own equipment, and fewer catamarans are needed. As Madras has expanded, the village has been swallowed up by suburban expansion, and many of the fishing community work in the city.

Activity A

1 Why is fishing called a primary activity?

2 **Either** describe the fishing methods used by the villagers of Minakuppam; **or** draw labelled diagrams to show how they fish.

3 Look at fig 30. Write about the recent changes which have affected fishing in Minakuppam under the headings of: **a** occupations, **b** nets, and **c** boats.

Fishing methods in villages like Minakuppam

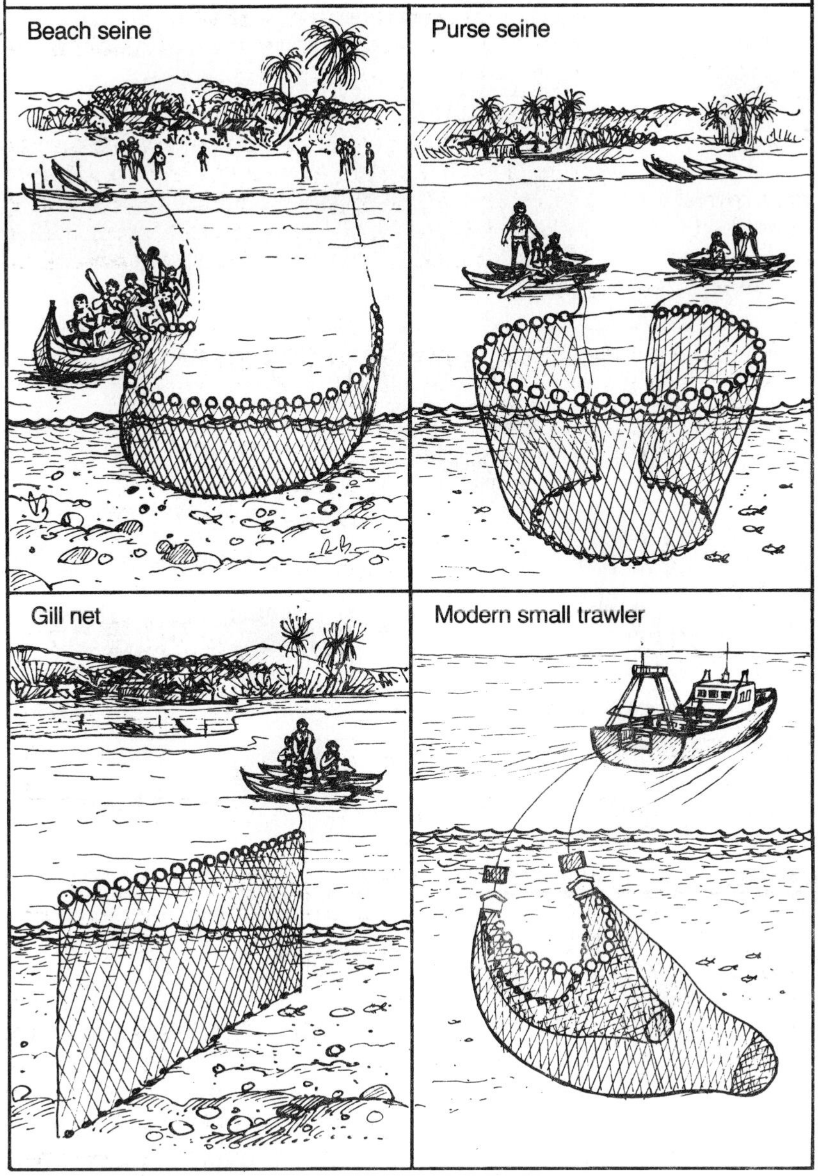

fig 31

Beach seine

Purse seine

Gill net

Modern small trawler

Fishing is important to the Japanese economy. It is an island nation with very limited amounts of farmland to feed its people. Japan's yearly catch in 1982 was 11.4 million tonnes, nearly five times as much as India. Nearly half a million people work in activities concerned with fishing.

The industry is highly organised, efficient, and uses the benefits of modern technology. It is so advanced that there is important 'fish farming' or **aquaculture** both in marine and inland waters.

Japan's fishing in 1982

Fishing boats	
Total number	445,000
motorised	415,000
(small vessels under 5 tonnes	380,000)
(large vessels over 200 tonnes	2,000)
not motorised	30,000

Fish caught	
Marine	
Tuna	347,000 tonnes
Sardine	3,290,000 tonnes
Mackerel	718,000 tonnes
Alaska Pollack	1,567,000 tonnes
Crab	90,000 tonnes
Squid	182,000 tonnes
Aquaculture	
In coastal waters (mainly shellfish)	938,000 tonnes
In inland waters (eels, carp and trout)	219,000 tonnes

Types of fishing	
Deep sea or Pelagic	18%
Offshore	54%
Coastal	18%
Aquaculture	10%

Whaling	
4,987 whales were caught	

Japan is the world's largest fishing nation and its vessels sail every ocean. Fish are caught as far away as the North Atlantic and Antarctica; however, over 75 per cent of the fish is caught in Japan's home waters.

Eating fish and shellfish is such an important feature of the Japanese way of life that it makes up nearly half of all animal protein eaten, about 100 grammes per person per day on average.

Japan imports fish from abroad. In 1982, this amounted to 1.2 million tonnes of which shrimps were 33 per cent, salmon and trout 10 per cent, tuna and swordfish 8 per cent. Others included squid, crab and octopus.

Activity B

1 Use the table to design a large wall chart picturing Japan's fishing industry by different graphs.
2 What is **aquaculture**?
3 With the help of your atlas, draw a small sketch map of Japan's home and nearby fishing waters, naming the seas where 75 per cent of the catch is made.
4 In about 100 words, explain how important the fishing industry is to Japan.
5 Add any new words to your dictionary of geography.

photo 16: Trawler, Japan

Soil Erosion

The unforeseen results of farming may include the removal or destruction of the soil. The diagrams and photos show examples of this **soil erosion.** It can make the land useless to farmers.

Soil can be destroyed in the following way:

- where the vegetation (such as trees or crops) is removed, the soil is not protected from the weather. Rain can blow or wash away the top soil which contains most of the plant foods
- without the top soil the land becomes useless to the farmer. The sub-soil left behind cannot support plants
- the top soil may be blown or washed into other areas, where it may even cause a hazard

The elements of nature work in a delicately balanced system, where this system is upset soil erosion can be the result. Soil erosion is likely in the following situations:

- where there is a low or variable rainfall e.g. the Great Plains, USA
- where the results of agriculture change are not foreseen e.g. Bakolori Dam project, Nigeria
- where there is heavy population pressure and the land is over-used by farmers

Soil erosion need not happen: if the land is farmed with appropriate methods the soil need not be damaged.

Activity

1 Look at fig 32. List the ways that vegetation cover may be removed from the land by farming and forestry.

2 Draw simple sketches of the photos and label them with the type of soil erosion that they show.

3 List the effects on the environment outside the area where the vegetation is removed.

4 Can you think of several ways in which natural vegetation protects the soil and helps maintain soil fertility? Describe what they are.

photo 17

photo 18

photo 19

fig 32

Soil erosion

Bare soil is exposed by the removal of vegetation:

OVERGRAZING DEFORESTATION SOIL EXHAUSTION POOR FARMING METHODS

The exposed soil is affected by normal weathering, but as there is no cover it is speeded up, to result in soil erosion:

WIND EROSION soil blown away SHEET WASH Rain washes top soil away GULLY EROSION Increased water in stream gives it power to cut deeply into soft rocks

The effects are not only felt in the area of erosion:

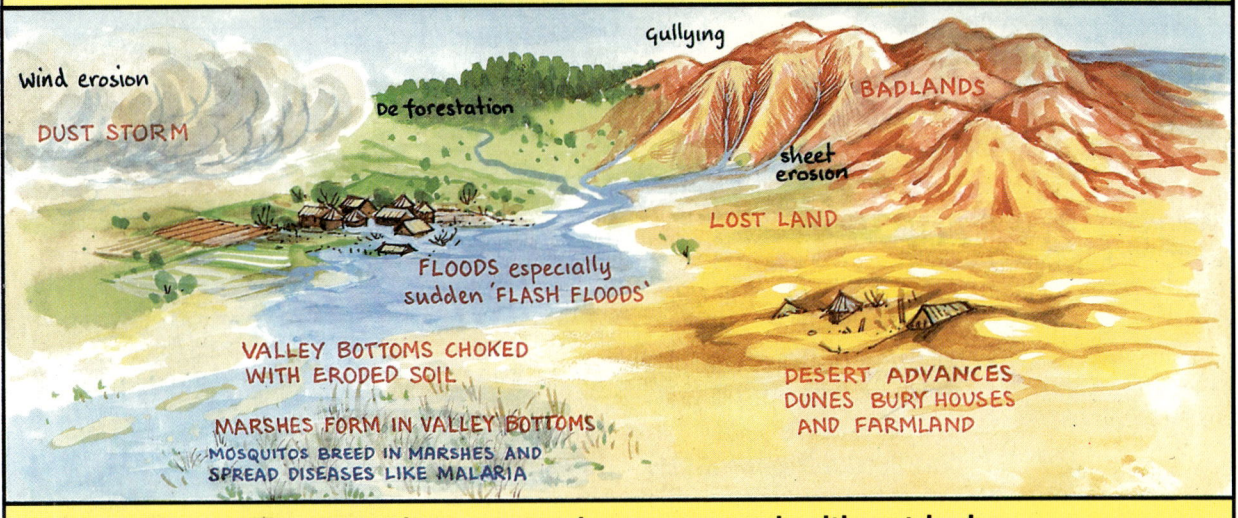

Wind erosion DUST STORM Deforestation Gullying BADLANDS sheet erosion LOST LAND FLOODS especially sudden 'FLASH FLOODS' VALLEY BOTTOMS CHOKED WITH ERODED SOIL MARSHES FORM IN VALLEY BOTTOMS MOSQUITOS BREED IN MARSHES AND SPREAD DISEASES LIKE MALARIA DESERT ADVANCES DUNES BURY HOUSES AND FARMLAND

The results cannot be removed without help.

Research task. How can soil erosion be prevented, and the 'lost land' regained? (Clues: shelter belts, contour ploughing, strip cropping, reafforestation, farming techniques)

The Effects of a Dam

The map shows the location of two dams in Nigeria.

One is the large-scale project on the river Niger at Kainji. The second is the more recent one at Bakolori on the Sokoto river in the far northwest.

The Bakolori dam is in the Sokoto valley. Before the dam was built farming used to be very closely related to the climate. It is in a tropical savanna region, with warm dry winters and hot wet summers, even so, the yearly total of rainfall is only moderate and some is lost due to evaporation.

Farms are mainly of the intensive, peasant, arable type. There was a type of farming here that made the best use of the moderate water supply from rainfall and the summer floods of the river. Two types of crop-growing were practised:

- on the dry, unflooded land above the river floodplain, food crops like millet and sorghums were grown by traditional peasant methods once a year
- on the lowest riverside plains which became flooded, there was **double-cropping**. First, in the wet season flooding, rice was grown. Then in the following dry season when the soils were still damp, cassava and cash crops

(like cotton, groundnuts as well as others) are grown. This system is known as **fadama**

Fishing is a traditional activity along the Sokoto river too. About one in 20 of the 50,000 people living in the villages of this area were engaged in fishing. They fished for Nile perch, Tigerfish, Trunkfish and Catfish. This was usually done in the drying pools of the floodplain in the winter dry season.

The Bakolori dam was built here and completed in 1978 to control the flooding. The irrigation scheme (to use the reservoir water and expand the agricultural production of the valley) was finished in 1984.

The building of the whole scheme changed the agriculture of the area, but had effects on the environment that were quite unforeseen and accidental.

fig 33

Sokoto

Area of Bakolori Dam Project

• Kano

Lake Chad

R. Rima

NIGERIA

Kainji Reservoir

Kainji Dam

R. Niger

R. Benue

Lagos

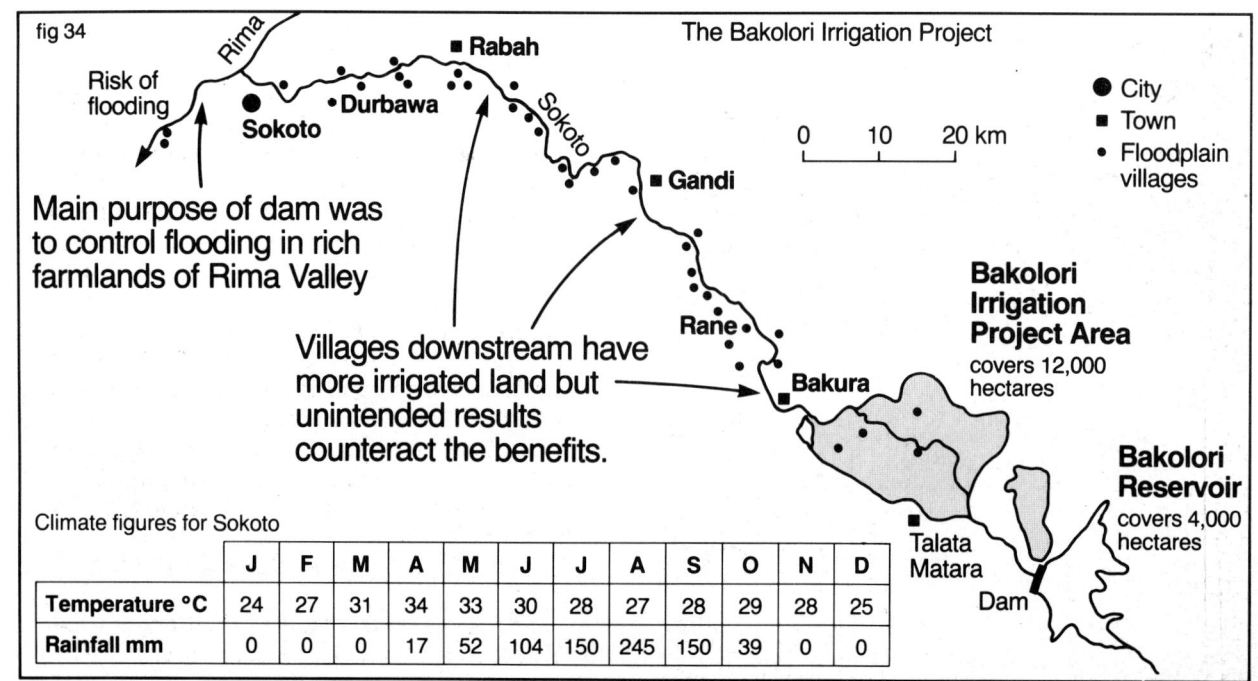

fig 34

The Bakolori Irrigation Project

Risk of flooding

Rima

■ Rabah

• Durbawa

● Sokoto

Sokoto

■ Gandi

Rane •

■ Bakura

Talata Matara

Dam

Main purpose of dam was to control flooding in rich farmlands of Rima Valley

Villages downstream have more irrigated land but unintended results counteract the benefits.

			● City
0	10	20 km	■ Town
			• Floodplain villages

Bakolori Irrigation Project Area
covers 12,000 hectares

Bakolori Reservoir
covers 4,000 hectares

Climate figures for Sokoto

	J	F	M	A	M	J	J	A	S	O	N	D
Temperature °C	24	27	31	34	33	30	28	27	28	29	28	25
Rainfall mm	0	0	0	17	52	104	150	245	150	39	0	0

The Bakolori irrigation project

fig 35

	Intended results	Actual results
Scheme	Irrigation of 30,000 hectares	Irrigation completed but cost of project 25% more than predicted
	Expansion of commercial farming for sugar and tomatoes	
	Loss of some farm land flooded by reservoir	Very high resettlement costs of people displaced by flooding
	Reservoir fishing to replace traditional river fishing	Virtually none created
	Water storage for dry season farming	Possible health hazard (as at Kainji Dam)
Downstream	Increased range of crops	Decreasing range of crops as fadama plots no longer naturally flooded (less rice, yams, cassava, tomato, peppers, tobacco and onions)
	Control of downstream flooding near Sokoto to increase rice production	Flooding reduced so much that rice can no longer be grown
	Irrigation water would replace natural flood water so there would be no loss of crop production	Supply of irrigation water does not make up for loss of natural flood water. Production of wet season crops severely reduced
	Loss of downstream fishing made up by fishing in new reservoir	Fishing declined in all villages, and stopped all together in some. Not made up for by new fishing in reservoir
General Benefits	Redevelopment of the economy of Sokoto valley	Downstream effects outweigh predicted benefits

The Bakolori project should have brought major benefits to the whole Sokoto valley region. These were to be in the new irrigation areas, and in the farming areas on the floodplain downstream as far as the town of Sokoto itself.

As in many development projects, the results were not entirely what was planned. The results are shown in fig 35.

Certainly the project did provide a 30,000 hectare irrigation area.

However, in the downstream areas the project has had unfortunate effects:

● it reduced the size of the wet season floods on which the system of fadama cultivation depended

● this meant that the rice and cash crops could not be grown in the same way

● this meant a change to the poorer food crops instead like millet and sorghums in the wet season

● there was a reduction in the production levels of dry season crops too

● fish numbers fell and fishing decreased greatly

The villagers downstream were not able to produce as much as before the dam was built.

The project might not have gone ahead at all if the losses of production had been realised at the start.

photo 20: Dam, Nigeria

Activity

1 Use your atlas to find the latitude and longitude of the town of Sokoto.

2 How far is it in kilometres from Lagos, Kano and the Tropic of Cancer?

3 Which main river does the water of the Sokoto river eventually join?

4 Use the statistics in fig 34 to draw a climate graph for Sokoto. Describe the climate by labelling your graph.

5 Outline in a few sentences the types of traditional farming in the Sokoto valley before the dam at Bakolori was built.

6 Find out what the crops of cassava and sorghums are like and what they are used for.

7 What were the unintended results of the Bakolori dam?

8 How were the villagers downstream affected by it?

9 Add to your dictionary of geography the words: fadama and double-cropping.

Hidden Treasures

Manufacturing industry is a **secondary** activity. It relies on primary activities because it needs raw materials.

Some of these are provided by agriculture and forestry. Many, however, are obtained from the rocks of the earth's crust. These are **mineral resources.**

A **mineral** is a non-living substance found in nature, which has specific and unique properties depending on its chemical composition. Rocks are made up of minerals. Only a small proportion are useful or valuable enough to be mined or quarried.

At different times in our history different minerals have been useful. The variety of minerals useful to people in the Stone Age were very different from all those that are now useful to people in the Space Age. Some like silica, have been used at all ages.

In order to be used in manufacturing, these useful minerals have to be extracted from the rocks of the earth. The photos on this page show three examples of minerals being mined: like agriculture and forestry, this is a **primary activity.**

Activity A

1 Describe, in about 50 words for each, what the photos show.

2 Find out from your local libraries the following two things

a the past and present uses of the following well-known minerals: quartz (or silica), diamond, kaolin, sulphur, galena, cassiterite, bauxite, magnetite, gypsum and halite.

b the following methods of mineral extraction: adit, drift, shaft, pumped well, solution, open-cast, strip, quarrying, hydraulic.

3 You might like to start a collection of minerals and build up a record of details about them.

photo 21: Limestone quarry, United Kingdom

photo 22: Gold mining, South Africa

photo 23: Coal mining, Nigeria

The minerals which are extracted from the earth are in many different forms. Only rarely are they pure enough naturally to be used without some form of initial processing. The industries which use them are often not nearby.

As a result, mining (like other primary activities) depends on a system of supporting services of tertiary activity to work. It relies on an international system of business organisations, transport and trade.

This is so because:
● minerals can be found anywhere, from the cold, barren wastelands of the Arctic Tundra to the depths of the ocean floors; and on the whole, they are not used where they are found
● minerals will only be worked where their value in quantity and quality outweighs the cost of extracting and transporting them; the more hostile the region, the more value they must have before they will be worked

However, not all minerals are **resources**:
● they only become potential resources when a use for them is discovered and they are located
● when they are found, they may not be exploited at once; the richer, more accessible and easily worked sites are mined first
● exploitation may have to wait until the technology is developed to extract them
● as mining methods improve, the more difficult and lower grade sites will be used as the richer ones run out; any that are not yet mined are known as **reserves**

Fig 36 shows some examples of the wide range of minerals that we use. But at any mine they will in the end run out: they are **exhaustible or finite resources.**
The mining industry is one which sees the continuing decline of some sites and the need continually to open up new ones.

fig 36 Use	Industries	Nature of material	Examples of minerals (in italic) and mining products
Construction	building	building blocks	rocks for building blocks
	building, road making	aggregates	sand, gravel, granite, chippings
	cement, bricks, tiles, plaster	processed materials	limestone, clay, *gypsum*
Metal working	iron and steel	ferrous metals (contain iron)	iron ores such as *haematite, magnetite, limonite*
	smelting for other metals	non-ferrous metals	other metal ores such as *bauxite, cassiterite, galena, malachite*
Fuel and power	nuclear power	inorganic minerals	*pitchblende* (uranium ore)
	electricity, domestic heating, gas, industrial furnaces, oil refining	organically formed (from animals and plants)	peat, lignite, coal, anthracite, petroleum (oil), natural gas
Chemicals	heavy industry: chemicals, fertilizers, drugs, cosmetics, paints	inorganic minerals	*anhydrite, halite, nitrates, potash, sulphur, barytes*
	fertilizers, synthetic fibres, plastics, drugs, cosmetics, paints	organically formed	petroleum (oil), natural gas, coal
Precious materials	jewellery, currency	metallic	*gold, silver, platinum*
	jewellery, objets d'art	non-metallic	*jet, diamonds,* other gems such as *topaz, garnet, ruby, amethyst*
Other industries	abrasives, fluxes, ceramics, glass	to make industrial processes	*silica, corundum, diamonds, fluorspar, kaolin, felspar*
	pottery, glass, salt, cosmetics	consumer products	*silica, kaolin, felspar, halite, talc*

Since the distribution of minerals is governed by geology, it is not related to the pattern of countries. Every country has its own mineral resource base depending on what is found within its borders. This partly affects the prospects for industry.

The random or accidental pattern of minerals also promotes trade between countries. This is a further example of the need for all the supporting services without which mineral extraction could not take place.

Activity B
1 Add to your dictionary of geography definitions of these words: mineral, reserves, exhaustible or finite resources.
2 **Group project work** Organise a class exhibition of minerals and mining. You could use the information from a library and produce wall-charts, picture displays, slides, models, and mineral samples (if you have any or can collect some).

Nigeria's Minerals

Nigeria's different minerals are very important to the economy of the country. Fig 37 shows that:

- only a very low percentage of Nigeria's workforce is actually employed in the mining industry
- minerals make up a quarter of the total earnings of the country from all activities
- by far the greatest importance of minerals is that they earn nearly all the country's money from sales abroad; oil alone provides 95 per cent of all Nigeria's export trade

Minerals have earned money for Nigeria for a long time. The three main ones have been coal, tin and oil. At no time have they been as vital as they are now. Coal and tin are no longer produced as much as they were. Oil has become the mainstay of the economy. Nigeria depends almost completely on the money it earns.

Nigeria has many minerals; there are fossil fuels, metal ores, radioactive minerals and non-metallic minerals. Despite this range of types, few of them are of any great importance:

- some are not yet mined at all, such as radioactive uranium and thorium
- some are mined in very tiny quantities, like many of the metal ores
- some are mined only for local uses in many places, such as limestone, marble and sandstone, all for the building industry; and phosphates, pottery clay and glass sand
- columbite mining is very small at 600 tonnes a year but this is 95 per cent of the world total

Fig 38 shows the more important minerals, some of these are declining: tin ore is mined on the Jos Plateau, but since the peak year of 1968 it has fallen in output to under 4,000 tonnes a year.

The hard black coals at Enugu are now well under half their peak level of 1960; less than 300,000 tonnes a year is mined. The coal is not good enough for metal-smelting and is used for the railways and a local chemical industry.

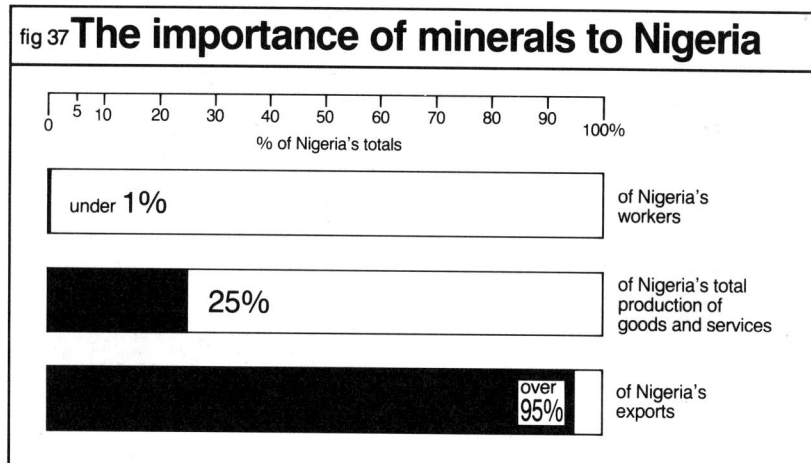

fig 37 **The importance of minerals to Nigeria**

% of Nigeria's totals

under 1% — of Nigeria's workers

25% — of Nigeria's total production of goods and services

over 95% — of Nigeria's exports

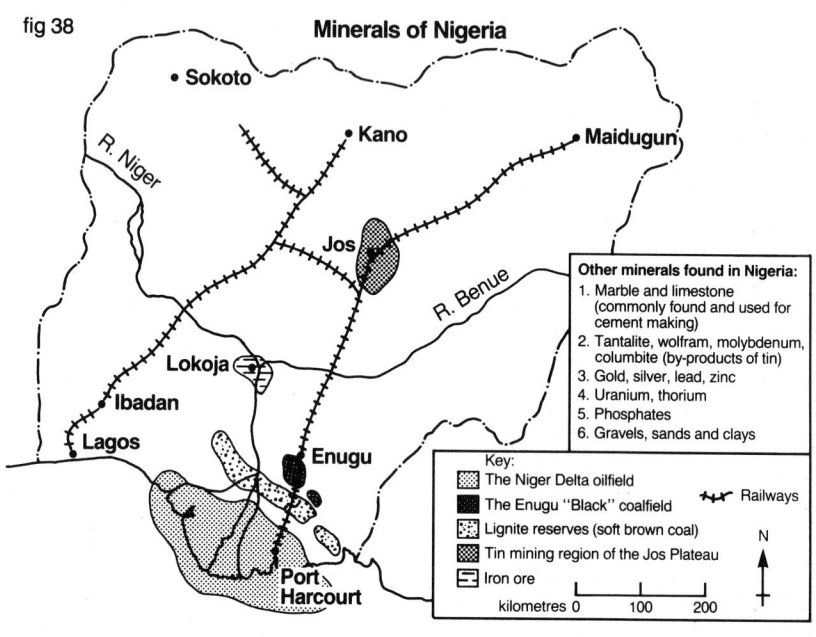

fig 38 — **Minerals of Nigeria**

Other minerals found in Nigeria:
1. Marble and limestone (commonly found and used for cement making)
2. Tantalite, wolfram, molybdenum, columbite (by-products of tin)
3. Gold, silver, lead, zinc
4. Uranium, thorium
5. Phosphates
6. Gravels, sands and clays

Key:
- The Niger Delta oilfield
- The Enugu "Black" coalfield
- Lignite reserves (soft brown coal)
- Tin mining region of the Jos Plateau
- Iron ore
- Railways

kilometres 0   100   200

The lignite (or soft, brown coal) is not yet mined on a large-scale but has large reserves. It is powdery and poor in quality, but it can be used in furnaces and for making chemicals. Iron ores are now being explored and developed as a new steel project gets under way.

Oil of the Niger Delta oilfields is the most important mineral by far. Several multi-national companies as well as a Nigerian state firm are extracting crude oil here, and prospecting for more offshore and in the Benue valley. At present only 15 per cent is refined in Nigeria. Only 2 per cent of the gas found with the oil is used, most is burnt as a waste product.

Nigeria's mineral potential is very large, but at present it is a large exporter of minerals and not really a large user of them. The country does rely on earnings from them rather heavily.

Nigeria's minerals vary in their area of importance:

- some are important only to the local area, such as pottery clay and glass sand
- some have a country-wide value, such as the lignite resources
- some are important in West Africa as a whole, such as coal for the railways in Nigeria and its neighbouring countries
- some such as tin and oil are of world-wide importance

Nigeria's minerals have been of different values at different times. For example, the oil resources shown in fig 39 were not located in large supplies until 1956. By 1965, oil overtook cocoa as Nigeria's leading export. By today, 95 per cent of all exports by value are made up by oil.

Clearly, oil is vital to Nigeria today. But despite its value there are drawbacks: not everyone benefits from the wealth it brings. It can lead to difficulties when:

- high wages are paid to oil-workers
- people from the countryside are attracted to the oil towns
- less food will then be produced
- the richer town dwellers can pay more so that food prices rise quickly
- country dwellers cannot afford the higher food prices
- more people leave for the towns because of growing poverty in the countryside
- even less food is then produced in the rural areas

In this way country dwellers and farm workers actually become poorer. This is why over the last few years, Nigeria has had to spend much of its earnings on an emergency farm development plan called **Feed the Nation.**

There is another problem for a country like Nigeria too. Since it does not have the technology or money to develop expensive mineral reserves, these must be borrowed from more advanced countries: tin on the Jos Plateau was developed during British colonial rule. Much of the oil is being developed by multi-national companies. Some of the profits therefore go to these companies and are lost to Nigeria.

The people of a country do not always benefit from the wealth that mining can create.

photo 24: Oil rig workers, Nigeria

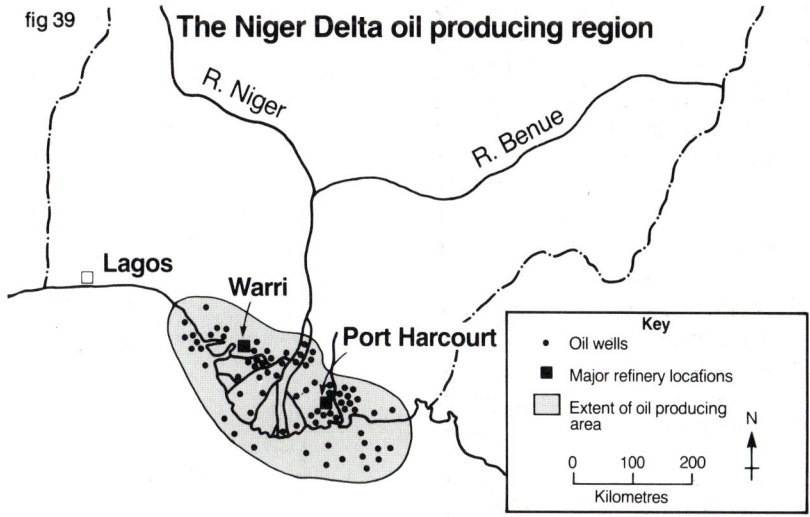

fig 39

The Niger Delta oil producing region

R. Niger

R. Benue

Lagos

Warri

Port Harcourt

Key
- Oil wells
- ■ Major refinery locations
- Extent of oil producing area

0   100   200
Kilometres

N

Activity

1 Look at all the minerals named on these pages. Draw a copy of the following chart and try to fill in each mineral in the correct column:

Fossil fuels	Metal ores	Radioactive minerals	Non-metallic minerals

2 What is mined at the following places: Jos, Lokoja and Enugu?

3 Briefly describe the pattern of minerals shown on the map.

4 What connection do Port Harcourt and Warri have with the mineral industry?

5 In about 100 words, describe why country dwellers and farm workers can become worse off when a large mineral resource is developed.

6 Briefly write down the advantages and disadvantages to Nigeria of allowing multi-national companies to develop some of its oil resources.

7 **Library work.** Try to find out the uses of columbite, molybdenum and phosphates.

South Africa's Minerals

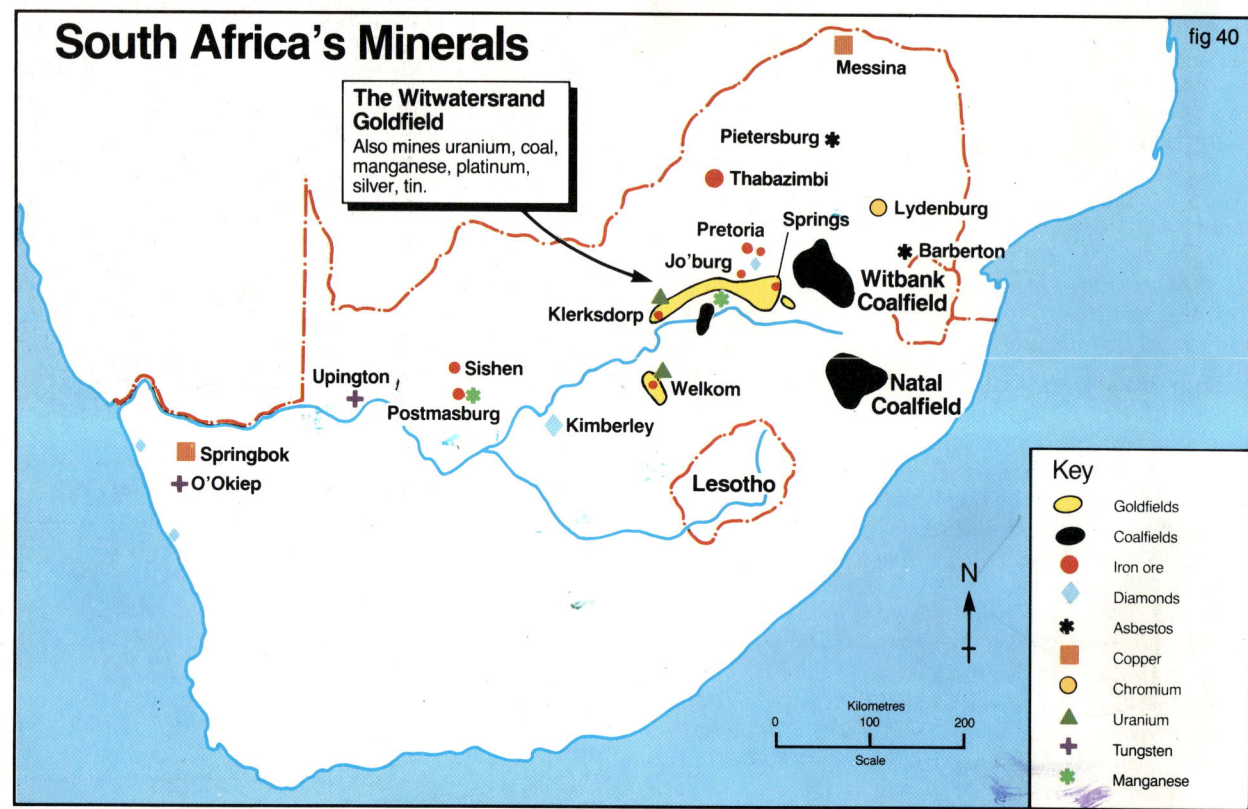

South Africa's development has been mainly the result of its minerals. This country of 26 million people has reserves of almost every commercially valuable mineral, except oil.

It produces nearly a half of all the minerals of the whole continent of Africa.

The pattern of the most important minerals and their locations are shown on fig 40. The importance of these minerals includes:

- nearly 70 per cent of the world's yearly gold output
- massive coal reserves which can last for at least 1,500 years at the present rate
- production of more gem diamonds than any other country
- the world's largest known deposits of platinum, chrome, vanadium, manganese, and fluor spar
- massive cheap open-cast resources of iron ore

Many of the less valuable minerals are not shown on the map. Altogether minerals provide the foundation of the country's wealth.

Minerals have

- earned large amounts of money from exports
- helped to pay for necessary imports of other goods
- kept the country from depending on outside supplies for its growth
- provided raw materials for industrial expansion
- helped maintain high standards of living, at least for the white population

The contrast with Nigeria is very striking. Exploiting its minerals has been the main cause of South Africa's present level of development.

Like most aspects of life in South Africa, the mining activities show the effects of the policy of separate development. The people who provide the labour to mine the wealth do not share much of its benefits. As one example of this, most mining settlements have two very different housing districts: the White town and the Black compound. It is perhaps in the mining settlements that the policy of racial segregation has been most marked.

Activity A

Look at fig 40 and an atlas.
1 Name the following:
a the two main goldfields.
b the sites of iron ore mining.
c two non-ferrous metals.
d the distance from Thabazimbi to Pretoria where there is a large steelworks.
2 Complete a table for South Africa's minerals like the one you did on page 39 for Nigeria.
3 In your atlas, find out the names of the provinces of South Africa. Use them to make a list of the minerals found in each one.
4 What can you now say about the pattern of minerals in South Africa?
5 List four ways that minerals have helped the growth of the country.

photo 25: Raw gold, South Africa

photo 26: Refined gold, South Africa

Among the workers in South Africa's mining industry a high proportion come from other countries in southern Africa. The foreign workers, who are mainly young men, leave their families to live and work in the Republic of South Africa for a fixed period of time. They then return to their home countries. These **migrant** or **guest workers** have to send a proportion of their earnings to their families. Whilst in South Africa, they live in hostels or camps which often are very over-crowded and unpleasant. The men find it difficult to live apart from their families.

Fig 41 shows the countries from which the 350,000 migrant workers came from in 1983. In addition there were probably about one and a half million other foreign workers who had entered the country illegally.

Most of the migrants work in the mining industry where they make up just over 30 per cent of the workforce. The proportion of the mining workers that are migrants has been going down steadily since the 1960s when no less than 60 per cent of the miners were migrants. The reasons for this decline are:

- international hostility to South Africa because of its racial policy
- the desire of South Africa to be independent of foreign workers
- increasing modernisation of the mines reduces the need for cheap labour and reduces the total workforce

Not only do the migrants benefit by earning money and acquiring new consumer goods and services, often at a much higher rate than they could at home, but they also gain new skills. The economy of the countries which border South Africa are dependent on the income from their migrants. Lesotho, for example, could only provide employment for 25,000 of its total labour force in 1983, however 150,000 citizens were employed in South Africa; over 50 per cent of Lesotho's earnings came from migrants working in South Africa.

There is, in addition, movement of workers within South Africa from the rural homelands to the cities and mines. Nearly 800,000 people are involved in this.

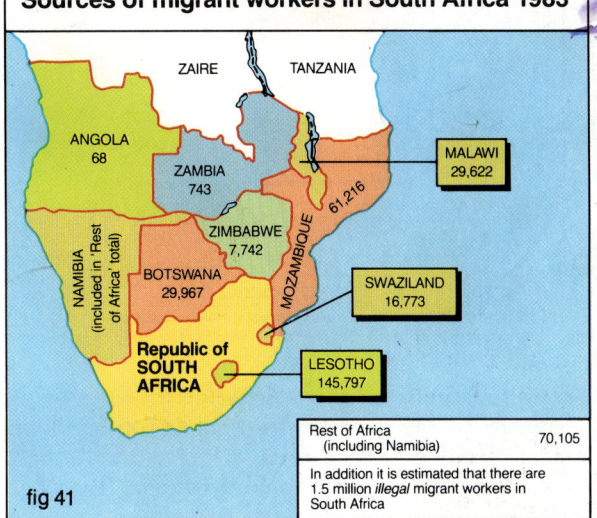

Sources of migrant workers in South Africa 1983

fig 41

ZAIRE TANZANIA

ANGOLA 68

ZAMBIA 743

MALAWI 29,622

61,216

ZIMBABWE 7,742

MOZAMBIQUE

NAMIBIA (included in 'Rest of Africa' total)

BOTSWANA 29,967

SWAZILAND 16,773

Republic of SOUTH AFRICA

LESOTHO 145,797

Rest of Africa (including Namibia) — 70,105

In addition it is estimated that there are 1.5 million *illegal* migrant workers in South Africa

Activity B

1 Use the information on this page to answer these questions:

a why do foreign workers work in South Africa?

b what do they do with a proportion of their earnings?

c where do they live when they are in South Africa?

d what percentage of mine workers are migrant workers?

e has this gone up or down since 1960?

f give three reasons why the proportion has changed.

g how is Lesotho's economy affected by the workers it sends to South Africa?

2 What do you understand by the term 'migrant worker'? Add it to your dictionary of geography.

3 Look at fig 41. Draw a bar graph to show the numbers of migrants to South Africa from each of the countries shown. Colour each bar in the same colour as the country on the map.

The Industrial System

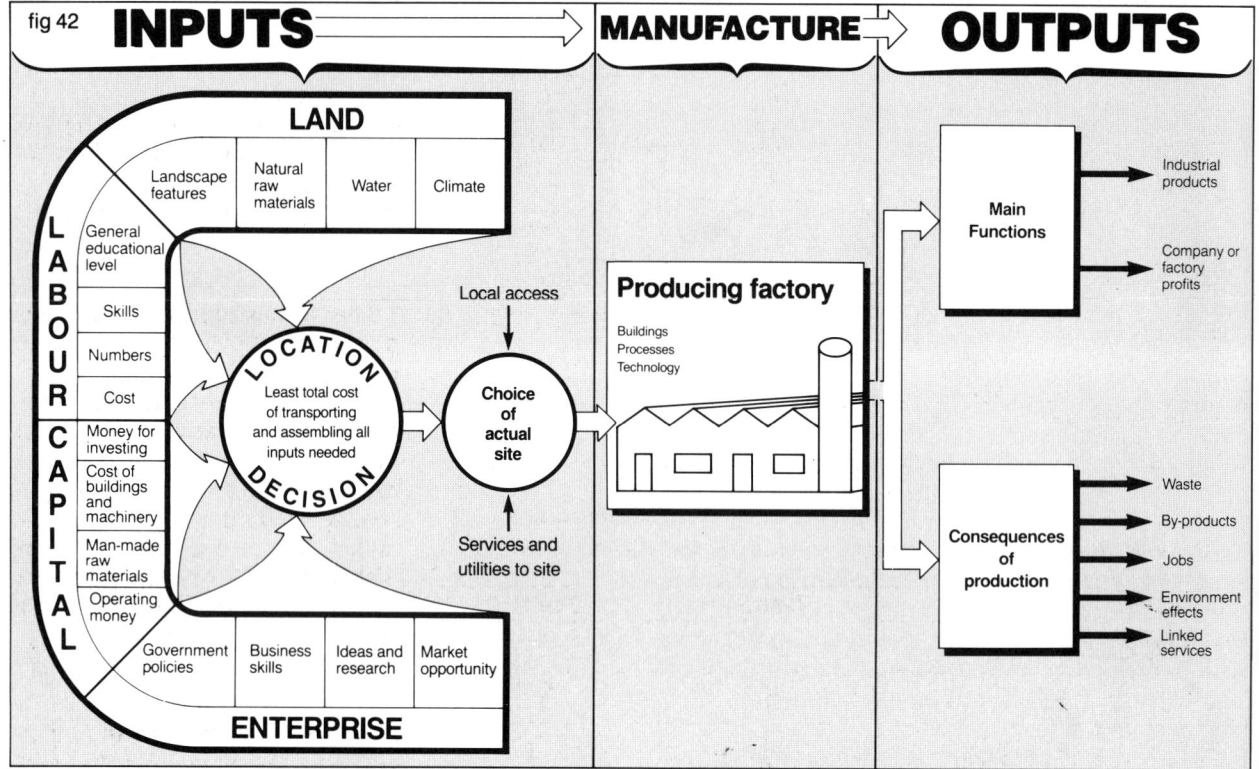

fig 42

INPUTS → **MANUFACTURE** → **OUTPUTS**

INPUTS:

LAND
- Landscape features
- Natural raw materials
- Water
- Climate

LABOUR
- General educational level
- Skills
- Numbers
- Cost

CAPITAL
- Money for investing
- Cost of buildings and machinery
- Man-made raw materials
- Operating money

ENTERPRISE
- Government policies
- Business skills
- Ideas and research
- Market opportunity

LOCATION DECISION — Least total cost of transporting and assembling all inputs needed

Local access → **Choice of actual site** ← Services and utilities to site

MANUFACTURE:

Producing factory — Buildings, Processes, Technology

OUTPUTS:

Main Functions
- Industrial products
- Company or factory profits

Consequences of production
- Waste
- By-products
- Jobs
- Environment effects
- Linked services

Secondary activities use materials from primary activities like farming, fishing and mining. They often take place in factories. A factory can be thought of as a system: it has inputs, components, flows and outputs.

The decision to locate a factory in a place must take account of where all the inputs come from and where all the output will go.

The **inputs** shown in fig 42 can be grouped into:
- **land** natural raw materials, water supply and some other features of the physical environment
- **labour** the numbers, skills and other characteristics of the workforce
- **capital** the money needed to finance all aspects of the setting up and running of the factory
- **enterprise** the business skills needed to develop ideas for products and to manufacture and market them successfully

The **components** are the buildings, equipment, processes and technology which transforms the raw materials into the finished articles.

The **flows** are the actual processes at work as manufacturing occurs, for example the main assembly line in a car plant.

Outputs are not just the products made by the factory but include other things like by-products, waste, jobs for workers and effects on the surrounding environment.

A **location** for a factory is chosen where the total costs of bringing all the inputs together, producing the

goods and distributing the product to the markets, allow the factory to make a profit. When a location is decided, an actual piece of land is selected as the **site** of the factory.

Different factories will have different types of inputs and outputs. In some cases the input of natural raw materials is the most important feature. In other cases other inputs or outputs will be more vital. Three examples of these could be:

- a local supply of skilled specialist workers
- nearness to the market where the outputs are sent
- available buildings, grants and services on a government trading estate or area of assistance

As a result of these different factors, factories in different industries will have different locations. The combination of all these locations leads to **spatial patterns** of industrial regions.

Activity A

1 Draw a large display version of fig 42, replacing the labels with simple sketches of your own or small pictures you may collect.
2 Describe in about 150 words, what your chart tells you about how a factory works.
3 Compare the input/output chart of a factory with that of a farm on page 8. What similarities are there in the inputs and outputs of a farm and a factory?

Changing Locations Exercise

fig 43

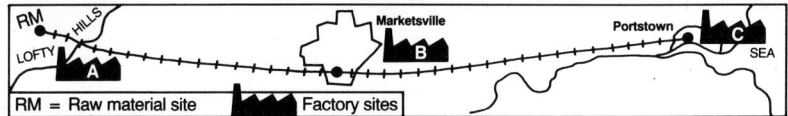

RM = Raw material site   ▲ Factory sites

1   Raw materials come from the Lofty Hills, and the products are sold in the city of Marketsville.

Each cost is cost per tonne	Site A	Site B	Site C
Cost of getting raw material	10	25	35
Cost of other inputs	5	5	5
Cost of production	10	10	10
Cost of distribution of product	10	5	10
Total costs			
Price at market	50	50	50
Profit or loss			

Preferred factory location is at [　　　　　　　]

2   Raw materials from the Lofty Hills are now exhausted. Raw material must be imported through the docks at Portstown.

Each cost is cost per tonne	Site A	Site B	Site C
Cost of getting raw material	35	25	10
Cost of other inputs	5	5	5
Cost of production	10	10	10
Cost of distribution of product	10	10	10
Total costs			
Price at market	50	50	50
Profit or loss			

Preferred factory location is at [　　　　　　　]

Spatial patterns of industry do not stay the same. Over a period of time factories in some locations are closed down and new factories are built in new places. These changes happen because there are changes in:

- the type or source of one or more of the inputs
- the technical processes making up the components of the producing factory
- the size, type or position of the market for the outputs of the factory

Sometimes when inputs and outputs change the factory remains in production at the same location. This is because there are other more important advantages at that place, or it would be too costly to move. The factory may simply change its sources of supply of raw materials or other inputs. It may distribute its products to new or different markets from the same site.

Therefore the pattern of industry in a country may show three types of change as time passes:

- some factories in some places will close down
- factories may be built in new locations
- some factories remain in their original locations, but may change their working arrangements as inputs and outputs alter

photo 27 Bridgend industrial estate, United Kingdom

Activity B

Look at fig 43: it shows a map of an imaginary area. There are plans to build a large, heavy industrial factory in the area. It will use raw materials from the Lofty Hills and sell its products in the city of Marketsville. There are three possible locations which could be used for it.

1   Draw a copy of Chart 1. Work out the total costs of production and the profits or loss at each of the three locations and enter them in your chart.

2   Where would you locate the factory at this stage?
Fill in your answer on your chart.

3   The results of a change in the input of raw materials are shown in Chart 2. Make a copy of this and complete it in the same way.

Study all the information on these two pages.

4   What other changes could happen which would alter the possible location of the factory?
5   Why do some factories remain in the same place even when there are changes in their inputs and outputs?
6   Describe the features shown in the photo.

Minerals and Industry

Some industries make **capital goods:** these are goods which are used in the manufacture of other goods. **Heavy industry** produces capital goods on a large-scale.

A mineral is often one of the raw materials used in heavy industry. Most such industries however, need more than one mineral as a raw material. For example, the iron and steel industry is a heavy industry, it uses three main minerals:

- **coal** which is used to make **coke** as a source of heat and to react with the iron ore
- **iron ore** various types are used since the qualities of the finished steel partly depend on the type of ore
- **limestone** to act as a flux making the iron melt more easily, and to absorb some of the impurities from the ore

The whole process shown can take place at a **raw material assembly** site. If all processes occur at the one place it is known as an **integrated works.** Sometimes the different processes are at different locations, like blast furnaces, steel furnaces, rolling mills, foundries and forges.

All the minerals needed by an iron and steel factory may not be mined at the same place. They have to be **assembled** at the blast furnace. The raw or 'pig' iron is then refined further, with new material inputs, in a steel furnace. Then the raw steel is shaped according to its final use. This production flow from mineral input to manufactured output is shown in fig 44.

An example of heavy industry producing capital goods is the steel industry of India.

fig 44

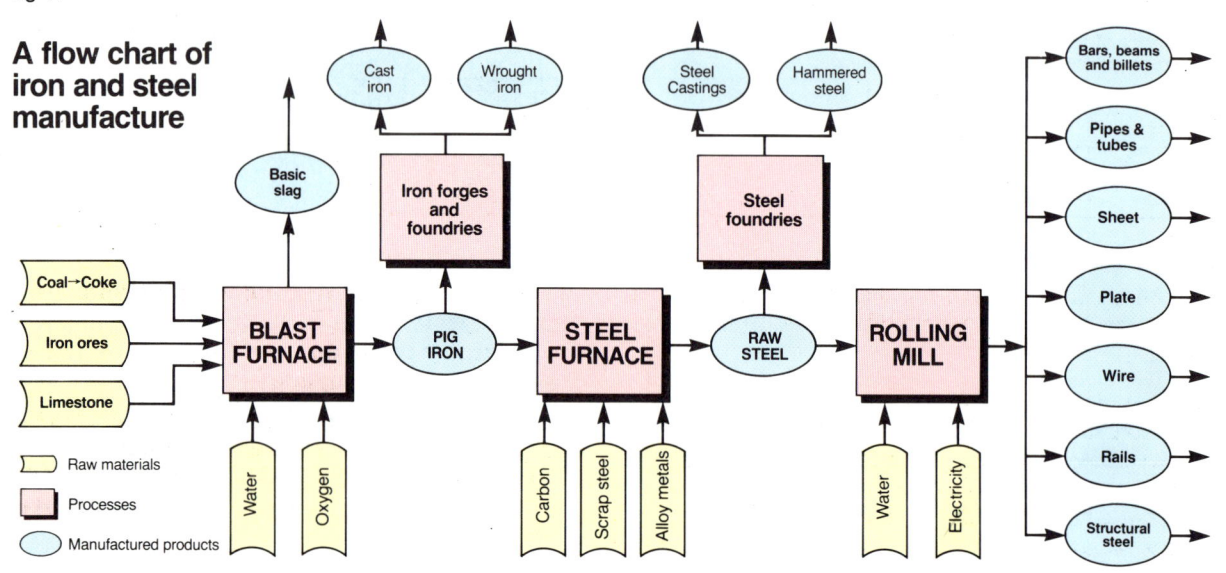

A flow chart of iron and steel manufacture

photo 28: Durgapur steel plant, India

Activity A

Look at fig 44.

1 Draw your own version of iron and steel manufacture.

2 Shade in on your diagram in three different colours the boxes that show inputs, production processes and outputs.

3 Look around your classroom and school and list all things made of steel.

4 Try to find out the properties of steel that make it such a useful material.

5 What disadvantages does steel have compared with modern plastic compounds that are increasingly replacing it?

6 Add the words assembly and integrated works to your dictionary of geography.

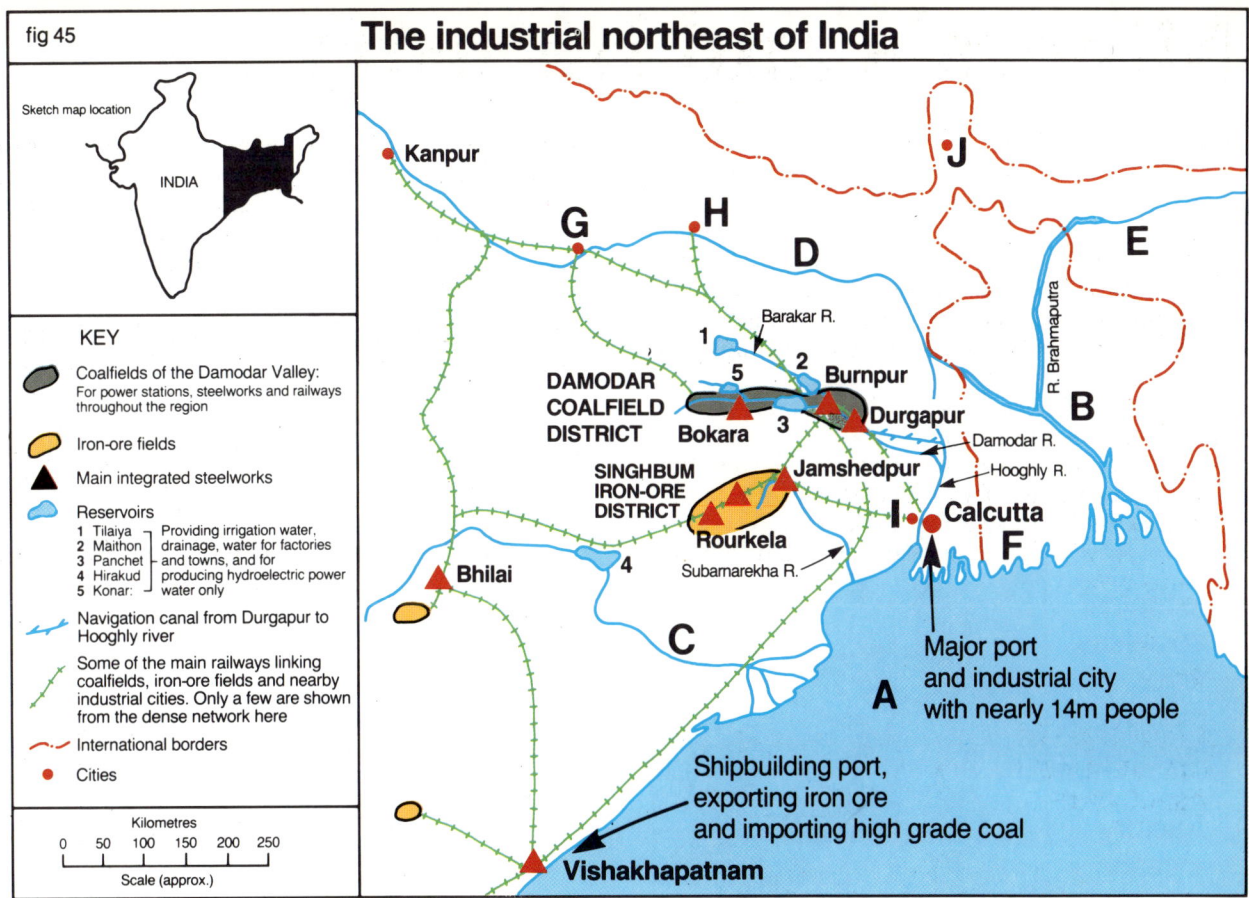

fig 45

The industrial northeast of India

Sketch map location

INDIA

KEY

- Coalfields of the Damodar Valley: For power stations, steelworks and railways throughout the region
- Iron-ore fields
- ▲ Main integrated steelworks
- Reservoirs
  1 Tilaiya ⎫ Providing irrigation water,
  2 Maithon ⎪ drainage, water for factories
  3 Panchet ⎬ and towns, and for
  4 Hirakud ⎪ producing hydroelectric power
  5 Konar: ⎭ water only
- Navigation canal from Durgapur to Hooghly river
- Some of the main railways linking coalfields, iron-ore fields and nearby industrial cities. Only a few are shown from the dense network here
- International borders
- Cities

Kilometres
0 50 100 150 200 250
Scale (approx.)

Kanpur

G H D J E

Barakar R.

1 5 2 Burnpur
DAMODAR COALFIELD DISTRICT Bokara 3 Durgapur
Damodar R.
SINGHBUM IRON-ORE DISTRICT Jamshedpur Hooghly R.
Rourkela I Calcutta
Subarnarekha R. 4 F

R. Brahmaputra

B

Bhilai

C

A

Major port and industrial city with nearly 14m people

Shipbuilding port, exporting iron ore and importing high grade coal

Vishakhapatnam

The photo shows one of India's largest steel plants. In 1984 India was the 15th largest steel producing country in the world (it made about two-thirds of the UK total).

The foremost steelmaking region is found in the east of the country, near to the city of Calcutta. This region can be called the Damodar Region, and its precise location is shown in fig 45. It has six integrated iron and steelworks. Out of India's total of 10.3 million tonnes, these integrated works made 8.7 million tonnes in 1983; the rest came from 147 mini-steel plants spread round the country.

As the map shows steel plants are found in mineral-rich regions, in two kinds of places:

- near **iron-ore resources** as is the earliest plant at Jamshedpur, and Bhilai and Rourkela today
- on **coalfields** as at Durgapur and Burnpur, and now Bokara

The money needed to build the plants was provided by assistance from the USSR, the UK and West Germany.

These steel plants can be called **raw material located** sites; it is particularly easy to assemble all the raw materials in this region because of the dense railway network. Raw material location (especially coal and iron ore) is traditional for steelmaking, and since steel-using industries grow there too, a large steel-making and steel-using integrated works often develops at these sites. However, more recently steelworks have grown up in other types of locations:

- at **low-grade iron ore** sites
- at points of **good transport connections** near a **market** for steel
- at **large coastal ports** where some of the raw materials may be imported

The major new integrated steelmaking works at Vishakhapatnam is such an example. It is not located on any raw material, but it is on a large shipbuilding port and it is well served by communication systems instead.

As the Damodar region shows, basic heavy industries, like steel, have large mineral inputs, and so they are usually located where these can be assembled cheaply. This is not true for all types of manufacturing.

Activity B

Look at fig 45 and your atlas:
1 Find the latitude and longitude of Calcutta.
2 How far is it from the town of Durgapur in the Damodar region?
3 Locate and name the features lettered A-J on the map.
4 Describe in about 75 words, the position of the two steelmaking areas of the Singhbum iron ore district and the Damodar coalfield.
5 From the map, list four reasons why iron and steelmaking grew up in these areas.

Industrial Location

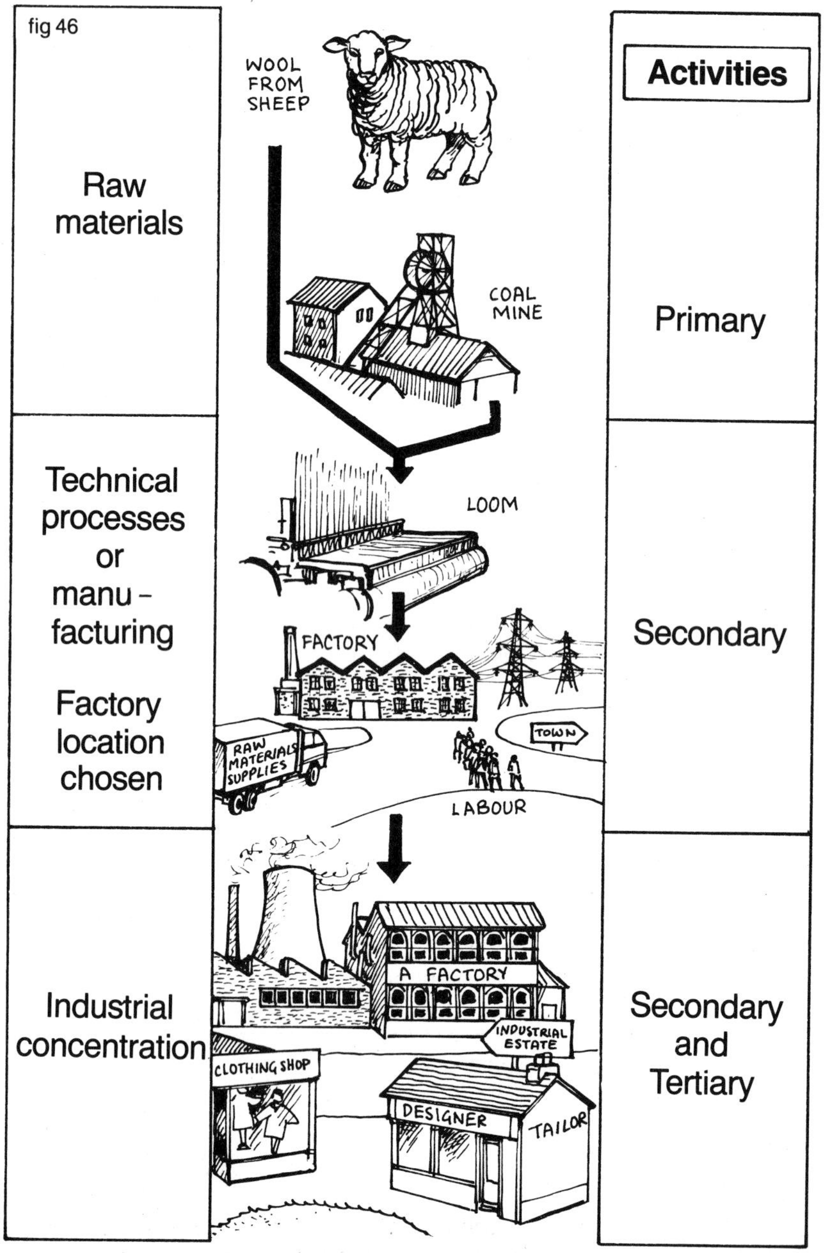

fig 46

		Activities
Raw materials	WOOL FROM SHEEP / COAL MINE	**Primary**
Technical processes or manu-facturing / **Factory location chosen**	LOOM / FACTORY / RAW MATERIALS SUPPLIES / TOWN / LABOUR	**Secondary**
Industrial concentration	A FACTORY / INDUSTRIAL ESTATE / CLOTHING SHOP / DESIGNER / TAILOR	**Secondary and Tertiary**

Manufacturing industries use raw materials which they then change into new products. They need factory space, machinery, power, and workers, as well as a wide range of services. Their output is then sold at the market.

Because raw materials, workers, and markets are not usually in the same place, a **decision** often has to be made as to where to build a factory. As a result **spatial patterns** often develop.

- similar industries choose similar types of places e.g. clothing manufacturing is found in most large cities, while oil-refining is found in deep-water harbours near heavily populated areas
- industrial concentrations grow up because many industries are linked e.g. the product of one factory may supply the raw material to another factory, and many factories may share common services
- some industries are widely dispersed, particularly where they rely on local workers e.g. 'cottage' industries in India are small scale and simple in technology, but require large inputs of labour

There are many ways of classifying manufacturing industry, fig 47 shows one example, based on the type of raw materials used.

photo 29: Aluminium plant near dam, India

photo 30: Kita-kyúshú industrial district, Japan

fig 47	Main material group	Type of resource	Category	Some examples
INDUSTRIAL CLASSIFICATION	Using mainly natural raw materials	Non-renewable exhaustible resources	Products of coal and oil	
			Chemicals	
			Metal refining	
			Bricks, pottery, glass, cement	
		Renewable resources	Food, drink and tobacco	
			Textile yarns	
			Leather and fur	
			Timber products	
			Paper and board	
	Using mainly already processed or man-made raw materials	Uses of already refined metals	Mechanical engineering	
			Instrument engineering	
			Electrical engineering	
			Ships and marine engineering	
			Vehicles	
			Other metal goods	
		Uses of already refined non-metals	Synthetic fibres	
			Textile goods	
			Clothing and footwear	
			Furniture	
			Printing and publishing	

photo 61 Making chicken baskets India

Activity
1 Describe the two different kinds of raw materials that industries use, from fig 47.
2 How does manufacturing change them?
3 List five things it needs to do this.
4 In about 100 words, describe how industrial regions may grow up.

Project work Make a large wallchart copy of fig 47. Fill in these examples :
computer manufacture, oil refining, newspaper publishing, iron and steel, confectionery, tractor making, textbook printing, canning, fruit , car assembly, and fertilizer making.
Add other examples you can think of. Collect pictures of factories and manufacturing to decorate your chart.

Locations

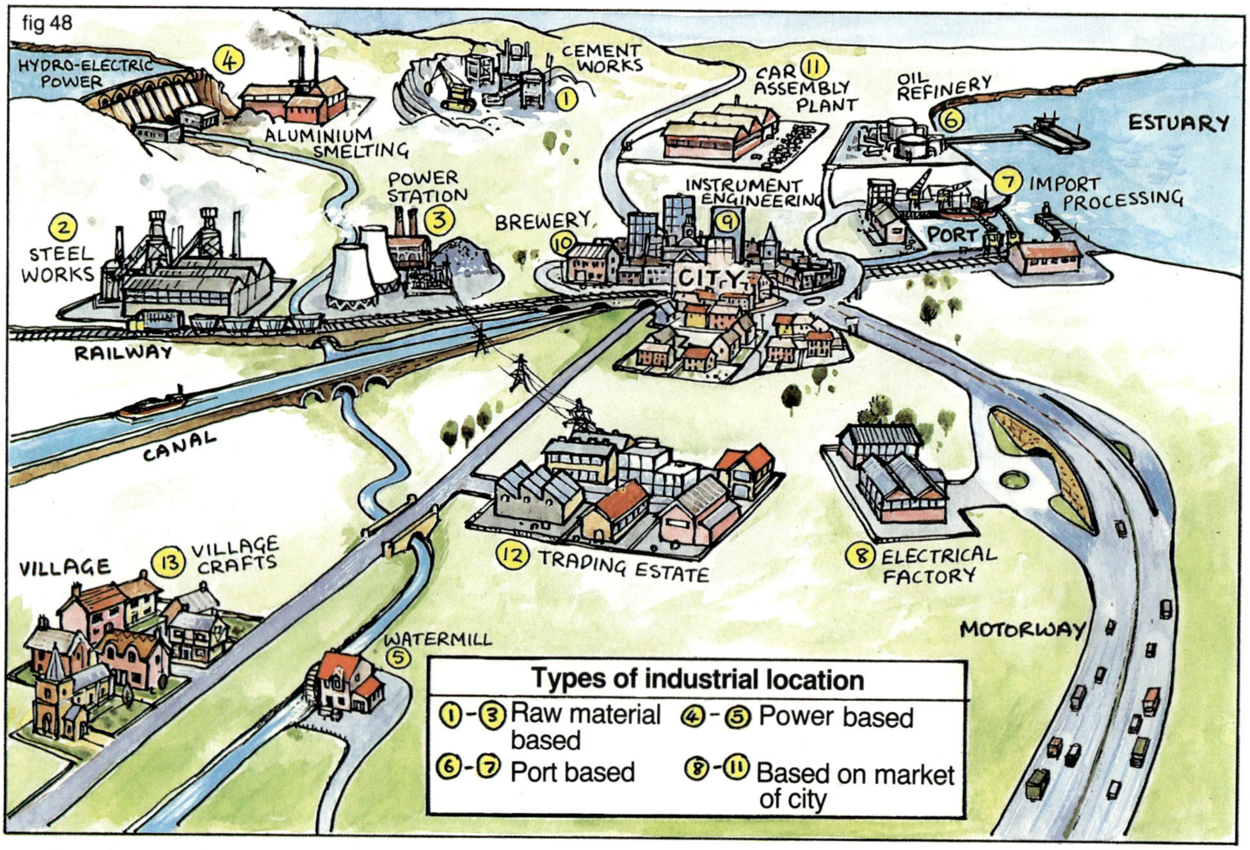

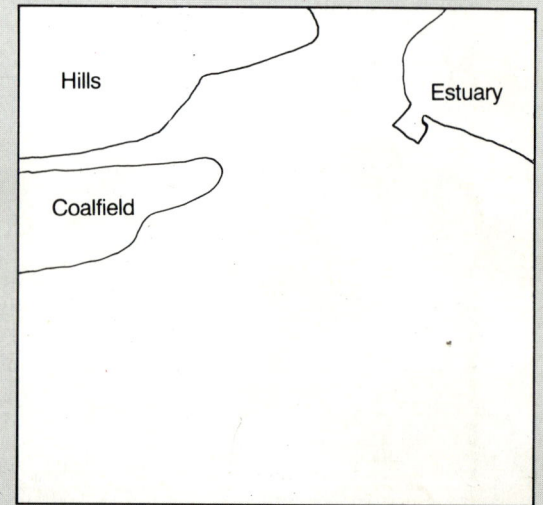

fig 48

Types of industrial location
- ①-③ Raw material based
- ④-⑤ Power based
- ⑥-⑦ Port based
- ⑧-⑪ Based on market of city

All industrial patterns result from the decisions to locate factories at particular places.

Fig 48 is a sketch picture of many different kinds of factory locations:

- **raw material locations** are illustrated by the cement works near a limestone quarry, and the steel works and electricity generating station on a coalfield
- **market locations** are either in a city or populated region, like the instrument engineering factory and the brewery; or on roads nearby, like the car assembly plant
- industries using massive amounts of electricity like aluminium smelting are **power located**
- industries relying on imported raw materials are **port located,** like oil-refining, flour-milling or soap-making
- some industries supply a large market area, and are located where they have good distribution facilities, such as along motorways like the electrical factory *Market located.*
- factories may be located in places where the government offers assistance in the form of grants or facilities, as on a **trading estate**
- **rural locations** are often based on local crafts using local raw materials and skills

The choice of these different locations depends on the type of industry and its various features and needs.

Activity A

1 Make a labelled map of the area drawn in fig 48 to show different types of industrial location. Use this outline as a guide to help you:

Hills

Estuary

Coalfield

2 List the types of locations shown on your map and try to give several examples of each type.

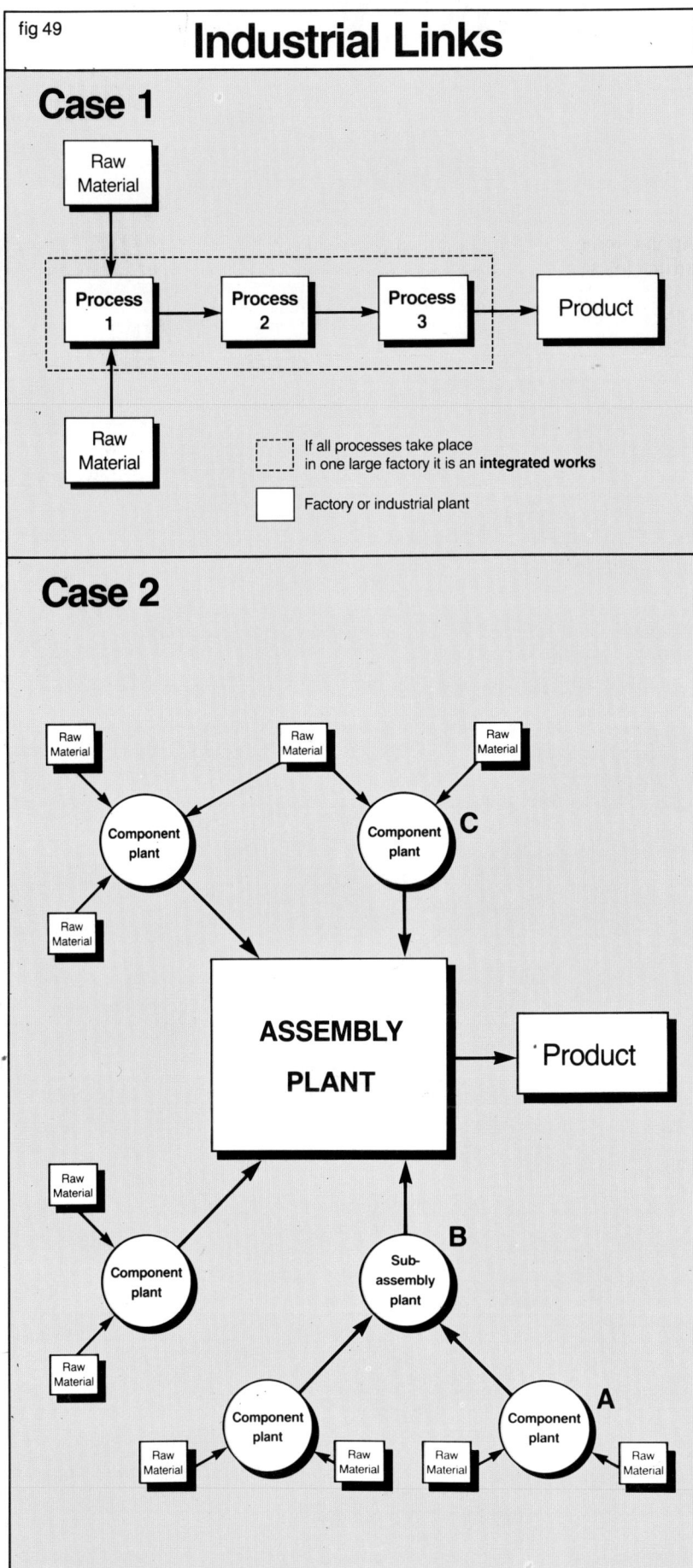

fig 49

Industrial Links

Case 1

Raw Material

Process 1 → Process 2 → Process 3 → Product

Raw Material

If all processes take place in one large factory it is an **integrated works**

Factory or industrial plant

Case 2

Raw Material · Raw Material · Raw Material

Component plant

Component plant **C**

Raw Material

ASSEMBLY PLANT → Product

Raw Material

Component plant

B Sub-assembly plant

Raw Material

Component plant · Raw Material · Raw Material · Component plant **A** · Raw Material

Industries are often concentrated into regions. An important part of the Indian steel industry is clustered in the Damodar Valley. Some individual plants may be in a separate location, such as the new Indian steelworks at Vishakhapatnam. However, firms generally gain advantages by being together: some may need similar services and facilities found in one region; some firms may depend on each other. Fig 49 shows two ways that industries may be organised and linked:

- Case 1 shows a sequence of manufacture starting from the raw materials through a series of processes to give the final product. Each process may take place in a separate factory. Where all these processes take place in one location the factory is an **integrated works.** For example the blast furnace, steel furnace, rolling mill and steel fabrication processes may be all in one big works, or in separate factories in different places
- Case 2 shows a different kind of linkage based on assembly processes, like the car industry. All the factories shown depend very closely upon each other; none of them can work separately from all the others

Concentrations of factories with these linkages are sometimes called regions of **agglomeration.** Some agglomerations specialise in a limited range of activities (like the Damodar Valley in India). Others have a wide number of different types (like the industrial conurbations of Japan).

Activity B

1 Look at the description in the text of Case 1 shown in fig 49. Write your own description of the linkages shown in Case 2 in a similar way.

2 How are factories A, B and C different from each other?

3 Add all new words to your dictionary of geography.

Japan's Car Industry

Japan has very few minerals. It lacks those that are essential for a modern industrial economy and so it has to import large quantities. As a result, the percentages of each which were imported in 1981 were: oil 99.8%; coking coal 83.9%; iron ore 99.7%; copper 96.5%; bauxite 100%; and nickel 100%.

Despite this lack of raw materials, Japan is a major industrial country and some of its industries are growing rapidly (see fig 50).

Most industry is concentrated in the Pacific Belt across the island of Honshu in large industrial conurbations. This pattern of industry has remained the same since the beginning of the Japanese industrial revolution in the 1880s. It is due to two main reasons:

- these are areas of the largest home markets for manufactured goods
- the areas are also close to the most important sheltered harbours, through which the vital imports are brought and exports sent abroad

Japan is now the world's largest manufacturer of cars. This industry is a good example of the distribution of manufacturing in Japan and the modern methods which help account for its success. Fig 51 shows the distribution of the ten major vehicle producing firms; they are plotted in the local government area or **prefecture** in which they are found.

- they are distinctly **clustered** into three main areas
- these clusters are very similar to the overall pattern of industry (shown on the map on page 59)

The main assembly plants buy over 70 per cent of the components they need from outside firms. There are over 8,000 of these, many of which are small, and most of which are found nearby in the same clusters.

fig 50	How Japan's industries have grown		
Item	**1970**	**1982**	**Increase 1970 – 1982**
Tractors No. produced	80,600	197,974	2.5 Times
Calculators No. produced	1,423,000	58,438,000	41 Times
Industrial Robots No. produced	1,660,000	24,782,000	14.9 Times
Computers No. produced	4,636,000	27,540,000	5.9 Times
Cars No. produced	3,179,000	6,882,000	2.2 Times
Watches and Clocks No. produced	495,500	146,232,000	29.5 Times

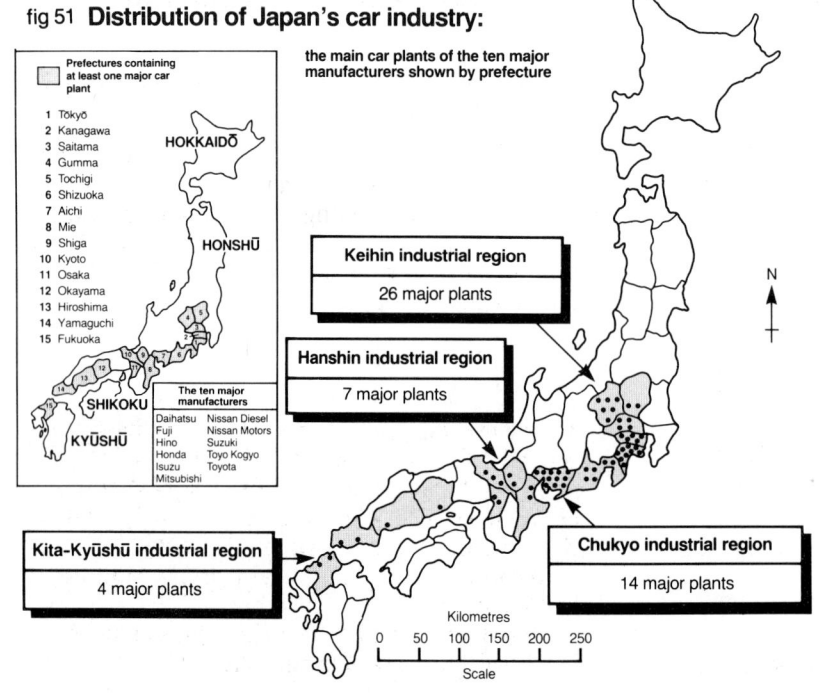

fig 51 **Distribution of Japan's car industry:**

Prefectures containing at least one major car plant

the main car plants of the ten major manufacturers shown by prefecture

1 Tōkyō
2 Kanagawa
3 Saitama
4 Gumma
5 Tochigi
6 Shizuoka
7 Aichi
8 Mie
9 Shiga
10 Kyoto
11 Osaka
12 Okayama
13 Hiroshima
14 Yamaguchi
15 Fukuoka

HOKKAIDŌ

HONSHŪ

SHIKOKU

KYŪSHŪ

The ten major manufacturers

Daihatsu | Nissan Diesel
Fuji | Nissan Motors
Hino | Suzuki
Honda | Toyo Kogyo
Isuzu | Toyota
Mitsubishi

Keihin industrial region
26 major plants

Hanshin industrial region
7 major plants

Kita-Kyūshū industrial region
4 major plants

Chukyo industrial region
14 major plants

N

Kilometres
0 50 100 150 200 250
Scale

Activity A

1 From fig 50, list the industries in their rank order of recent increase.

2 Why does Japan have to import large quantities of minerals?

3 What percentage of the following materials did Japan produce at home in 1981: coking coal, oil and iron ore?

4 Look at fig 51. Using the text to help you, describe the distribution the map shows.

5 Name each cluster from the map on page 59.

6 How many main vehicle plants are found in each of the main clusters?

7 How many main plants and how many component firms are there?

Most cars are made on an **assembly line.** Fig 52 is a simplified diagram showing how this may be done. Cars are built up stage by stage:

- raw materials are processed into simple components
- individual components are put together (or assembled) into larger parts called **sub-assemblies**
- the sub-assemblies are put together in a certain order along a main conveyor belt or assembly line

Nowadays much of this assembly work can be done by industrial robots as the photo shows.

photo 32: Robotic car assembly, Japan

fig 52   **How a car is made or assembled**

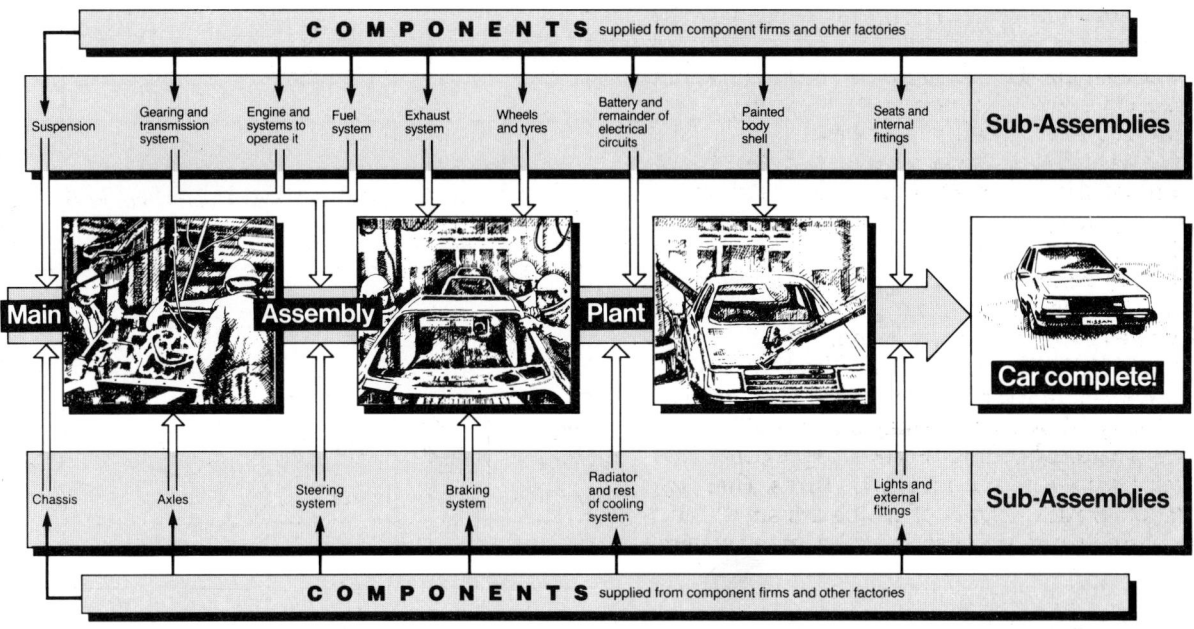

One simple example of how the assembly process works is the making of the car body:

- sheet steel is cut and pressed into body panels
- body panels are spot-welded, often by robots, into the body shell
- the body shell then goes through the painting process
- the body shell sub-assembly is then taken to the main assembly line, to be built on to the chassis of the car
- finally, the body fittings and fixtures are added

Since a car is made of many components and sub-assemblies, all the firms making them and the main plant assembling them are located near each other.

The reasons are:
- the assembly plant is the **market** for the component firms
- the component firms supply the **raw materials** for the assembly plant
- one assembly plant may get its components from very many smaller firms
- one component firm may supply several assembly plants in the same area

The links between all firms involved in the assembly line lead to a cluster. By being together, all the firms may also benefit from using common services, such as transport facilities, power supplies and skilled labour. A cluster of related industries like this is called an **agglomeration.**

Activity B

1 Draw a simplified version of fig 52 or use it to describe the stages in which a car is made.
2 Look at the photo. Can you suggest some advantages and disadvantages of using industrial robots on a car assembly line?
3 Write down the reasons why firms in the car industry are clustered together.
4 Add any new words, such as agglomeration, to your dictionary of geography.

Governments and Industry

fig 53

GRANTS AND SUBSIDIES

TRADING ESTATES

COSTLY SERVICES BUILT FOR INDUSTRY

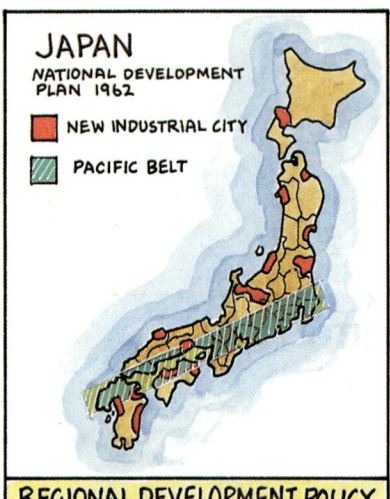

REGIONAL DEVELOPMENT POLICY

RESEARCH AND EDUCATION

TARGET PLANS

One of the most important influences on industrial location in the world today is government policy. It accounts for many changes in the spatial pattern of industries.

In many developing countries, like India, governments set up plans for investing money in future developments, such as industrial expansion. These plans usually set up targets for new production over a period of years. They do this because:

- industry creates wealth which can be spent on social improvements, such as health care, education and housing
- new industrial goods produced at home reduce the cost of importing expensive manufactured goods from abroad
- they hope that by starting some industries in a place, others will naturally follow because of linkages
- the overall effect of industrial expansion is to raise the general level of living standards throughout the country

Governments in the already industrialised countries are also involved in industrial planning. One of their main aims is often to re-distribute industry; the reasons why they do this include:

- some regions of a country may be less wealthy than others
- some regions have high rates of unemployment, especially where old, traditional industries have declined
- to prevent further congestion in existing industrial concentrations, such as in the Pacific Belt of Japan
- to reduce further pollution of heavily populated industrial regions
- in some countries, to spread industry more widely for reasons of defence

Some of the ways by which industrial locations are encouraged in new areas are shown in fig 53. Sometimes these types of encouragement are not enough: governments also discourage firms from expanding old plants, or locating new ones in existing industrial areas. This is often done by refusing planning permission.

The two-pronged efforts of governments to influence industry are sometimes called a **carrot and stick** policy.

photo 33: Cramlington New Town trading estate

Here is one pupil's record of a survey of the industrial site shown in the top photo. The survey was about the advantages and disadvantages of the sites for factories and the cause and results of government policies.

Activity

1 Look at fig 53.
a list some of the ways that governments influence industrial locations.
b suggest the reasons why governments might want to do this.
2 What do you understand by the phrase 'a policy of carrot and stick'?

Project work Do your own fieldwork. You may be able, with supervision, to conduct your own survey of some industrial sites in your own local area.

SITESCAN

Name of surveyor: Soqab Ali

Location: Trading estate in Cramlington New Town

Date: 14/2/87

	ADVANTAGES	DISADVANTAGES
INDUSTRIAL ENTERPRISE	1. Modern buildings. 2. Low rent and tax rates. 3. Modern amenities like roads. 4. Pleasant attractive environment. 5. Not congested.	1. Away from raw materials and markets. 2. Workers live a long way away, so firm provides buses.
PEOPLE	1. New jobs. 2. Pleasant working conditions. 3. Not near houses. 4. Plenty of parking space.	1. Long distance to come to work. 2. People needed to do training for new kinds of work.

Countries and Manufacturing

fig 55

			India	Nigeria	Republic of South Africa	Japan
	Income per capita 1980 (in £ sterling)		87	290	756	3471
	% of workers in manufacturing 1980		13	19	29	39
Group	Broad industrial group	Particular industries within group (see classification)	† = 1% of the workers in manufacturing industry			
I	Processing of agricultural produce except textiles	Food, Drink, Tobacco	††††††††† ††††††††	††††††††††† ††††††††††	†††††††††††††††	††††††††††
II	All textile goods	Yarns and synthetic fibres, Leather and fur, Textile goods, Clothing and footwear	††††††††††† ††††††††††† †††††††	††††††††††† †††††††††††	†††††††† †††††††††	†††††††††††††
III	All produce of forests	Timber products, Paper and board, Furniture	††††††	††††††† ††††††	†††††††††††	†††††††††††††
IV	Construction and ceramics	Bricks, Pottery, Glass and cement	†	†††††	††††††	†††††
V	Chemicals	Chemicals, Products of coal and oil	††††††††††	†††††††††††††	††††††††††	††††††††††
VI	All metal refining	Metal refining	††††††††	†	†††††††††	††††††
VII	Engineering and metal using industries	Mechanical engineering, Electrical engineering, Marine engineering, Vehicles	†††††††††††† †††††††††††	†††††††††† †††††††††	†††††††††††††† ††††††††††††††	†††††††††††††† †††††††††††††† †††††††††††††
VIII	Others not covered		†		†	††

The pattern of manufacturing industry varies between countries. These patterns are affected by the following features
- the **resource base** of a country: the raw materials available for manufacturing
- the size, skills and spending power of the country's population
- the trading pattern of a country
- the level of technology available in a country
- the history of a country's political and economic growth

Fig 55 shows the **manufacturing profiles** of India, Nigeria, South Africa and Japan. The relative wealth of each country is shown by their **per capita income.** This is the total earnings of the country divided by the total number of people. It is not the average income. Generally the more wealthy a country is the more people there are in manufacturing industry, especially in engineering and metal using industries compared with those connected to processing, agricultural and forest products.

- India has over half its manufacturing workers in the food, textile and wood product groups. It is industrialising, and the number in textiles reflects the policy of encouraging this industry countrywide. Metal and engineering industries are expanding
- Nigeria also has most manufacturing workers in food and textiles. There are very few in metals and heavy engineering. It does earn money from its oil resources, but although this makes the per capita income higher than India's, most people are not markedly better off
- South Africa has important minerals, and is an industrial country. However the majority of people

have little spending power and do not share in the country's wealth
- Japan is a highly advanced industrial nation with a high standard of living for all its people. Nearly one half of all its manufacturing workers are in the engineering and high technology industries on which its trade and development are based

All four different countries have workers in all the manufacturing classes, but their **manufacturing profile** or pattern is very different.

Activity A
Look at fig 55 and answer the following
1 What percentage of manufacturing workers are employed in:
a food, drink and tobacco industries in Nigeria.
b metal refining industries in South Africa.
c engineering industries in Japan.
d textile industries in India.
2 Place the four countries in order of highest to lowest for each of the following:
a per capita income.
b manufacturing workers as a percentage of all workers.
c textile workers as a percentage of all factory workers.
d engineering workers as a percentage of all factory workers.
3 In about 75 words, write down what conclusions you can make by comparing these four lists.

The manufacturing profiles of countries do not stay the same throughout their history. As a country industrialises, its manufacturing profile changes. Fig 56 shows this for Japan from 1920 to 1980, and indicates two different features:
- the percentage of the total workforce employed in manufacturing rose e.g. from 16% in 1920 to 39% in 1980
- the manufacturing profile changed e.g. the largest category in 1920 was textiles, and now it is engineering and high technology manufacturing

This shows the transformation of Japan into a competitive, major industrial nation over this period of time. The production of steel is a measure of this change:

Year	1920	1940	1945	1965	1979	1983
Raw Steel Production (million tonne)	1	8	1	41	111	97

The drop in 1945 was at the end of the Second World War, but after this you can see very rapid growth, until the early 1980s when world demand for steel fell slightly. Along with this industrial expansion, there were associated changes including a great growth of tertiary activities (or service employments) to support industry.

India, Nigeria and South Africa show much less dramatic change through this period. However, their manufacturing profiles have also changed over time.

- India's change is shown by the table in fig 56
- Nigeria's industrial growth and change has only started recently. In 1960 only 10% of the workers were in manufacturing, but this had nearly doubled to 19% to 1980. The first large integrated steelworks did not open until 1981
- South Africa has had 30% of its workers in manufacturing since 1950. However, some manufacturing has expanded faster than others. The greatest growth rates are at present in motor vehicles, textiles and clothing

In all four countries, the manufacturing profile is changing as they develop over time. Each one is at a different stage of development which is why the profiles are not the same.

Activity B

1 Look at fig 56 and answer the following:
a what percentage of Japan's workers were employed in manufacturing in 1920, 1960, and 1980?
b which category of manufacturing had the highest percentage of workers in 1920, and 1980?
c which categories of manufacturing employment have grown in importance since 1920? Which categories have fallen in importance?
d if the proportion of workers in a category has fallen, does it mean that the total output of that category has fallen too? Explain your answer.
2 Copy the line graph of Japan's manufacturing workers. Add in another colour a line for India, using the numbers given in the table.
3 a draw a bar chart, like the one for Japan, to show India's manufacturing categories in 1980.
b compare your graph with the two for Japan (1920 and 1980). Which of them is most like India's?
c what conclusion can you now make about India's industrial growth?

fig 56

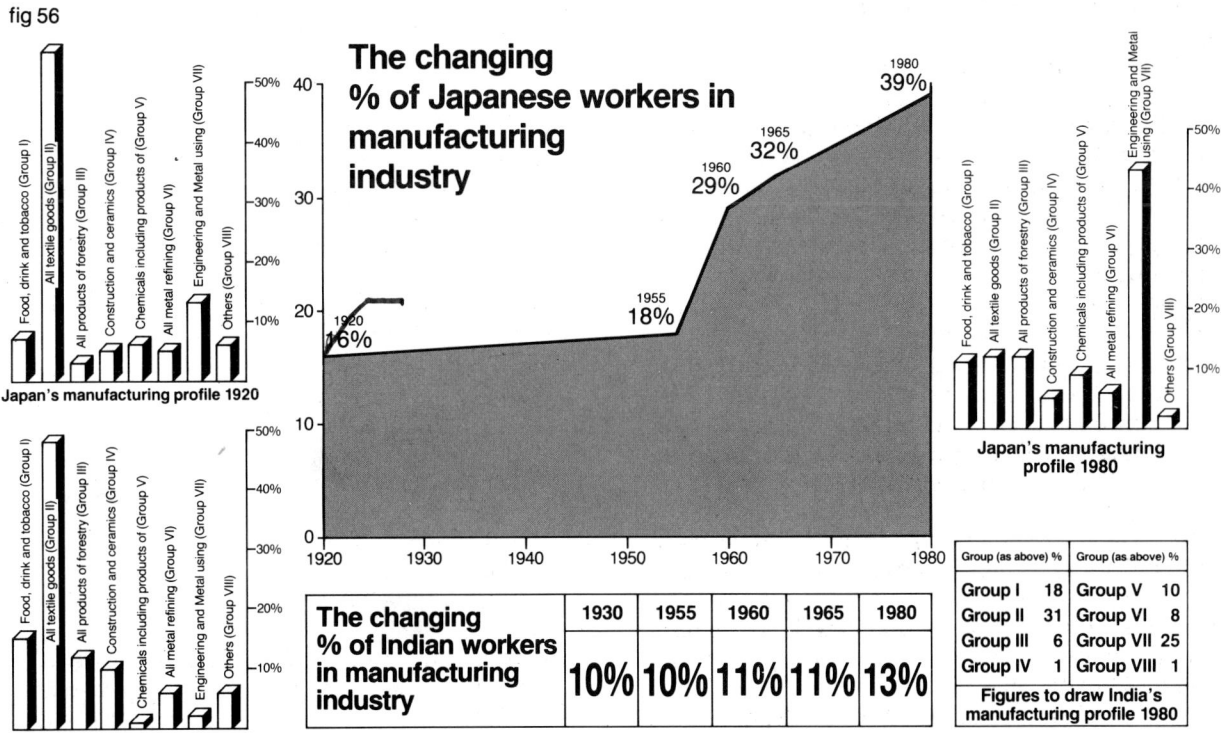

The changing % of Japanese workers in manufacturing industry

Japan's manufacturing profile 1920

Japan's manufacturing profile 1980

India's manufacturing profile 1920

The changing % of Indian workers in manufacturing industry	1930	1955	1960	1965	1980
	10%	10%	11%	11%	13%

Group (as above) %		Group (as above) %	
Group I	18	Group V	10
Group II	31	Group VI	8
Group III	6	Group VII	25
Group IV	1	Group VIII	1
Figures to draw India's manufacturing profile 1980			

South Africa's Industry

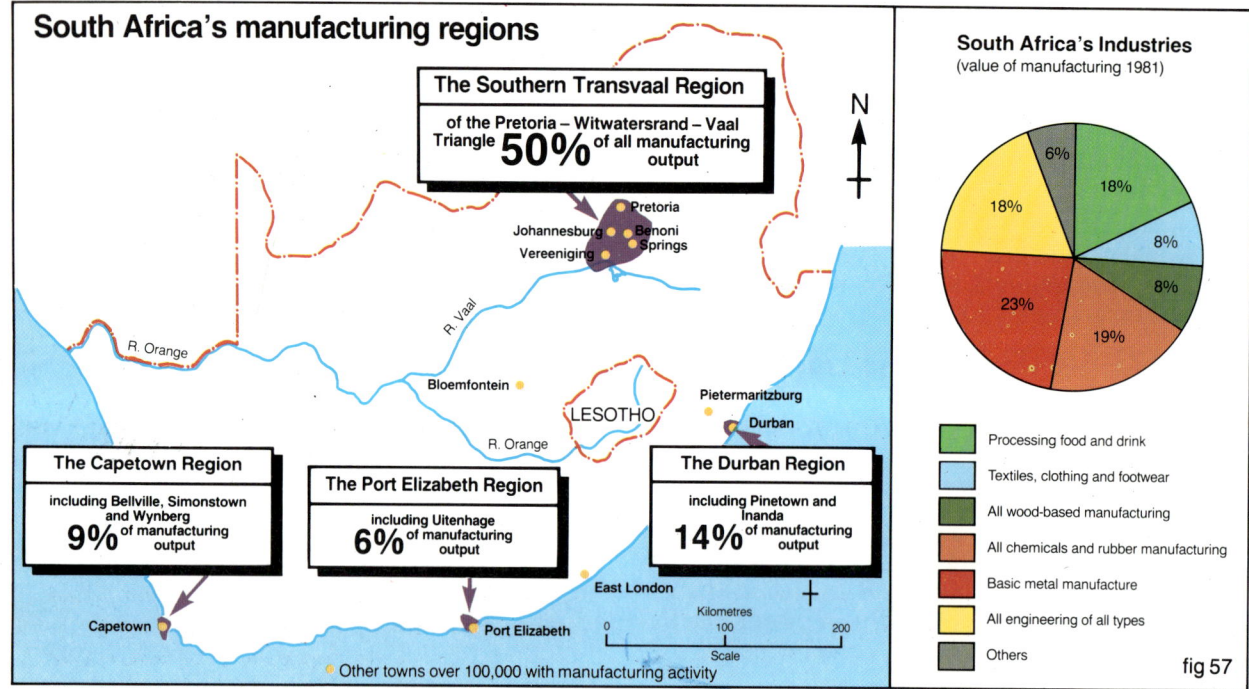

South Africa's manufacturing regions

The Southern Transvaal Region

of the Pretoria – Witwatersrand – Vaal Triangle **50%** of all manufacturing output

The Capetown Region

including Bellville, Simonstown and Wynberg **9%** of manufacturing output

The Port Elizabeth Region

including Uitenhage **6%** of manufacturing output

The Durban Region

including Pinetown and Inanda **14%** of manufacturing output

R. Vaal
R. Orange
Bloemfontein
LESOTHO
R. Orange
Pretoria
Johannesburg Benoni
Vereeniging Springs
Pietermaritzburg
Durban
East London
Capetown
Port Elizabeth

Kilometres
0   100   200
Scale

Other towns over 100,000 with manufacturing activity

N

South Africa's Industries
(value of manufacturing 1981)

6% • 18% • 8% • 8% • 19% • 23% • 18%

- Processing food and drink
- Textiles, clothing and footwear
- All wood-based manufacturing
- All chemicals and rubber manufacturing
- Basic metal manufacture
- All engineering of all types
- Others

fig 57

The demands of the black majority of South Africa's population for equal freedom, opportunity, and a fairer share of the wealth created by the country, are often in the news on television, or in the newspapers. Political unrest caused by the South African Government's policy of 'separate development' means that future changes in the pattern of activities are very uncertain. Details can change within a very short period of time.

South Africa has a wide range of manufacturing industries (see fig 57). The importance of manufacturing industry has grown in the last 50 years, this is because:

- gold resources (in the Witwatersrand region) earned money which could pay for industrial development, and at the same time this development provided a market for many manufactured goods
- massive coal reserves were available as power for industry
- a wide range of other minerals were also available for industry
- the agricultural regions produced a wide variety of food and raw materials for many processing industries
- there has been much foreign investment in the past (because of the large wealthy market, the cheap costs of labour and the cheap power from coal)
- Government policy encouraged home production and financed heavy industries, to make South Africa less dependent on imports (there is an unusual industry making oil from coal for this reason)

Fig 57 shows the distribution of South Africa's industries: it is concentrated into four areas. These areas have over three-quarters of all the country's manufacturing output. Three of them are only coastal port cities. The fourth, the Witwatersrand area of Southern Transvaal, usually just called **The Rand,** is different. It is the only real industrial conurbation.

The Rand alone has half of all South Africa's industry: it has large mineral wealth, easy communications on the grassy **veldt** landscape, cheap labour from the contract black labour force, and water from the river Vaal. The main city of Johannesburg, with over 1.25 million people, gives an idea of the range of industries: gold mining, banking, food processing, textiles, metals working, engineering and machinery, diamond cutting, paper and printing, chemicals, canning, electrical equipment, jewellery, timber working, and furniture.

The Rand is not without its industrial problems:

- new industries are now banned because there is a water shortage
- the Government policy of having separate homelands for black people means that some factories are located far away from their work force
- there is heavy environmental pollution
- there is increasing social unrest

Activity A

1 Make your own copy of the map in fig 57. Describe the pattern it shows.
2 Write out a list of South Africa's industrial groups in order from highest to lowest.
3 What reasons explain the growth of the country's manufacturing?
4 What facts would you give to show the types and importance of industries on the Rand?

Nigeria's Industry

Fig 58 seems to show quite a wide pattern of manufacturing industry in Nigeria. In fact its manufacturing industries produce only a small percentage of the earnings of the country. Nigeria really has no major industrial regions: industries are simply found in a number of towns scattered throughout the country. The manufacturing industries are very closely linked to the patterns of farming and mineral resources. A high proportion of them are in the food processing, textile, leather, and clothing industries. These types alone produce over 50 per cent of the value of manufacturing.

A summary of Nigerian industry might include some basic points:
- it provides a low proportion of the country's earnings and employment
- it is dominated by the consumer industries of food processing and textiles
- there is little large-scale heavy manufacturing industry
- there is very little overall manufacture of metals, machinery or engineering products
- the pattern of manufacturing is widely scattered to serve local needs
- Lagos dominates the totals of factories and jobs

Nigerian industry is held back by the low level of technology, investment money, and personal incomes. Despite this, it does have a large population and when incomes rise more, it could provide a large home market for many more manufactured goods.

Some developments and changes are happening:
- there is a new steelworks at Ajaokuta near the iron ore resources, although production is small at present
- the Government is investing more money in large power and water projects, and in industrial estates to encourage new factories to start
- imports of some goods are now banned to help home production to grow, as has happened in textiles

Nigeria's manufacturing industry is still at the stage where there is not yet enough production of heavy metal and machinery goods. There is little money to start them. Much of Nigeria's earnings are being spent on the more pressing problems of feeding a fast growing and large population.

Activity B

1 Draw an outline map of Nigeria and mark on it the three belts shown on the farming map on page 14. Add to it the pattern of industrial towns from fig 58.
2 What can you say about the distribution and types of industry your map shows?
3 Use your atlas to mark Nigeria's railways on your map. What do you notice now about the distribution of industrial towns?

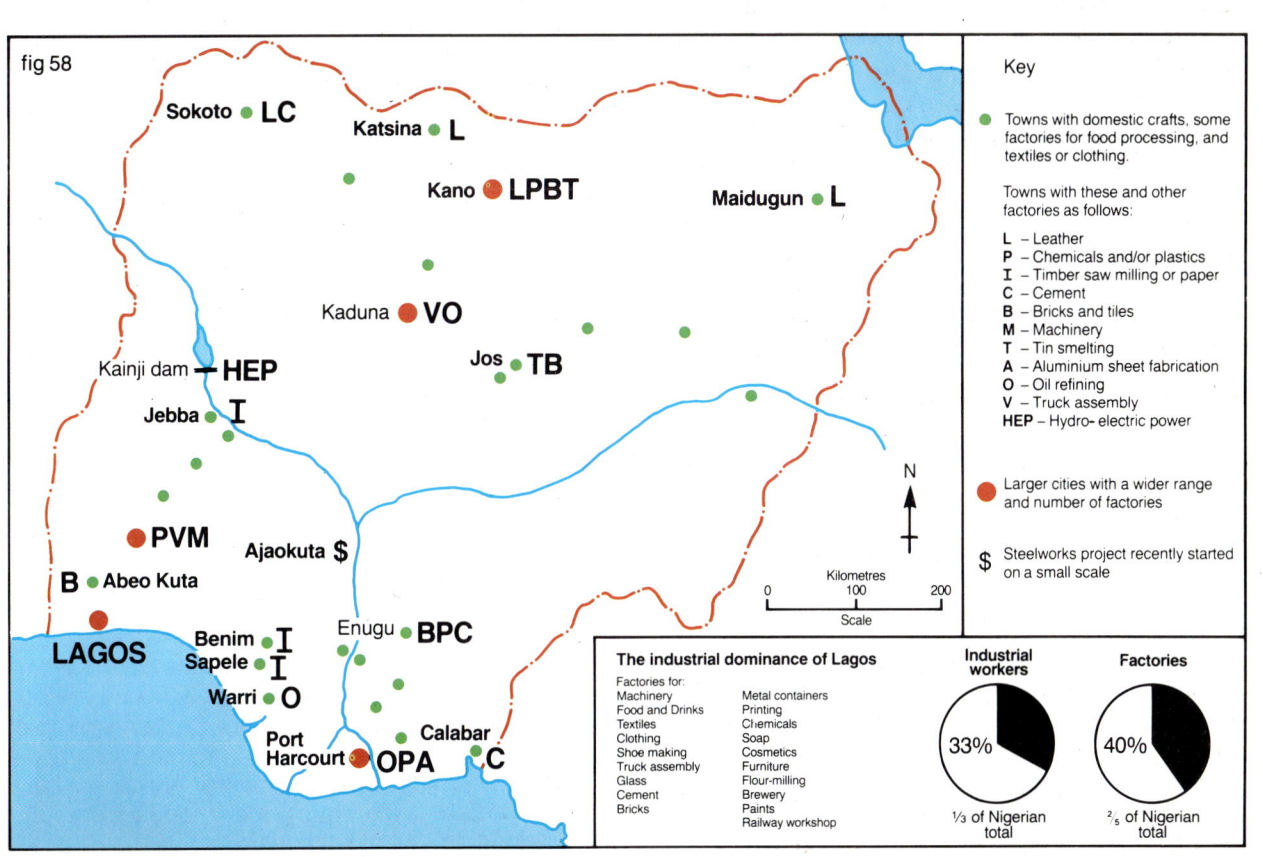

fig 58

Key

- Towns with domestic crafts, some factories for food processing, and textiles or clothing.

Towns with these and other factories as follows:

L – Leather
P – Chemicals and/or plastics
I – Timber saw milling or paper
C – Cement
B – Bricks and tiles
M – Machinery
T – Tin smelting
A – Aluminium sheet fabrication
O – Oil refining
V – Truck assembly
HEP – Hydro- electric power

- Larger cities with a wider range and number of factories

$ Steelworks project recently started on a small scale

Kilometres
0   100   200
Scale

N

The industrial dominance of Lagos

Factories for:
Machinery
Food and Drinks
Textiles
Clothing
Shoe making
Truck assembly
Glass
Cement
Bricks

Metal containers
Printing
Chemicals
Soap
Cosmetics
Furniture
Flour-milling
Brewery
Paints
Railway workshop

Industrial workers: 33% — ⅓ of Nigerian total

Factories: 40% — ²⁄₅ of Nigerian total

India's Industry

India has few regions where there is a large concentration of heavy manufacturing industries. Nor does it yet have a large proportion of its workers employed in this secondary activity. As a developing country, with a massive and rapidly growing population, it is still beginning its industrial development.

Fig 59 shows the pattern of industrial regions in India and brief details of each. Special points to note about this pattern are:

- there is only one major heavy industrial concentration based on mining, steel-making and heavy engineering found in the Chota Nagpur region

- except Chota Nagpur, all the other four regions are dominated by textile industries; they are hardly true industrial regions at all, just a few industrial towns reasonably near each other

- the Hooghlyside region is the densest industrial area and has the most industrial workers

- some of these regions are showing a wider range of industries. Bombay has a growing engineering sector, it now makes modern goods such as vehicles and electrical equipment; this gave rise to the use of hydro-electricity from nearby, and the building of India's first nuclear power station

- Bangalore is different from the other towns in its region, as well as having textile industries it has factories making aircraft, machine tools, cars, and telecommunications equipment

Industry is much more widely spread than the map might suggest: in fact, almost every large city in India has some food processing, pottery, small scale engineering, and textile industry workshops. Some towns have developed a special importance for industry, these are marked on the map:

- several cities like Amritsar, Meerut, Delhi, Agra and Kanpur in the Ganges Plain, have large and specialist textile industries selling at home and for export

- some railway towns like Nagpur, Jabalpur and Ajmer have a range of small scale engineering factories

- some towns have newer steelworks, like Bhilai and Vishakhapatnam

- some coastal ports like Madras and Cochin, have developed oil refining and chemicals to add to their traditional activities

For some time now the Indian Government has been trying to spread the distribution of new manufacturing industries and factories. This is so that wealth from industry can be available to many more of the poorer people. One aspect of this is the encouragement of **cottage industries** in the many villages and homes of rural areas. Industries on this very small scale are cheap to start and use local skills, crafts and raw materials: examples are spinning, weaving, pottery, food processing and soap making.

fig 59

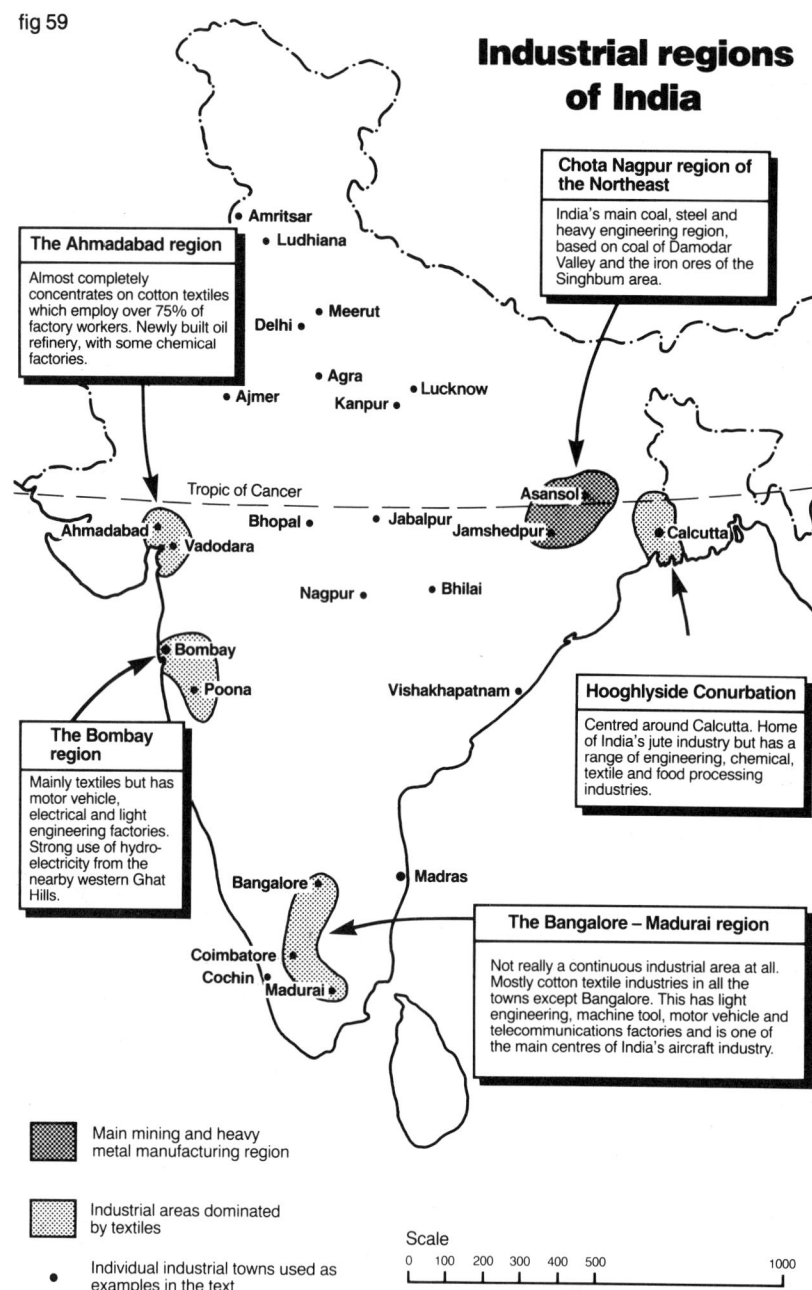

Industrial regions of India

Chota Nagpur region of the Northeast
India's main coal, steel and heavy engineering region, based on coal of Damodar Valley and the iron ores of the Singhbum area.

The Ahmadabad region
Almost completely concentrates on cotton textiles which employ over 75% of factory workers. Newly built oil refinery, with some chemical factories.

The Bombay region
Mainly textiles but has motor vehicle, electrical and light engineering factories. Strong use of hydro-electricity from the nearby western Ghat Hills.

Hooghlyside Conurbation
Centred around Calcutta. Home of India's jute industry but has a range of engineering, chemical, textile and food processing industries.

The Bangalore – Madurai region
Not really a continuous industrial area at all. Mostly cotton textile industries in all the towns except Bangalore. This has light engineering, machine tool, motor vehicle and telecommunications factories and is one of the main centres of India's aircraft industry.

Main mining and heavy metal manufacturing region

Industrial areas dominated by textiles

Individual industrial towns used as examples in the text

Scale
0 100 200 300 400 500   1000
Kilometres

Japan's Industry

Japan is one of the world's industrial giants. It is the world's largest maker of motor vehicles. It is also a leading manufacturer of products ranging from **heavy capital goods** like steel, ships, and industrial machines, to **high technology goods** like computers, telecommunications equipment, and consumer electrical goods.

Unlike India, its manufacturing regions are highly concentrated. There are many links and connections between firms and factories which make their location near each other very important.

Fig 60 shows four main regions of concentration; each one is on a coastal plain with deepwater, sheltered harbours. This is vital because of Japan's need to import the vast majority of its raw materials and fuels, needed by its industries. Most of the minor districts are also coastal for the same reasons.

Japan's industrial success is illustrated by the following table:

Machinery produced in 1981	Japan's position in the world
Tractors	3rd (after the USSR and USA)
Cars	1st
Washing machines	1st
TV sets	2nd (after the USA)
Watches	1st

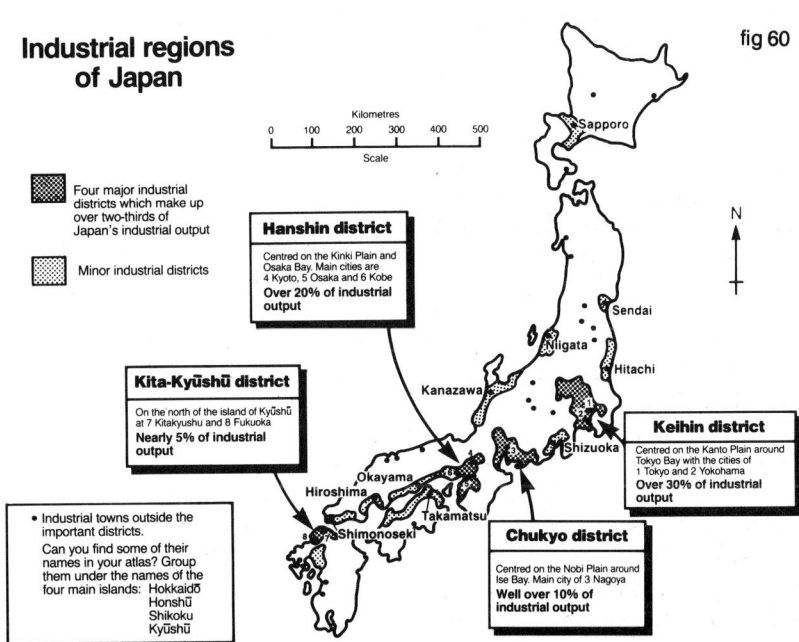

Industrial regions of Japan

fig 60

Scale — Kilometres 0 100 200 300 400 500

Four major industrial districts which make up over two-thirds of Japan's industrial output

Minor industrial districts

Hanshin district
Centred on the Kinki Plain and Osaka Bay. Main cities are 4 Kyoto, 5 Osaka and 6 Kobe
Over 20% of industrial output

Kita-Kyūshū district
On the north of the island of Kyūshū at 7 Kitakyushu and 8 Fukuoka
Nearly 5% of industrial output

Keihin district
Centred on the Kanto Plain around Tokyo Bay with the cities of 1 Tokyo and 2 Yokohama
Over 30% of industrial output

Chukyo district
Centred on the Nobi Plain around Ise Bay. Main city of 3 Nagoya
Well over 10% of industrial output

• Industrial towns outside the important districts.
Can you find some of their names in your atlas? Group them under the names of the four main islands: Hokkaidō, Honshū, Shikoku, Kyūshū

Sapporo, Sendai, Niigata, Hitachi, Kanazawa, Shizuoka, Okayama, Hiroshima, Takamatsu, Shimonoseki

photo 34: Container wharves, Japan

These give a brief idea of Japan's success. It has resulted from the effective use of all the skills, inventiveness and business enterprise of all of its people. Workers, managers, businessmen and government all combine in their different ways to use the available human resources to the full.

Activity

1 Make your own copy of fig 59. Add to it labels to show the industries of the towns outside the five main areas.
2 Draw a graph to show the following figures:

Industrial region	Approx. number of workers in industry
Chota Nagpur	150,000
Hooghlyside Region	600,000
Bombay Region	600,000
Ahmadabad Region	275,000
Bangalore-Madurai	200,000

3 List the types of industries for which Japan is famous.
4 Describe the photo and say how it represents Japanese industrial success.
5 Suggest in about 100 words, the differences you notice in the industrial patterns of India and Japan.
6 How do their patterns compare with those of Nigeria and South Africa?
7 Add any new words to your dictionary of geography.

Death at Midnight

fig 61

The full extent of the suffering caused by Monday's gas leak at the Union Carbide pesticide plant at Bhopal, in India, is now becoming known. As the death toll now exceeds 2,000, reports from Bhopal illustrate the enormity of the disaster.

Thousands of dead cattle lie bloated in the streets, babies cry for milk. The leaves on the trees are yellow and shrivelled. Turnips and spinach in the fields are chemically scorched and covered with a fine white film. Ponds are discoloured and lurid.

The stench of death hangs over the city mingled with the smoke of funeral pyres. Grave-diggers open mass trenches. Tailors are stitching shrouds. Doctors are struggling to prevent a second tragedy: an epidemic.

The 900,000 people are stunned and grieving for the victims of the poisonous gas. Many of them, poor and ignorant and illiterate, still fail to understand what happened in their slums of mud, thatch and rubble opposite the pesticide plant. Many said that they did not know that something terrible could happen, and that when they heard the factory siren they should run for their lives.

In Jaiprakash Nagar across the street, more than 200 people died. At least half were children too weak and under-nourished to outrun the white cloud of gas, too frail to fight the effects of the poison.

Many of the dead were discovered when the authorities broke down shanty doors bolted from within. The people had tried to hide from the fumes which turned their shacks into gas chambers.

Hundreds died in their sleep and hundreds more were overcome as they fled, coughing and vomiting. They stampeded out of the city. Some were run over by cars and buses in the panic.

"We were choking and our eyes were burning. We could barely see the road through the fog, and sirens were blaring. We didn't know which way to run," Ahmed Khan said. "Everybody was very confused. Mothers didn't know their children had died, children didn't know their mothers had died and men didn't know their whole families had died," Major Girish Tiwari of the local police said. "Anyone who was left alive ran away blindly."

Abdul Karim said, "It is a sin to bury two bodies in one grave but we must bury three or four and more together. I pray Allah I never have to do this again."

At the Choia Ghat cremation ground, bodies were burnt in stacks of 25 because there was not enough firewood. Flames filled the sky on Tuesday, and workers were calling it the "devil's night" as hundreds of corpses were burnt. Victims' faces were marked with ink for identification.

As he carries his son, Daya Ram says: "We never expected anything like this. But even so, there's no way for us to live anywhere else. Even now, where is the land? Where is the money?"

A band of angry young students calls the factory an evil which must be removed. "If the factory is not removed from India, we will set it on fire," said one. "We are right next door. How can we live in the shadow of death?"

60

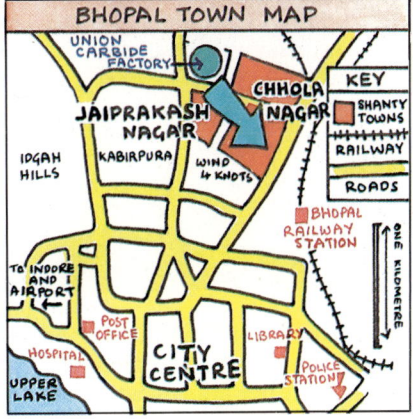

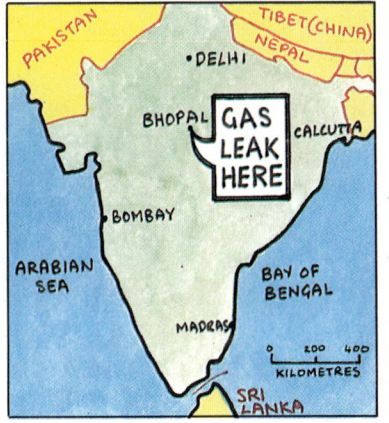

①	Union Carbide factory
②	'Scrubber' where leak occurred
③	Wind at 4 knots blowing towards shanty towns
④	Lethal fumes escape into the air
⑤	Four lane highway
⑥	Shanty towns of Jaiprakash Nagar and Chhola Nagar.
⑦	Heavier than air, the escaped gas drifts over the shanty towns

fig 62

One of the unintended outputs of the industrial system is the effect of industrial production on the environment of surrounding areas. Sometimes these are so extreme that they cause disasters, like the Chernobyl incident in the USSR in 1986.

The newspaper account shows another example of how disastrous the effect on people can be.

The chemical factory in Bhopal was a branch of the USA company, Union Carbide. This is a **multi-national company** with factories in many countries including the USA, France, the United Kingdom and India. It is well known for making, amongst other things, the Ever Ready dry cell batteries.
The Bhopal chemical factory in India manufactured mainly fertilizers and pesticides. It was built there partly because of the vast need for these products as the **Green Revolution** developed in India. It also was there to take advantage of government assistance and the very cheap costs of labour.
When it was built in 1975, it was placed nearly three kilometres away from the city. This was because it needed to be on an isolated site for safety reasons. However, make-shift houses or 'jhuggis' were built around the factory by poor people looking for work. In this way the shanty towns of Chhola Nagar and Jai-prakash Nagar grew up; the factory was therefore no longer on an isolated site.
The disaster of December 6th, 1984 resulted from a leak of toxic gas from the pesticide part of the plant built in 1980. The leaking gas was heavier than air, and was blown that day by chance in the direction of the shanty towns. The effects are clearly illustrated by people's experiences reported in the newspaper. Even now, the real suffering is still being counted and some people will bear the results for life. 200,000 people were injured or bereaved, and 50,000 people are still developing medical complications.

Despite the terrible effects it must be remembered that the Union Carbide factory made many useful products for India, and provided a lot of work. Six months after the accident in June 1985, the workers held a sit-in protest against the proposed closing of the factory. However, it did close down on July 11th, 1985.

Activity

1 Use all the details on these two pages to prepare a TV news report on the Bhopal tragedy. Write out your script and draw some maps and diagrams. Present your report as an illustrated two minute talk to your class.
Note: You might like to use your libraries to look at back copies of newspapers for the dates of the 6th to the 9th, December 1984.
2 Find out about other examples of industrial disaster, using old newspapers and other library material.

A National Problem

Damage to the environment by industry does not just mean a disaster like the one at Bhopal. It can build up slowly over a period of time, especially where there are dense concentrations of people and industry. Such environmental effects are usually called **pollution.** The photo shows an example of common urban pollution.

Pollution of the environment has been happening for the whole of human history; it has increased dramatically since the large-scale development of industries. Only in recent years has the importance of the problem been recognised.

Japan, like other advanced, industrial countries, has seen a growth of public concern about the problem. The pie chart in fig 64 gives the proportion of complaints about pollution to local authorities in 1982. It shows there is pollution of:
● land
● water supplies, rivers, lakes and seas
● air
● other aspects of peoples' living conditions

The effects can be unpleasant, irritating and uncomfortable, or extremely dangerous.

Japan has particularly suffered from the effects of pollution because:
● there is only a limited amount of flat land
● people and industry are heavily concentrated, in confined lowland plains in the Pacific Belt
● its industrial growth has been very rapid
● as in many other countries, industrial growth has taken place without people realising at first what damage could be done

In the 1960s there were four well-known court cases in Japan which illustrated the growing effects of pollution, and the worries about it. Each case was about risks to health caused by pollution building up over a number of years. The incidents were:
● people suffered from mercury poisoning along the Agano River, in Niigata prefecture

photo 37: Pollution, Japan

● people living near the petro-chemical factory at Yokkaichi, in the Chukyo industrial region, started suffering badly from asthma after it was built in 1955
● people in Toyama suffered from a disease called **itai-itai** (it hurts-it hurts) which was caused by cadmium poisoning in the soil. This had built up in the soil since the 1930s, and contaminated the rice grown here along the Jintsu River

fig 63

No. of patients suffering from environmental pollution diseases in Japan

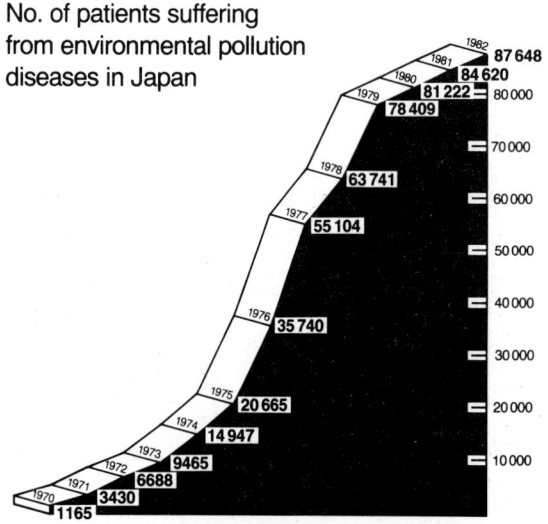

fig 64

Pollution in Japan 1982

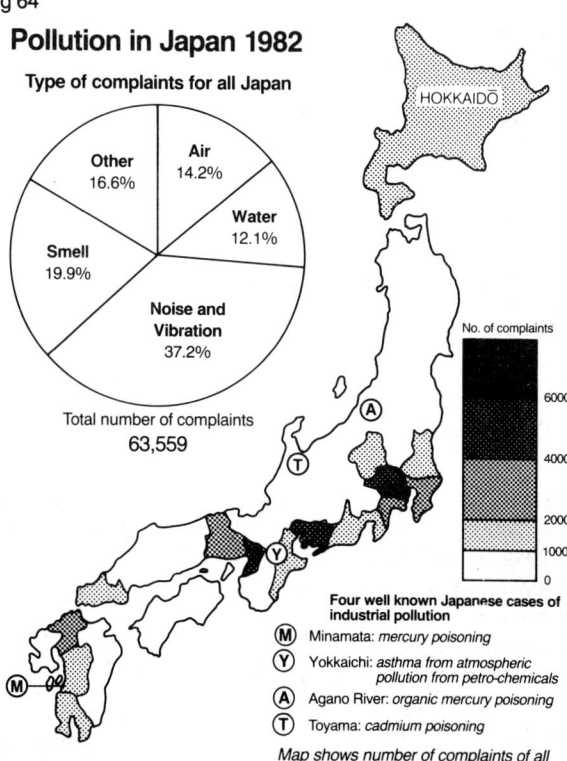

Type of complaints for all Japan

Other 16.6%
Air 14.2%
Water 12.1%
Smell 19.9%
Noise and Vibration 37.2%

Total number of complaints
63,559

HOKKAIDŌ

No. of complaints

6000
4000
2000
1000
0

Four well known Japanese cases of industrial pollution

Ⓜ Minamata: *mercury poisoning*
Ⓨ Yokkaichi: *asthma from atmospheric pollution from petro-chemicals*
Ⓐ Agano River: *organic mercury poisoning*
Ⓣ Toyama: *cadmium poisoning*

Map shows number of complaints of all types by local government areas.

● at Minamata in western Kyushu people got Minamata disease, also due to mercury poisoning. This was first noticed in the 1950s. It was caused by eating fish that were contaminated by pollution in the seawater

All the court cases resulted in the victims getting compensation. Since then, the monitoring of air and water pollution has been much more strict. The map in fig 64 shows that the pattern of these complaints matches the pattern of industrial regions in Japan. The island of Hokkaido is the exception, although it does contain much of Japan's coal-mining.
The number of complaints has nevertheless risen sharply in the years 1970 to 1982. This reflects the way in which people are now more aware of the problem. It also explains why Japan as a country has developed a range of anti-pollution measures.

fig 65 **Japanese action against pollution**

Public pressure for a nationwide policy led to

1967 BASIC LAW for ENVIRONMENTAL POLLUTION CONTROL

National Environmental Agency
established for total control of anti-pollution measures

Coping with present pollution	Preventing future pollution	Compensation
Daily monitoring of water and air by local governments	Laws against pollution	
	Strict national standards enforced by courts	Principle of
Scientific survey of existing problem	Car emission laws	**'Polluter pays'**
	Grants given to all businesses taking pollution-preventing measures	firms found guilty of pollution must compensate victims and pay for their continuing medical care.
Health research centres for pollution-related diseases	Planning controls on location of new enterprises and research on to effects of new industries	(70,000 people in 1981 got compensation)
Active measures to clean up environment		
	Environmental conservation measures	

National spending per person on anti-pollution measures highest of any country in the world (2% of Japan's total earnings in 1981)

AIMING FOR 'ENVIRONMENTAL PRESERVING SOCIETY'

Worries about the effects of pollution are not new. The dense killer smogs, of the large cities of the United Kingdom in the 1950s, led to the creation of urban smokeless zones and the production of smokeless fuels.
Nowadays, there is a growing concern about poisonous lead additives in petrol which are passed through a car's exhaust into the air. Car manufacturers are researching and developing more efficient engines to use lead-free petrol. There are many more examples of the concern about pollution dangers in the modern world.
Japan as a country has paid more attention to anti-pollution measures than most. Its attempts to develop an **environmental preserving society** are outlined in fig 65.

Activity A

1 What do you understand by the word pollution?
2 Give four reasons why Japan has particularly suffered from it.
3 What pollution happened at Minamata?
4 What is itai-itai and why did it happen?

Look at fig 63.
5 State the number of people in Japan who suffered from pollution-linked disease in 1970, 1975, and 1982.
6 Between which two years was there the greatest increase?

Project work. Pollution happens everywhere. Try to set up a **pollution watch.** Use local newspapers and any other source of information to collect and record examples or complaints connected with pollution in your local area.

Activity B
Library research

1 Use your local library to find out about the London smogs of the 1950s.
2 What was this smog?
3 Are there other different types now?

Look at fig 65.
4 When did the Japanese pass the Basic Law for Environmental Pollution Control?
5 What did this law establish?
6 What three categories of action were then taken?

7 What do you understand by the 'polluter-pays' principle?
8 List the anti-pollution measures taken to prevent future problems.
9 How much do the Japanese spend on all pollution control?
10 What do you think an environmental preserving society is?

A Worldwide Problem

The three photos on this page show different kinds of environmental damage.

- damage to the land: the destructive and harmful effect of mining on the landscape in South Africa
- pollution of the air: in Tokyo
- pollution of the water: results of the contamination of natural water supplies in India

These examples from different countries show that the environmental impact of industry is a worldwide problem. There is a clear difference between pollution, and other destructive and harmful effects on the natural world (shown on fig 66). Remember that agriculture, forestry and fishing activities can also cause various different types of environmental damage and pollution.

The overall problem of all these different impacts on the environment is very important because:

- we share this planet with many other living things
- the wellbeing of future generations depends on how we use the Earth now
- continuing growth of population will put further pressure on the available resources

All business and economic activities and enterprises need to make use of the world's resources carefully, so as not to cause irreversible damage.

Perhaps the ideas of the 'polluter pays' principle and the 'environmental preserving society' are important for the future. They are ways of making sure that all the people and nations now, and in the future, have the full benefit of the resources the Earth can provide.

photo 38: Gold mine waste dump, South Africa

photo 39: Smog in Tokyo, Japan

photo 40: Polluted water, India

Some environmental impacts of industry

fig 66

DESTRUCTIVE OR HARMFUL EFFECTS ON LANDSCAPE	INDUSTRIAL ACTIVITY	POLLUTION OF THE ENVIRONMENT
LOSS OF LAND DERELICT ABANDONED SITES WASTE AND SPOIL HEAPS SUBSIDENCE RESOURCES USED UP DESTROYS APPEARANCE OF SCENERY	**MINING AND QUARRYING** 	POISONING OF SOIL NOISE AND VIBRATION DUST
WASTE DISPOSAL SPOIL HEAPS EFFECT ON CLIMATE AND WATER DE-OXYGENATED RIVERS & LAKES OIL SLICKS DUMPING OF WASTE AT SEA LOSS OF WILDLIFE HABITATS LOSS OF LAND FOR RESERVOIRS	**PRODUCTION OF POWER FROM FUELS** 	DUST NOISE AND VIBRATION SMELL SMOKE AND TOXIC FUMES RADIOACTIVE CONTAMINATION ACID RAIN PHOTO-CHEMICAL SMOG
DERELICT SITES DUMPING OF INDUSTRIAL WASTE POISONED RIVERS, LAKES & SEAS LOSS OF LAND LOSS OF WILDLIFE HABITATS DEFORESTATION	**PROCESSING AND MANUFACTURING** 	DUST TOXIC FUMES AND GASES POISONOUS LIQUIDS TOXIC METALS POISON SOIL ACID RAIN SMELL SMOG NOISE AND VIBRATION
DEAD LAKES, RIVERS & SEAS FROM SEWAGE CONTAMINATION DOMESTIC WASTE AND RUBBISH DISPOSAL (NON-ROTTING PLASTICS) UNSIGHTLY WASTE HEAPS URBAN SPRAWL POPULATION EXPLOSION OF SOME SPECIES (PESTS)	**CONSUMPTION OF INDUSTRIAL PRODUCTS** 	DUST BACTERIA AND DISEASES FROM UNTREATED SEWAGE NOISE AND VIBRATION SMOG LEAD IN AIR FROM CAR EXHAUSTS AEROSOLS

 All these may affect the workings of the atmosphere, landscape and natural world.

Do you know of any more effects?

 All these risk life and health of all living things.

Activity

Look at fig 66.
1 What destructive and harmful effects do mining and quarrying have on the landscape?
2 What types of pollution result from the use of fuels and the production of power?
3 What do you understand by the words 'toxic fumes and gases'?
4 Try to record, honestly, the ways that your family and household contributes to pollution and damage to the environment.
5 Add any new words from your work on environmental damage to your dictionary of geography.
6 **Either** Design a poster to inform the public about the problems of environmental damage.
or Design a short TV commercial to make people think of how they could help overcome local problems of pollution.

Services

fig 67

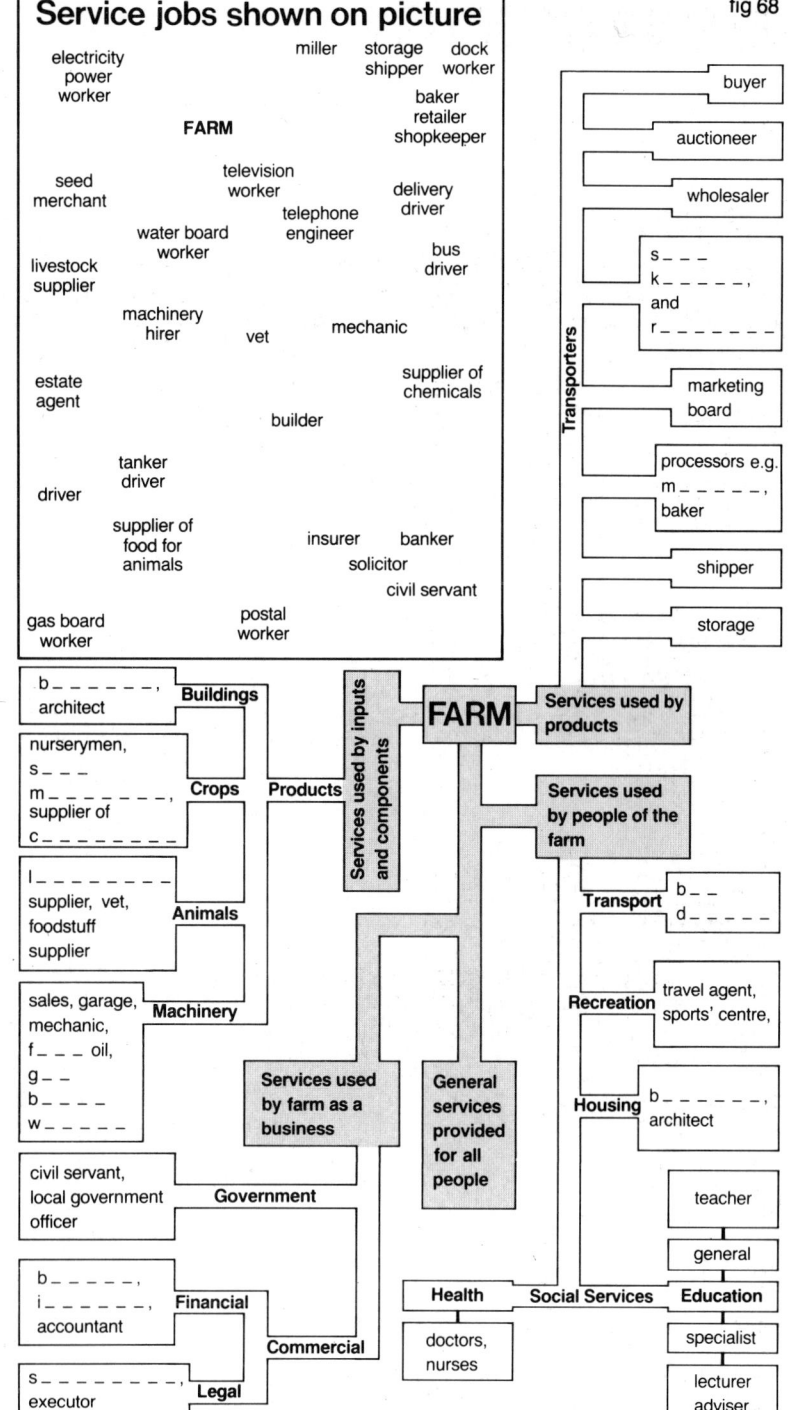

All primary and secondary activities produce material goods. However, in order for the pattern of these activities to function, they need many supporting services. These are the **tertiary** activities. They do not make particular products, but supply a service and keep the economic and business system going.

To think about the range of services that are needed by other activities, we shall look first at those which support a farm.

The picture of the farm (fig 67) was started by thinking about which visitors would visit a farm. The artist has drawn the **mental picture** we **visualised**. Once you have a picture like this in your mind, then it is possible to make rough notes of what you see or visualise. After this you can organise the rough notes into an ordered arrangement, like the flow diagram in fig 68. This method develops your understanding by a simple thinking skill. It allows you to look at a complicated set of facts about the real world, and change them into a more simplified pattern of ideas called a **model**. A model reduces a confusing mass of information down to the essential, underlying ideas. See if you can find similar models in this book.

Industrial factories, like farms, also need a large number of supporting services. The chocolate bar factory described on pages 4 and 5 could be used as an example. All the services it needs can be worked out from fig 2 on that page. Can you **visualise** a picture like fig 67 to show all the services it needs?

Service jobs shown on picture

fig 68

electricity power worker / miller / storage shipper / dock worker

FARM

baker / retailer / shopkeeper

seed merchant / television worker / delivery driver / telephone engineer / water board worker / bus driver

livestock supplier / machinery hirer / vet / mechanic

estate agent / supplier of chemicals / builder

tanker driver / driver

supplier of food for animals / insurer / banker / solicitor / civil servant

gas board worker / postal worker

Transporters — buyer / auctioneer / wholesaler / s _ _ _ k _ _ _ _ _ , and r _ _ _ _ _ _ _ / marketing board / processors e.g. m _ _ _ _ _ , baker / shipper / storage

Buildings — b _ _ _ _ _ _ , architect

Crops — nurserymen, s _ _ _ m _ _ _ _ _ _ , supplier of c _ _ _ _ _ _

Animals — l _ _ _ _ _ _ _ supplier, vet, foodstuff supplier

Machinery — sales, garage, mechanic, f _ _ _ oil, g _ _ b _ _ _ _ w _ _ _ _

Government — civil servant, local government officer

Financial — b _ _ _ _ _ , i _ _ _ _ _ _ , accountant

Legal — s _ _ _ _ _ _ _ , executor

Commercial

Products / Services used by inputs and components / FARM / Services used by products

Services used by people of the farm

Services used by farm as a business / General services provided for all people

Transport — b _ _ d _ _ _ _ _

Recreation — travel agent, sports' centre,

Housing — b _ _ _ _ _ _ , architect

Health — doctors, nurses / Social Services / **Education** — teacher / general / specialist / lecturer adviser

---

Activity A

1 Make your own copy of the farm services chart in fig 68.
2 Try to fill in the empty boxes by using the details shown in the picture in fig 67.
3 Can you think of any more farm services that might be added to the chart?
4 The visualised farm in fig 67 is likely to be in an advanced, industrial country of the developed world. What range of services do you think would be available to farms in a developing country, like the farms you looked at in Nigeria on pages 14 and 15?

Activity B

1 Make rough notes of your mental picture of the chocolate bar factory and its services.
2 Use your notes to draw a services chart for a factory like the one for a farm in fig 68.
3 How different are services needed by a factory and a farm?

Group work

In groups, decide on a visualised or mental picture of the services for a factory, like the one for a farm. Draw it out as a wall mural. Divide the work up so that each person draws a part of it.

The Service Types

Tertiary activities are essential to the operation of all businesses. They allow all other productive activities to function because they provide the links between

- **inputs:** the things that a business needs from outside
- **components:** the production features of the business
- **outputs:** the goods or products obtained or manufactured by the business

Tertiary activities permit and supply the flows of energy, materials, and information within a business system.

Classifying tertiary activities is difficult because there are so many, especially in an advanced, industrial country.

Fig 70 shows a simplified way of representing them. Public services are those that are provided by, or on behalf of, national or local government. These can be supplied directly by government agencies, or according to government guidelines by private firms. They include:

- **public utilities** such as water, power and waste disposal
- **social services** such as education, health care, housing and recreation
- **public administration** which organises and runs all the others

Commercial services are largely run by private firms. They are concerned with buying and selling the products of primary and secondary activities. They are businesses themselves, but look after the interests of people and other businesses:

- **retailing** and **sales** services include not only shops, but all the storage, maintenance, wholesale and marketing activities which selling activity needs
- **legal services** exist to make sure that all activities and business transactions can take place according to the agreed rules and laws of the country concerned. All branches of law are represented by different legal services
- **financial services** are for personal or business transactions including banks, insurance firms, and the post office

Leisure services provide recreation opportunities for people, sometimes they are public services and sometimes commercial services.

Transport and communication link places. They provide for exchange and trade. They allow the necessary flows of goods, people, and ideas between places, and are vital in all human activity.

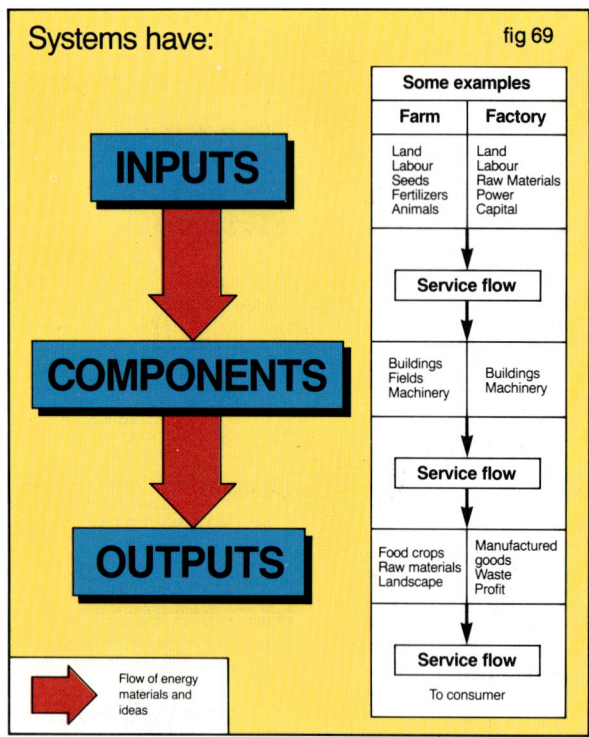

Systems have: — fig 69

Some examples	
Farm	**Factory**
Land Labour Seeds Fertilizers Animals	Land Labour Raw Materials Power Capital
	Service flow
Buildings Fields Machinery	Buildings Machinery
	Service flow
Food crops Raw materials Landscape	Manufactured goods Waste Profit
	Service flow
	To consumer

INPUTS

COMPONENTS

OUTPUTS

Flow of energy materials and ideas

Photo 41: School, Mauritius Island

fig 70	Main groups	Types		Users	Some examples
Service types	Public	Utilities		Personal and business	Water, power, gas, waste disposal
		Social		Personal	Education, health, recreation
				Business	Trading estates, training centres
		Administrative		Local government	City hall services, public housing, libraries
				National government	Job centres, training centres
	Commercial	Retail and sales		Personal	Shops, department stores
				Business	Wholesale warehouses, storage, maintenance services
		Legal		Personal and business	Solicitors, estate agents, surveyors
		Financial		Personal and business	Banks, insurance, post office, stock exchange
		Leisure		Active	Golf courses, sports clubs, adventure holiday centres
				Passive	Professional football, cinemas, bingo
	Transport and communication	Passenger		Personal and business	Rail, air and shipping, road services
		Freight		Personal and business	Rail, air and shipping, road services, post office
		Information		Personal and business	Telephone networks, post office

Service activities occur in all societies and nations at all stages of their history. However, the types and importance change. As a country develops, and as places and activities become more specialised, there is a greater need for more services. The following statistics suggest how this is true. They show the percentage of workers in the different types of activities in 1981:

Country	Percentage of workers in		
	Agriculture	Industry	Services
India	71	13	16
Japan	12	39	49

As a country develops, it may show changes in many aspects of life which result in the growth of services. Some of these changes might be:
- increasing production in all primary and secondary activities requires more supporting services
- increases in internal and external trade (trade within, and in and out of the country) requires more services
- improvements in peoples' living conditions leads to the growth of public services and utilities
- the rising of wages and living standards means that people begin to spend more on consumer goods and services
- a reduction in the hours of work per week and an increase in paid holiday time means that there is much more demand for leisure, recreation and tourist services
- as the economy and society becomes more complex an expansion in public welfare and administrative services will be necessary

- as the spiral of rising national wealth goes on more and more is invested in research, to expand further development, trade and wealth
- all these changes increase movement of all kinds, and the need for new transport and communication services grows rapidly

The overall result of all these changes, and many more, is the growth of the business system of the country. Services have also had to grow to contribute to the country's position within the world community and the world's business system.

Activity
1 A cinema can be called a 'passive, leisure, commercial' type of service. Write a sentence describing each of the following: water supply, post office, education, golf course, and department store. Use fig 70.
2 Work out what these words mean: utility, administration, retailing, information services, and social services.
Add them to your dictionary of geography, along with any of the other words you did not know.
3 Draw two suitable graphs to show the percentage employments in Japan and India in 1981.
4 How is the pattern for Japan different from that of India?
5 Write down in sentences four reasons to help explain the differences you have noticed.
Project work Collect small pictures of different kinds of services from magazines and make a large pictorial wallchart version of fig 70.

Australia

Australia has a large proportion of its workers employed in service activities. The precise figure in 1981 was 61 per cent. To show how service industries grow, we will look at one example: the growth of the railways in Australia.

Australia was first settled and colonised from a number of separate coastal ports, and as the economy grew it required more and more services to link the ports with the expanding producing areas inland of them.

Soon some of the earliest coastal ports became the capitals of the new states, and as they grew they expanded their hinterlands into the interior of the country. Railways expanded because they represented the transport and communication services needed to carry farm products, minerals and people over longer distances.

fig 71

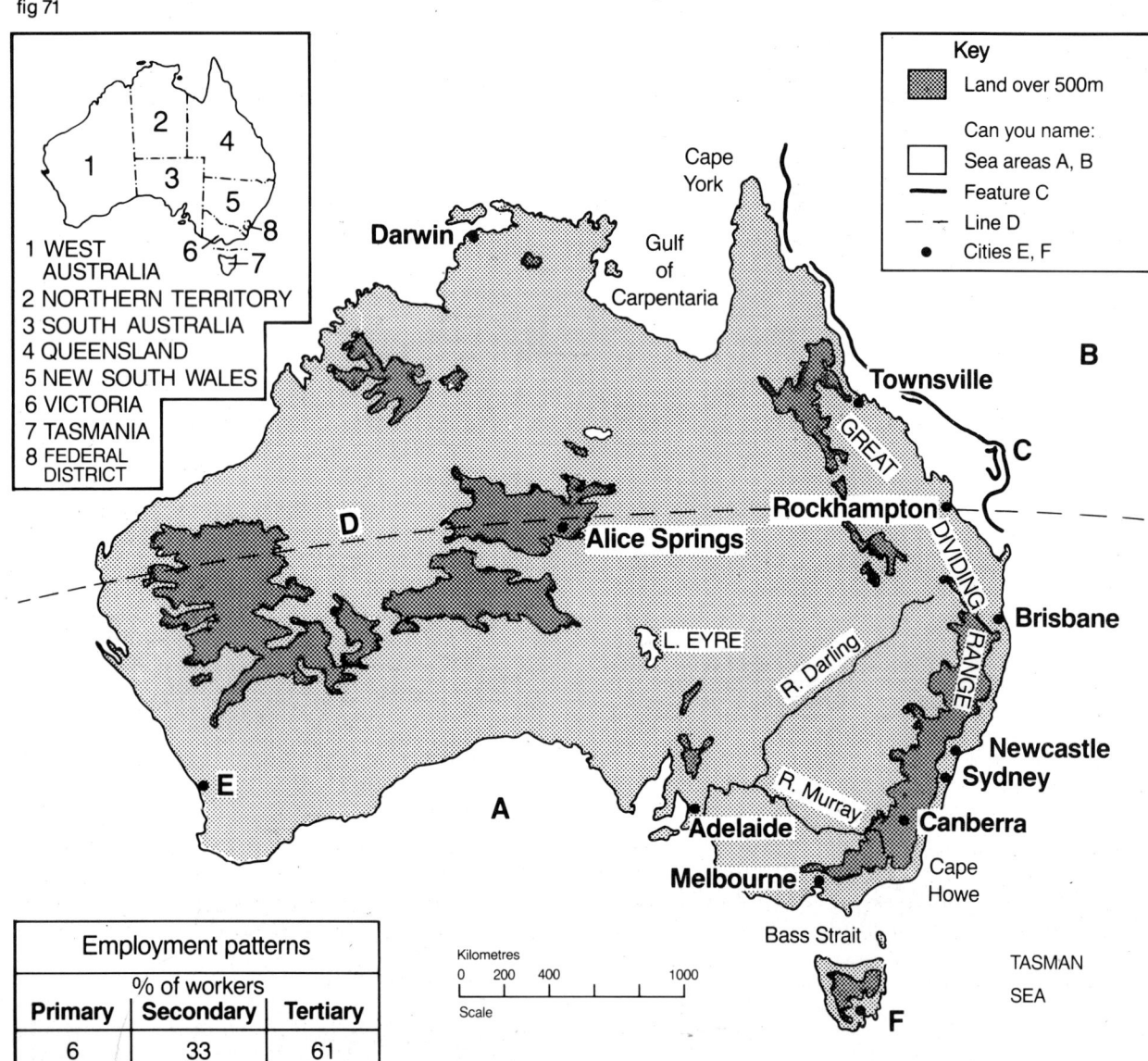

Key

Land over 500m

Can you name:
Sea areas A, B
Feature C
Line D
Cities E, F

1 WEST AUSTRALIA
2 NORTHERN TERRITORY
3 SOUTH AUSTRALIA
4 QUEENSLAND
5 NEW SOUTH WALES
6 VICTORIA
7 TASMANIA
8 FEDERAL DISTRICT

Employment patterns		
% of workers		
Primary	Secondary	Tertiary
6	33	61

Kilometres
0   200   400   1000
Scale

Activity A

Look at fig 71 and your atlas.

1 Make your own copy of the map.

2 Find out and add to your map key the names of the features lettered A to F.

3 Find and write down the latitude and longitude of Canberra, Adelaide, Alice Springs, Wellington and Suva. How many are in the Tropics? For comparison, find the latitude and longitude of your nearest city.

4 Use the statistics to draw two graphs to show the employment structure of Australia and New Zealand.

5 Describe in about 50 words what these graphs tell you about the importance of service activities in these countries.

fig 72

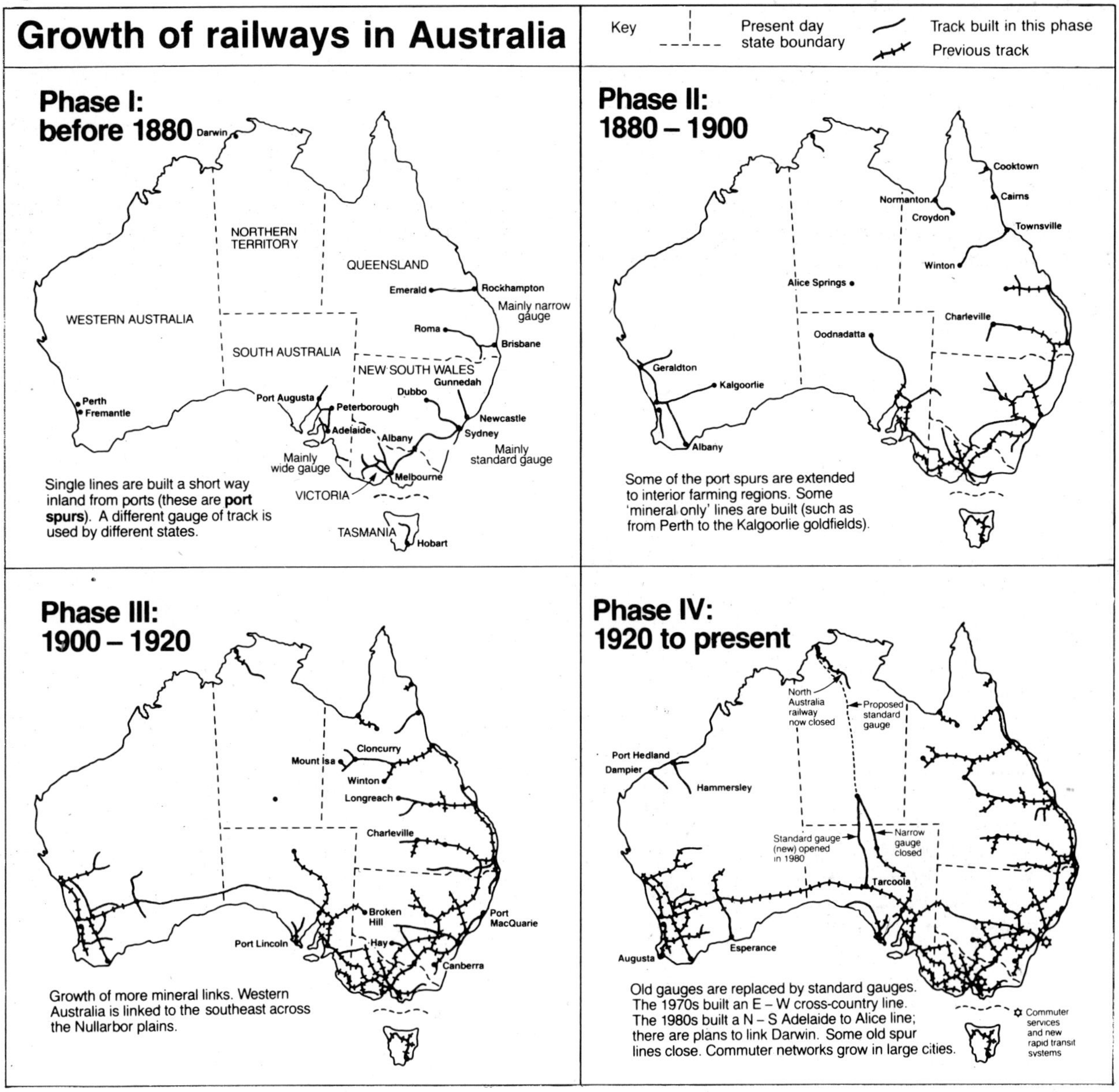

Growth of railways in Australia

Key | Present day state boundary | Track built in this phase | Previous track

Phase I: before 1880

Darwin

NORTHERN TERRITORY

QUEENSLAND

Emerald
Rockhampton

Mainly narrow gauge

Roma

Brisbane

WESTERN AUSTRALIA

SOUTH AUSTRALIA

NEW SOUTH WALES
Gunnedah
Dubbo

Port Augusta
Peterborough
Adelaide
Albany
Newcastle
Sydney

Perth
Fremantle

Mainly wide gauge

Mainly standard gauge

Melbourne

VICTORIA

TASMANIA
Hobart

Single lines are built a short way inland from ports (these are **port spurs**). A different gauge of track is used by different states.

Phase II: 1880 – 1900

Cooktown
Normanton
Cairns
Croydon
Townsville

Winton

Alice Springs

Charleville

Oodnadatta

Geraldton

Kalgoorlie

Albany

Some of the port spurs are extended to interior farming regions. Some 'mineral only' lines are built (such as from Perth to the Kalgoorlie goldfields).

Phase III: 1900 – 1920

Cloncurry
Mount Isa
Winton
Longreach

Charleville

Broken Hill
Port MacQuarie
Hay

Port Lincoln
Canberra

Growth of more mineral links. Western Australia is linked to the southeast across the Nullarbor plains.

Phase IV: 1920 to present

North Australia railway now closed
Proposed standard gauge

Port Hedland
Dampier

Hammersley

Standard gauge (new) opened in 1980
Narrow gauge closed

Tarcoola

Augusta
Esperance

Old gauges are replaced by standard gauges. The 1970s built an E – W cross-country line. The 1980s built a N – S Adelaide to Alice line; there are plans to link Darwin. Some old spur lines close. Commuter networks grow in large cities.

Commuter services and new rapid transit systems

Fig 72 shows the phases of railway growth since the first line was built from Melbourne in 1854. As time passed, more and more of the country was made accessible as new lines were built. We could say therefore, that as the railways penetrated more of the country the **service frontier** expanded.

The service frontier is advancing further and further inland. At the same time, the growth of the large cities (especially the state capitals) has expanded not only the transport service, but all types of service activity.

Activity B

Use your atlas and all the information on this page to help you answer the following:

1 List the termini in 1880 of the railways from Sydney, Melbourne, Brisbane and Adelaide.

2 Work out the greatest distance inland that any of these lines reached.

3 Describe the routes of any two of the penetration lines built between 1880 and 1900.

4 Write down how the railways expanded in the years 1900 to 1920.

5 When and where were commuter networks established?

6 Name the phase of present railway change.

7 Describe how the line north from Adelaide has changed and what future plans there are.

8 What do you understand by the phrase the service frontier?

9 Write in about 100 words how you think the growth of railways in Australia illustrates the expansion of the service frontier.

The Alice to Adelaide

Alice Springs and Adelaide are two different towns in Australia. These two towns have contrasts in their service provision, related to their size and history.

Alice Springs (or 'The Alice') started as a telegraph station, in 1872, based in the interior, over 1,300 km south from Darwin. In 1929 it was connected to Adelaide by railway. It began to develop into a town providing services to its **hinterland.** In 1981 it had a population of 22,000. Alice Springs has an unusually high number of services because of its role as a central point in the interior. As well as providing very special services, such as the Flying Doctor and the School of the Air, it has become a base for tourism in recent years. Even so it has many fewer services of all types than Adelaide.

Adelaide began as a settlement in 1836. It was built as a coastal port, in a natural harbour near good farming land. It has grown to become the state capital of South Australia. It is the 4th largest city in the continent. In 1981 Adelaide has a population of over 882,000. The city provides many different services for a wide region around called its **hinterland.** Some of these services are connected with public administration, as it is the state capital. Some of them are the financial and business services needed by firms operating in South Australia. There is a very large range of service types, and many examples of each type.

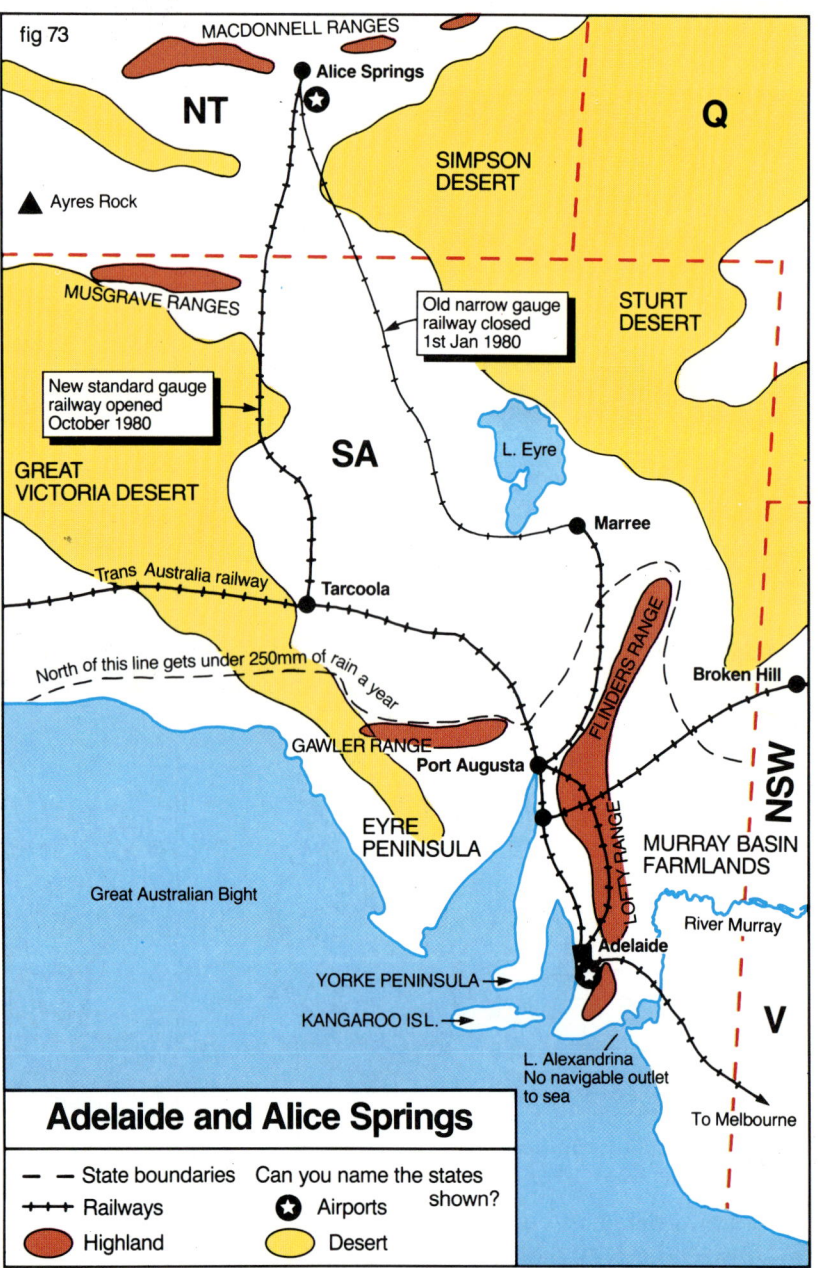

fig 73

Adelaide and Alice Springs

- – State boundaries
- +–+ Railways
- Highland
- Airports
- Desert

Can you name the states shown?

Activity

Look at fig 74 and the photos.

1 Count up the services of Alice Springs under the following headings: education, government administration, health, tourist accommodation, and sports facilities.
Make a graph of your results.

2 Which of these services are likely to be found only in Adelaide, which only in Alice Springs, and which in both: supermarket, large theatre, School of the Air, post office, university, chemist shop, state parliament, and commuter railway.

3 In about 100 words, try to explain your answer to question 2.

Research project You might like to do your own survey of services near your school to see if small centres have different services than large ones.

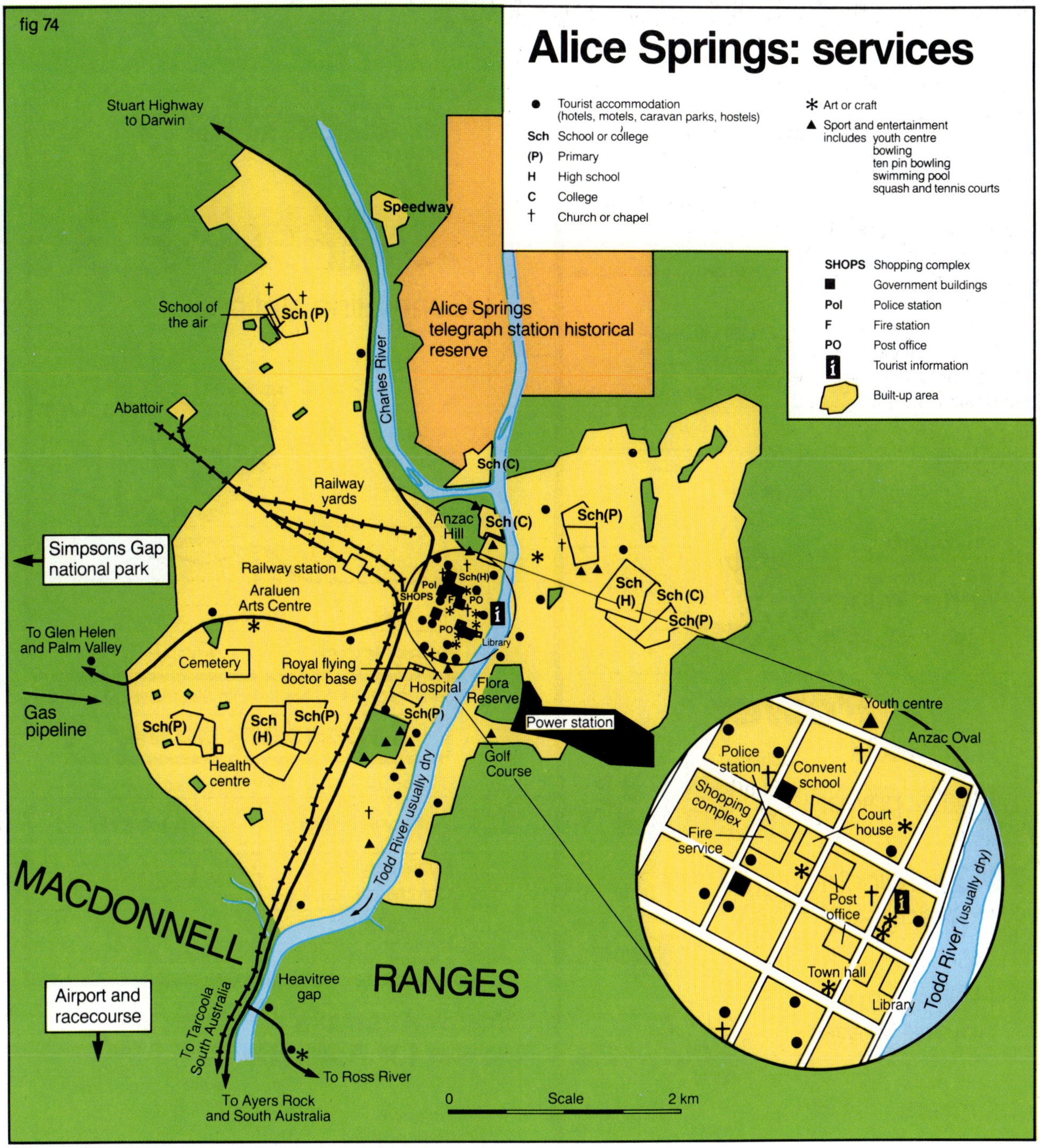

fig 74

Alice Springs: services

● Tourist accommodation (hotels, motels, caravan parks, hostels)
Sch School or college
(P) Primary
H High school
C College
† Church or chapel

∗ Art or craft
▲ Sport and entertainment
includes youth centre
bowling
ten pin bowling
swimming pool
squash and tennis courts

SHOPS Shopping complex
■ Government buildings
Pol Police station
F Fire station
PO Post office
[i] Tourist information
▨ Built-up area

Stuart Highway to Darwin

Speedway

Alice Springs telegraph station historical reserve

Charles River

School of the air

Sch (P)

Abattoir

Railway yards

Sch(C)

Anzac Hill

Sch(C)

Sch(P)

Sch(C)

Sch(P)

Simpsons Gap national park

Railway station

Araluen Arts Centre

Sch(H)

Pol

SHOPS

PO

PO

[i]

Library

Sch (H)

To Glen Helen and Palm Valley

Cemetery

Royal flying doctor base

Gas pipeline

Hospital

Flora Reserve

Power station

Sch(P)

Sch (H)

Sch(P)

Sch(P)

Health centre

Golf Course

Todd River usually dry

MACDONNELL

RANGES

Airport and racecourse

Heavitree gap

To Tarcoola South Australia

∗

To Ross River

To Ayers Rock and South Australia

0   Scale   2 km

Inset

Youth centre

Anzac Oval

Police station

Convent school

Shopping complex

Court house

Fire service

∗

Post office

[i]

Town hall

Library

Todd River (usually dry)

photo 42: Alice Springs, Australia

photo 43: Adelaide, Australia

73

People and Power

fig 75

Fuels

Exhaustable and finite

Coal → coke →
gas
others →

Oil and oil products → fuel oil →
petrol →
others →

Gas →

Nuclear →

Other minor fuels e.g. peat →

Power

Renewable

Water power

Hydro-electric power →

Human and animal power

Others

solar	geothermal
wind	wave
wood-burning	

When energy is used directly it is called

Primary power

used for

Primary activities	Secondary activities
Mining Forestry Farming	Manufacturing

Electricity

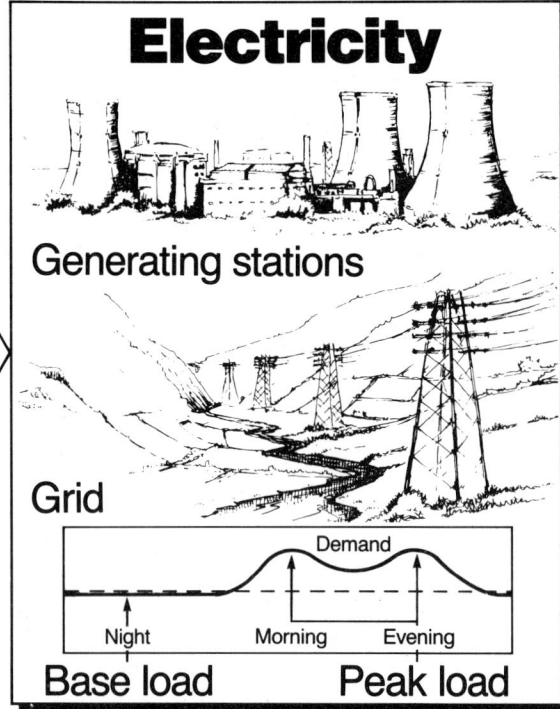

Generating stations

Grid

Demand

Night — Morning — Evening

Base load — Peak load

When energy is converted into electricity it is called

Secondary power

used for

Tertiary activities	Domestically
Public services Commercial services	Homes
Transport	Personal transport
Leisure	

South Australia – power for Adelaide

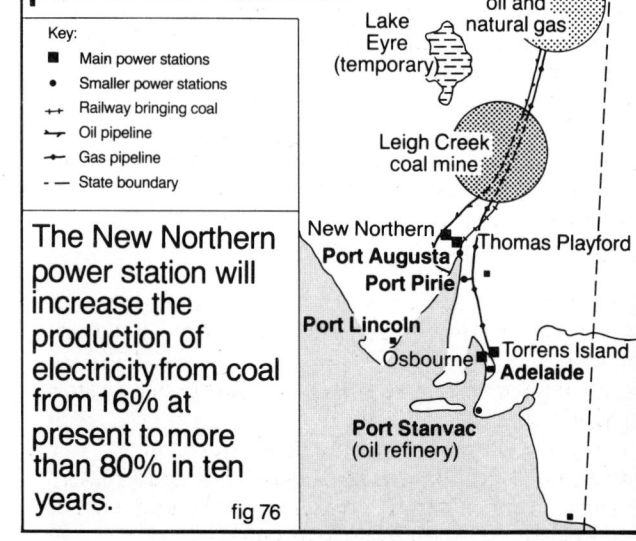

Key:
- ■ Main power stations
- • Smaller power stations
- ⊢⊣ Railway bringing coal
- ⊸ Oil pipeline
- ⊸ Gas pipeline
- - - State boundary

The New Northern power station will increase the production of electricity from coal from 16% at present to more than 80% in ten years.

Cooper Basin oil and natural gas
Lake Eyre (temporary)
Leigh Creek coal mine
New Northern
Port Augusta
Thomas Playford
Port Pirie
Port Lincoln
Osbourne
Torrens Island
Adelaide
Port Stanvac (oil refinery)

fig 76

fig 77

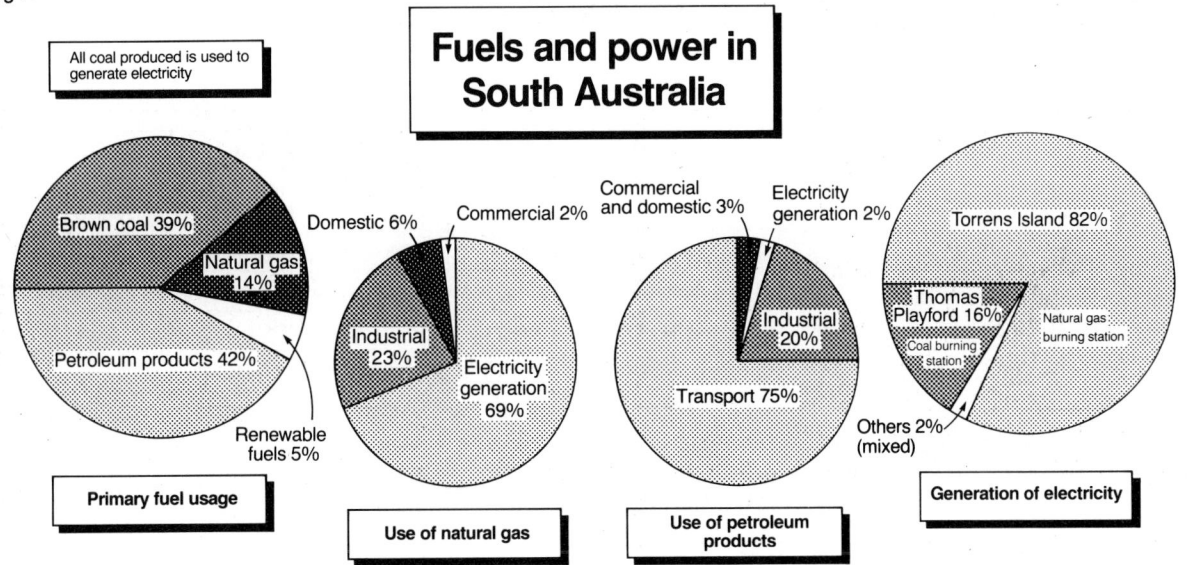

Fuels and power in South Australia

All coal produced is used to generate electricity

Brown coal 39%
Natural gas 14%
Petroleum products 42%
Renewable fuels 5%

Primary fuel usage

Domestic 6%
Commercial 2%
Industrial 23%
Electricity generation 69%

Use of natural gas

Commercial and domestic 3%
Electricity generation 2%
Industrial 20%
Transport 75%

Use of petroleum products

Torrens Island 82%
Natural gas burning station
Thomas Playford 16%
Coal burning station
Others 2% (mixed)

Generation of electricity

Figures for year 1982/3

All human activities need energy. As a country becomes more developed its need or demand for energy rises very rapidly, that energy can come from many sources, as fig 75 shows:

- by unlocking the energy stored in non-renewable fossil fuels like coal, oil, gas and peat
- by unlocking the energy of the atom from non-renewable radioactive minerals like uranium
- from running water
- from renewable biological sources like wood, animals and people
- from natural physical sources such as direct from the sun, or from heat underground, or from waves and wind

The energy from these sources can be used directly in which case it is called **primary power.** Alternatively, the energy locked up in these sources can be converted into a different form, like electricity, which is called **secondary power.**

Just like all activities we have seen, there are spatial patterns to energy.

- a spatial pattern of supply: the fuel resources are not evenly distributed, nor are the sites of secondary power generation
- a spatial pattern of demand: where the power is used

Because each has a separate pattern, there is a need for a **distribution system** to link them. This is often in the form of a network of transport lines and pipelines, and an electricity transmission grid.

There is also another pattern. This is the pattern of power use in time. The amount of energy used is not the same at all times of the day or in the different seasons. For example, this is why electricity supply is divided into two parts.

- **base load:** the amount used all the time
- **peak load:** the extra amount used at certain times such as morning and evening peaks, and winter demand compared with summer demand

Demand for energy is very rarely supplied from one source. Most places rely on a mixture of sources. Supplying energy therefore requires careful planning of a suitable **energy mix.** The energy mix for South Australia is shown in fig 77.

Activity

1 Here is the start of a pupil's personal energy diary for a day. It records the activities which needed energy:

Time	Date: 4th June Activity	Energy source
07.30	Got up—put on light	electricity
07.40	Washed in hot water	gas
07.45	Breakfast cooked	gas
07.55	Lit fire for Mum	wood/coal
08.15	Bus to school	petrol

Try to write out your own energy diary for the whole of one particular day.

2 How many types of energy did you use?

3 Try to work out the periods in the day when you used these sources of energy most.

4 Work out definitions of the following and add them to your dictionary of geography: primary power, secondary power, base load, peak load, and energy mix.

5 List the primary power sources of South Australia.

6 Name the base load power stations of South Australia and then those supplying peak load only.

7 How would your energy needs be different from those of a school pupil living in Adelaide and a peasant farmer in Nigeria?

Leisure

Leisure	Recreation			Examples	fig 78
Non-working time	Indoor	Active	Home-based	DIY, model making, knitting, sewing, carpentry	
			Outside home involving travel	Sports centres, indoor swimming pools, 10 pin bowling, ice skating, squash, amateur drama	
		Passive	Home-based	Watching TV, listening to records, radio, reading	
			Outside home involving travel	Visiting library, museums, pubs, theatres, concerts	
		Mixed	Outside home involving travel	Disco, youth clubs	
	Outdoor	Active	Home-based	Gardening, car maintenance	
			Outside home involving travel	BMX, hill walking, jogging, football, netball, fishing	
		Passive	Home-based	Sitting in garden, sun bathing	
			Outside home involving travel	Visiting zoos, car trips, family excursions, watching football	
		Mixed	Outside home involving travel	Picnics, family trips to seaside, window shopping	
Tourism	Indoor and outdoor	Mixed active and passive	With a day's travel, involving no stay	Visiting local tourist attractions	
			Short stay	Weekend stay, short residential courses	
			Long stay	Cycle touring, walking expeditions, annual family holiday	

photo 44: Sunbathing on holiday

photo 45: Walking expedition

Tertiary activities provide services for primary and secondary activities, while people are at work. Some tertiary activities also provide services to cater for the times when people are not at work. Non-working time is called **leisure**, the way that people use this time is called **recreation.** Each person's pattern of leisure and recreation is different, it depends on their different circumstances, personality, and situation. **Tourism** has become one of the major growth industries of the twentieth century too (the movement of people to visit other places in their leisure time). This is for several reasons:

- the length of the working week is decreasing
- annual paid holidays are getting longer
- personal incomes are rising
- more people can afford to buy private transport

- the tourist industry has become geared to catering for large numbers of people at reasonable cost
- people are now able to travel to very distant places easily

There is though a·very important difference between various parts of the world:

- in the industrial countries of the developed world, the majority of people are gaining more leisure time and opportunity
- in some of the developed countries the income from tourists is a vital part of the economy
- in the poorer developing countries tourism for foreigners is encouraged, as it is a means of growth, increases wealth, provides jobs and earns money for investment in economic and social development

fig 79

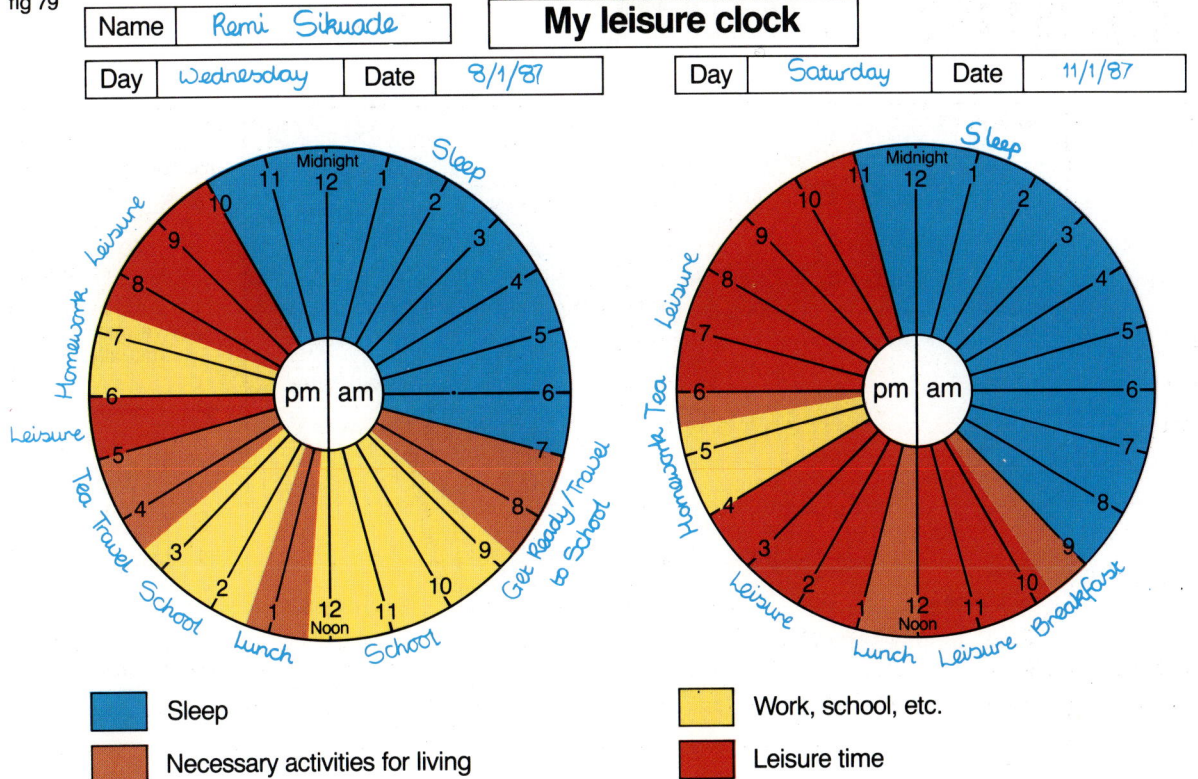

| Name | Remi Sikuade | | My leisure clock | | | | |

| Day | Wednesday | Date | 8/1/87 | Day | Saturday | Date | 11/1/87 |

My leisure clock

Left clock labels: Midnight 12, Sleep, Get Ready/Travel to School, School, Lunch, School, Travel, Tea, Leisure, Homework, Leisure

Right clock labels: Sleep, Breakfast, Leisure, Lunch, Leisure, Homework Tea, Leisure

- 🟦 Sleep
- 🟧 Necessary activities for living
- 🟨 Work, school, etc.
- 🟥 Leisure time

photo 46 : Playing dominoes

Recreation takes many different forms. The types are arranged in fig 78.

It can be pursued:
- either indoors or outdoors
- actively, passively or as a mixture of both
- at different times such as weekdays or evenings, weekends or in different seasons

Since there are many different types of recreation and tourism, there are also many different service industries which provide the facilities for it to take place.

Activity

1 Define the words leisure, recreation and tourism and add them to your dictionary of geography.

2 List at least five reasons why people have their own individual leisure pattern.

Look at fig 79.

3 Draw your own leisure clocks like these, one for school, and one for a day at the weekend or in the school holidays.

4 How different is your pattern from that of your friends?

6 Look at fig 78. Make your own copy of the chart but leaving the example column blank. Now try to fill in this column with your own individual leisure activities. Make sure that they are classified in the correct spaces using the examples in the chart to help you.

The Red Centre

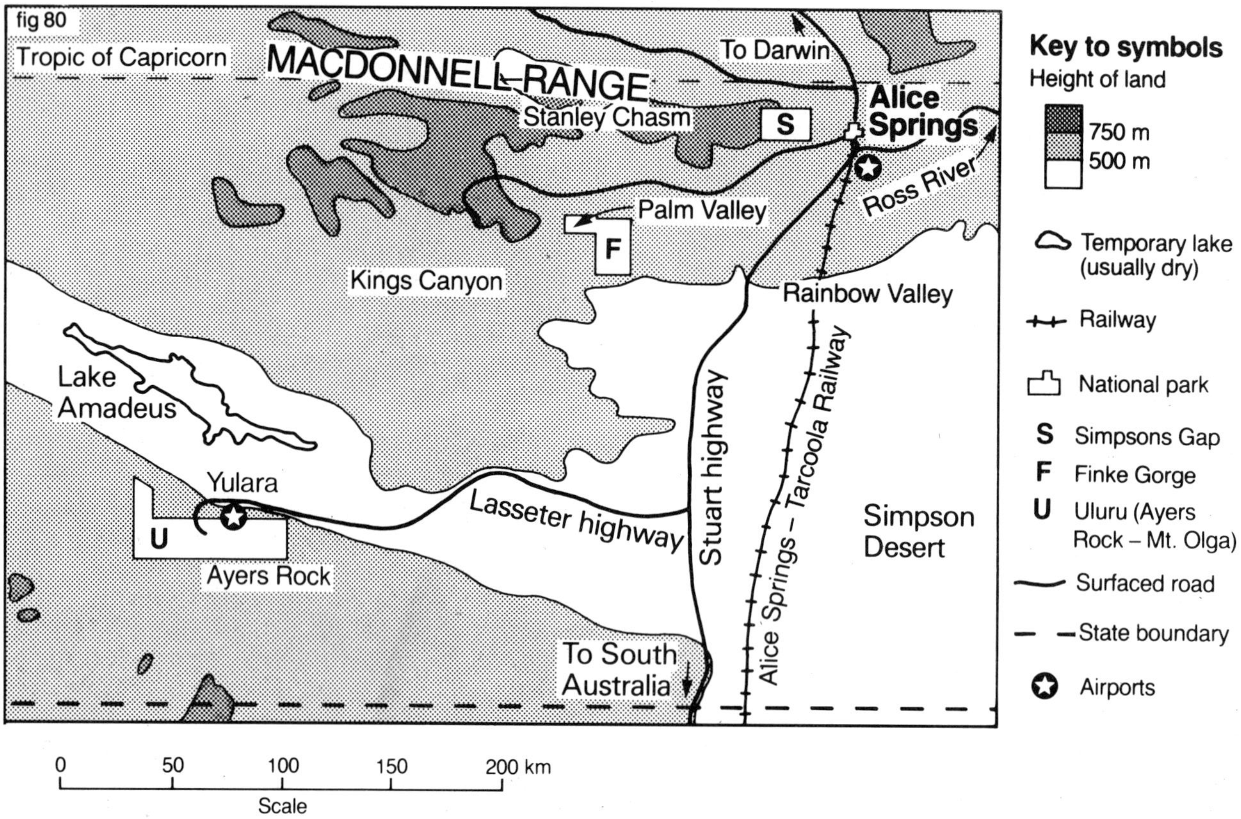

fig 80

Tropic of Capricorn

MACDONNELL RANGE

To Darwin

Stanley Chasm

S

Alice Springs

Ross River

Palm Valley

F

Kings Canyon

Rainbow Valley

Lake Amadeus

Yulara

U

Ayers Rock

Lasseter highway

Stuart highway

Alice Springs – Tarcoola Railway

Simpson Desert

To South Australia

Key to symbols

Height of land

- 750 m
- 500 m

- Temporary lake (usually dry)
- Railway
- National park
- **S** Simpsons Gap
- **F** Finke Gorge
- **U** Uluru (Ayers Rock – Mt. Olga)
- Surfaced road
- State boundary
- Airports

Scale: 0 50 100 150 200 km

photo 47: Stanley Chasm, Australia

photo 48: Kings Canyon, Australia

photo 49: Ayers Rock, Australia

As a case-study example of leisure, tourism offers a wide range of important ideas. It is not like many of the daily and local recreational activities you have just looked at. This is because tourist holidays and visits usually have:
● both an **indoor** and an **outdoor** element
● both **active** and **passive** pursuits
● a long stay
● both **non-travel** and **travel** activities once the tourist has a place to stay for a period of time
Tourism is a tertiary service industry itself, but it also requires many other linked services if it is to be successful. The tourist development at Ayers Rock shows how this is true. It is in the hot, dry heart of Australia called 'The Red Centre'.

Fig 80 shows the area of Northern Territory south of the Tropic of Capricorn. It contains Alice Springs and the area south and west of it. Within a four or five hour car drive along the Stuart and Lasseter Highways is Ayers Rock, a very famous landmark of Central Australia.
The whole area has seen a great growth of the tourist industry in recent years. Some of the attractions of outstanding natural beauty in this part of Northern Territory are shown in the photos.
The attractions of the area are wide-ranging and very largely **natural** ones:
● the position in the heart of the continent
● the continuously hot dry weather
● the view of extensive desert landscapes, and features like Ayers Rock
● the desert wildlife
● some naturally preserved evidence of aboriginal life and culture such as the rock paintings

The attraction to a remote and unpopulated area like this, as well as some of the other remote areas of the world, gives people what has been called the **wilderness experience.**
However, tourism in such an area cannot take place in any real way without some form of development. To some extent this automatically means that it is no longer a wilderness if modern amenities are built, but the natural attractions still remain as long as they are carefully looked after.
This is why tourism in the whole area has been so carefully planned. The government of Northern Territory is responsible for:

photo 50: Yulara holiday resort, Australia

● helping set up and run **national parks**
● building the Lasseter Highway to give better access
● promoting tourism both inside Australia and abroad
● providing funds for developing facilities
● helping to **conserve** all the natural features
Much of this has been done in a controlled way since the setting up of the Northern Territory Tourist Commission in 1980.
One of the major new developments is near Ayers Rock, the greatest attraction in the Territory. An 'oasis in the desert' holiday resort has been built. It is called Yulara and is shown in its building phase in one of the photos. It is just on the edge of the Uluru National Park where Ayers Rock is found.
Yulara has many services linked to tourism:
● camping grounds for 3,600 people
● holiday cabins
● two hotels, one of 100 rooms and a large international one of 230 rooms
● shopping facilities
● an Aboriginal craft centre
● a visitor information centre with National Park rangers
● solar power for 70 per cent of the hot water and a sizeable gas-fired power station
● a sealed circuit road around Ayers Rock
● a new airport for internal air services from the main cities
Yulara was planned to cater for 6,000 people a day. With such a large number of people, there is a danger of environmental damage. This is why the whole project was so carefully planned from the beginning. Full protection measures are taken to preserve the environment and large areas have been left in their natural state, even within the town.
Yulara is a good example of the way that service industries can grow to use the natural resources of the landscape. They can be developed in such a way that environmental impacts are kept to the very minimum.

Activity
1 Look at fig 80 and your atlas.
a calculate the distance from Alice Springs to Ayers Rock.
b what is the latitude of Ayers Rock?
c why is Lake Amadeus usually dry?
d how many National Parks are there in the area shown?
e list the natural attractions shown on the map.
2 Choose any two of the photos. Draw your own sketches of each and label on them the features that you think are attractive to tourists.
3 List the reasons why tourists are attracted to the Red Centre.
4 In about 75 words, describe why Yulara was so carefully planned.
Project work Design and make a completed postcard that you might send home if you were staying at Yulara on holiday. Draw on one side a view or views, and write your impressions on the other.

Temples at Dawn

photo 51: Beach in Goa

photo 52: Hindu temple

photo 53: Pilgrims in the Ganges

photo 54: Taj Mahal in Agra

India has many **scenic attractions** for tourists, such as the tropical palm-fringed sandy coasts of Goa, and the spectacular mountain scenery of the Himalayan foothills. However, tourism is also a result of the human features of the country: the **cultural attractions,** some of which are shown above.

Activity A

1 Look at the pictures carefully. Use your atlas to mark all these places on an outline map of India.
How far apart are these places, approximately?

2 Work out a package holiday plan for a fortnight's holiday in India. Visit at least five places. Write it as though it was an itinerary for a tour in a travel brochure. Your plan should include details of the towns where you stay, and give times and distances. The tour starts and ends in Delhi. Use your library and tourist brochures from your local travel agent to help you.

International tourist visitors to Australia and India, in 1983, came from very different parts of the world. The origins of these tourists were as follows:

Percentage of international visitors (%)		
From	To Australia	To India
United Kingdom	16	10
Rest of Europe	13	18
North America	18	10
East Asia and the Pacific (e.g. Japan and New Zealand)	49	10
South Asia	1	41
Rest of the World	3	11

Most of Australia's visitors came from New Zealand (24 per cent alone), Europe, Japan and the USA, most of India's visitors came from Europe and South Asia.

Despite these differences in origins the similarity between the amount of international tourism in Australia and India is quite striking. In 1983, both had about the same earnings and numbers of overseas visitors. This table shows the details:

Country	Earnings from tourism in millions of £s	Number of overseas visitors
Australia	655	1.0 million
India	533	1.3 million

However, the benefits of the earnings from international tourism vary. They depend on the overall size of the home population. As Australia had 15.4 million people compared with India's 733.2 million, Australia's earnings per person were 57 times greater. In many developing countries like India tourism could be greatly expanded to help earn money for development.

fig 81

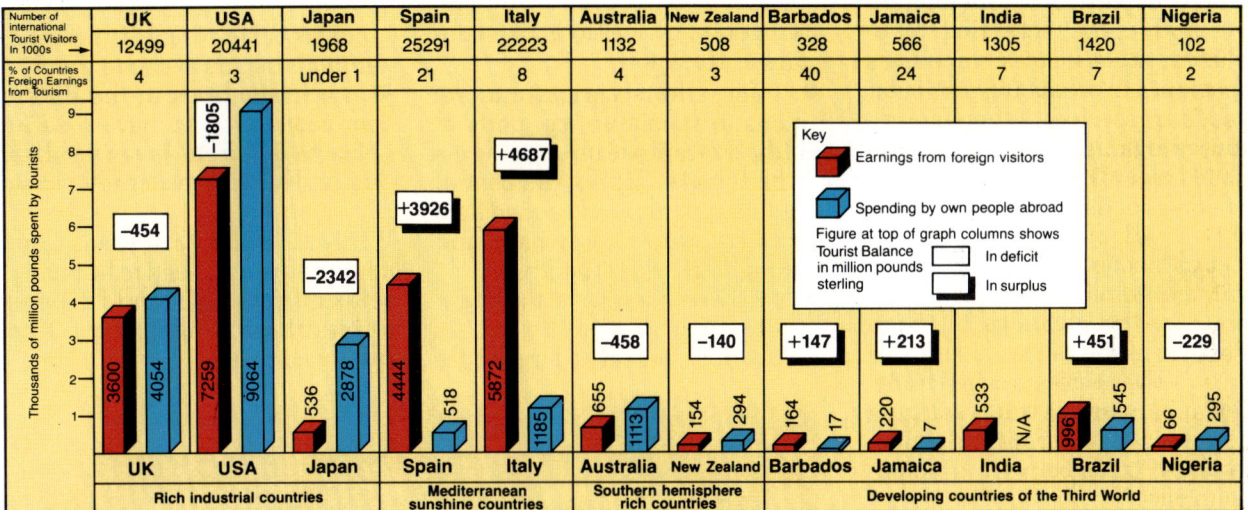

Fig 81 shows the **Tourist Budgets** of 12 selected countries. It compares, for each country, the money received from foreign visitors with the amount spent by its own people abroad.

Tourism is a fast growing industry around the world, especially in developing countries. Improvements in air transport have been a major factor in making this possible. Many developing countries are anxious to encourage tourism, and some, like Kenya, have deliberately tried to plan for this by building facilities, services and resorts. They hope that tourism will earn money to help pay for the development of agriculture, industry and services, and that it will provide jobs and improve living standards.

The provision of services, such as airports, roads and shops, are not only needed for tourism. Once built, they may benefit all the population, and encourage developments in other activities such as farming and industry.

Expanding tourism in a country can bring problems:

● the impact of tourism is usually **concentrated** at places such as coastal sites, and historical and cultural locations. Only some regions may benefit. The differences in wealth within a country can bring social and economic problems

● not all the earnings from tourism go to the country concerned. It may have had to borrow money to develop tourism. These loans have to be repaid with interest. Some multi-national companies finance and run airlines, hotels and package tours, and they will often take profits out of the country

Tourism can have major benefits for developing countries, but it is not always as straightforward and simple as it seems.

Activity B

1 Look at fig 81 and answer these questions in sentences.
a list in order from high to low the countries which earned a surplus from tourism.
b which ones had a deficit?
c suggest several reasons why the less developed countries might want to develop tourism.
2 Why does the text say that developing tourism in a developing country 'is not always as straightforward and simple as it seems'?

Trade and Exchange

We can think of the world as having various patterns:
- a pattern of natural resources
- a pattern of producing locations for each primary, secondary, and tertiary activity, using the natural resource base
- a pattern of population which produces and consumes goods and services, made available by all the activities

These patterns do not coincide in the same places completely. There are many kinds of regions with their own particular combination of production, activities, population, and resources: some areas specialise in producing particular goods or services, others are resource regions, and some are populated regions with few resources. Making goods and services available to all may provide all the factors needed for living where they are required. This can only be done by the **exchange** of them. This exchange of goods and services between areas is called **trade**. It can be **internal trade** within a country or **external or international trade** between different countries.

Trade connects different places and therefore:
- links different activities which depend on each other
- allows some areas to specialise in things they are best suited to produce and get other necessary goods by exchange
- creates patterns of activities by allowing raw materials to be brought into an area and goods and services to be distributed elsewhere
- creates jobs as part of the tertiary sector

Some examples of the links that trade gives are:
- raw materials are transported to manufacturing locations in other places e.g. Japan imports the bulk of its raw materials for industry
- manufactured goods are transported to markets e.g. they may be transported from Japan to other countries, such as the United

fig 82

Location		Location
Production of goods and services	**Trade** — Internal *within a country* / External *with other countries*	People needing goods and services
Spatial pattern of enterprise		Spatial pattern of demand

Kingdom, by methods like container transport
- trade allows agricultural regions to specialise e.g. parts of India concentrate on growing tea which makes up six per cent of India's exports; food needed here may be grown elsewhere and brought in by internal trade
- northern Nigeria is the main cattle area of the country, but the south does not have a large cattle industry, and so trade in meat and animals occurs between them
- the inequalities in the different economies we have seen in Nigeria, India and Japan result in individual trade patterns for each

Without trade, all areas and countries would need to be totally self-sufficient. Life would depend on only those things that could be produced there.

photo 55: Barges bringing iron ore, Goa, India

Activity A
1 Add definitions of exchange and trade to your dictionary of geography.
2 What is the difference between internal and external trade?
3 Find out how much you depend on world trade by drawing up a list of the countries of origin of food items and manufactured goods used by your family.
4 On a world outline map, shade and name all the countries in your list.
5 How many of the goods that you have listed come from developed countries and how many from the developing countries?
6 How does trade affect your life?

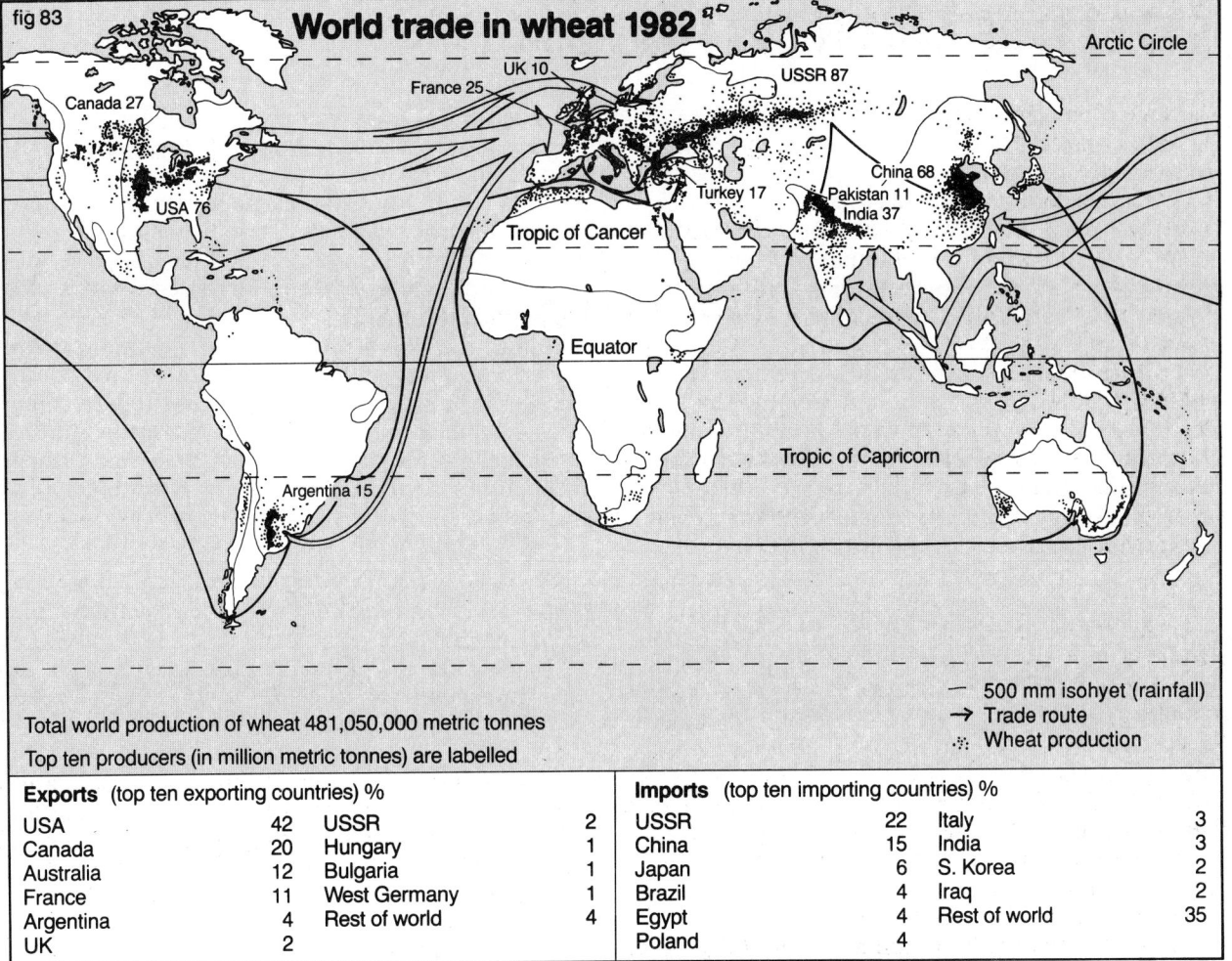

World trade in wheat 1982

Canada 27, USA 76, Argentina 15, UK 10, France 25, USSR 87, Turkey 17, China 68, Pakistan 11, India 37

Arctic Circle
Tropic of Cancer
Equator
Tropic of Capricorn

Total world production of wheat 481,050,000 metric tonnes
Top ten producers (in million metric tonnes) are labelled

— 500 mm isohyet (rainfall)
→ Trade route
Wheat production

Exports (top ten exporting countries) %			
USA	42	USSR	2
Canada	20	Hungary	1
Australia	12	Bulgaria	1
France	11	West Germany	1
Argentina	4	Rest of world	4
UK	2		

Imports (top ten importing countries) %			
USSR	22	Italy	3
China	15	India	3
Japan	6	S. Korea	2
Brazil	4	Iraq	2
Egypt	4	Rest of world	35
Poland	4		

The map shows that there are specialised areas of wheat production, where the conditions favour the growing of wheat on a large scale. These areas are mainly
● in temperate latitudes between 25° and 50° away from the Equator
● extensive lowland areas with gentle slopes
● of between 500 and 800 millimetres rain a year

The diagram names the top ten producing countries. Of the total world production of wheat, only about one-fifth enters international trade. Not all top ten **producing** countries are in the top ten for **exporting** wheat.

Ten exporting countries produce enough surplus wheat to make up 96 per cent of world exports. This is exported to areas of **demand,** most of which grow relatively little wheat themselves. The top ten **importing** countries, by comparison, account for only 65 per cent of the world total. This shows that the pattern of demand is much more widely spread than the pattern of **supply.**

Some unusual features of the trade are suggested by the figures:
● production of farm goods (like wheat) may vary greatly year by year and this may affect trade
● certain nations both import from some countries and export to others
● there are different varieties of wheat used for different bakery products, and a country may export one type of wheat that it grows and import another type that it needs

Wheat is just one trade commodity, any primary or secondary commodity may be traded and this is called **visible trade.** A country may also earn money from **invisible trade:** the exchange of information and services provided by tertiary activities.

Activity B
Use fig 83 to answer the following.
1 Write a list of the top ten wheat producing countries in their rank order from largest to smallest.
2 Draw a graph to show the top ten importing countries.
3 Make lists for the countries in the top ten for:
a production and export.
b production and import.
c production, export and import.
d import but not production.
4 Which two of these lists do you find unusual? Why?
5 Describe three reasons from the text which might help explain these unusual features.

Import/Export

India's trade pattern for 1981 is shown in fig 84. It indicates that the total value of imported goods exceeded the value of goods exported. India was in deficit on the **balance of trade** in goods.

It imported mainly manufactured goods with the exception of crude oil in large amounts. It has few oil resources of its own. Exports were mainly primary products, with some basic manufactures like textiles and clothing.

The **direction of trade** was mainly with rich developed countries. To them India sent well over half its exports. Exactly 50 per cent went to only five such countries. These same five countries provided 38 per cent of all imports.

Japan's trade, as in fig 85, was rather different. It had a surplus on its balance of trade in goods. It imported mainly the resources which Japan itself lacks. As the graph shows, just six of these accounted for 71 per cent of total imports.

Exports were almost completely manufactures, ranging from heavy goods like ships, steel and heavy machinery to consumer and high technology products like cars, electrical appliances, computers and scientific equipment.

Although the USA is the main trading partner, Japan exported to a very wide range of countries with both developed and developing economies. Imports came from an equally wide range of sources, though the pressing need for oil was shown by the proportion of imports from Middle Eastern countries and Indonesia.

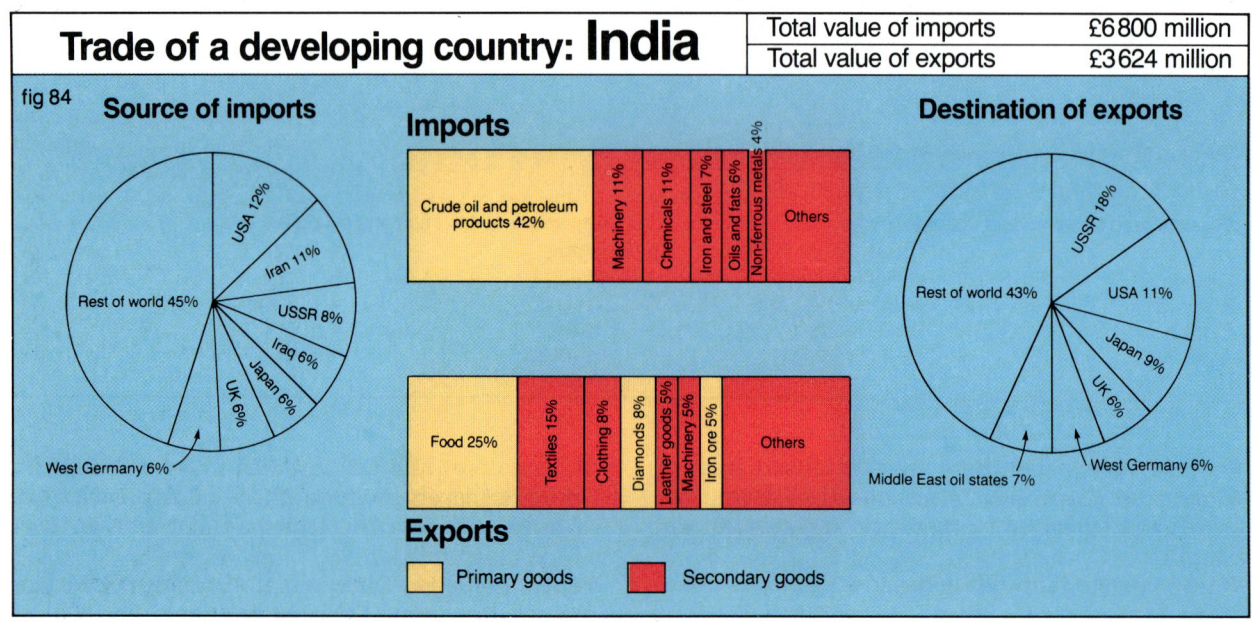

Trade of a developing country: India

| Total value of imports | £6 800 million |
| Total value of exports | £3 624 million |

fig 84

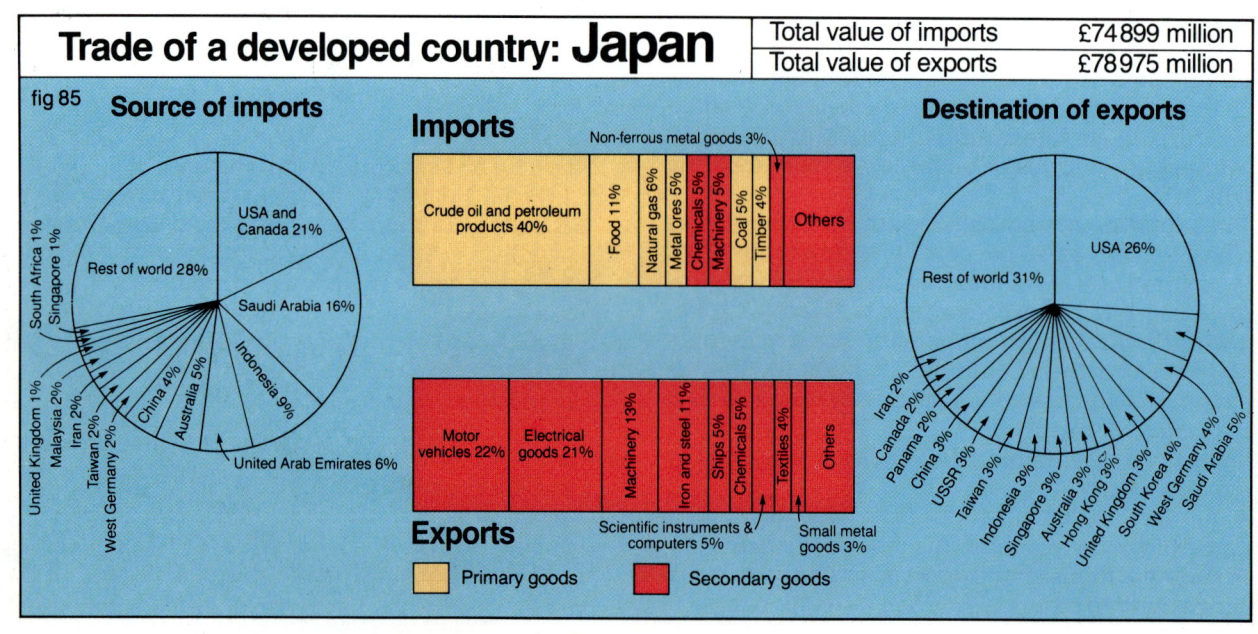

Trade of a developed country: Japan

| Total value of imports | £74 899 million |
| Total value of exports | £78 975 million |

fig 85

Similarities between the trading patterns of India and Japan are few:

- both import oil, which makes up nearly the same large percentage of the total
- textile goods are a significant percentage of exports in both cases

Differences in their trading patterns are much more noticeable:

- Japan's total value of all import and export trade is 15 times greater, even though its population is only about one-seventh
- Japan's imports are primary raw materials, while India's are mainly manufactures

- Japan's exports are dominated by a wide range of manufactures, while India's include mainly primary goods and only basic manufactures
- the direction of Japan's trade appears to be more worldwide

These differences reflect the contrast between developed and developing countries. Developed countries tend to be **exporters of manufactures** while developing countries are often **providers of food and raw materials.**

The worldwide pattern of these contrasts is shown on fig 86. It is perhaps no great coincidence that this division based on economic activities and trade is the same as the division based on standards of living.

fig 86

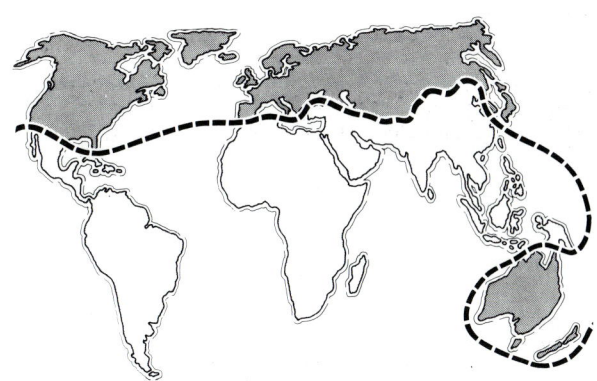

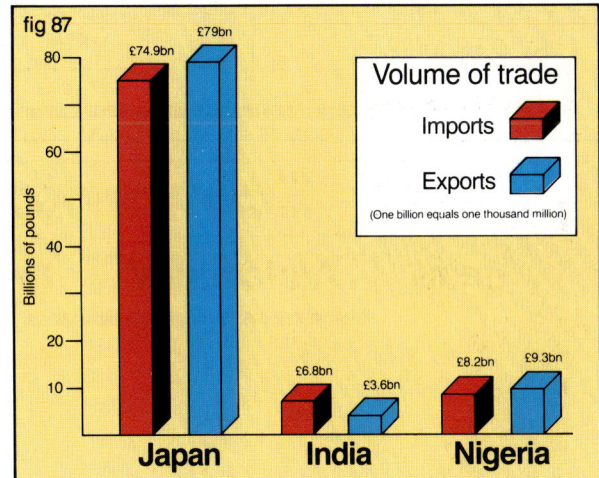

Activity

1 Copy this comparison chart of Japanese and Indian trade. Complete it from the figures on page 84.

	Japan	India
Value of imports		
Value of exports		
Balance of trade in goods		
Primary imports over 5%		
Secondary imports over 5%		
Primary exports over 5%		
Secondary exports over 5%		
Five main countries imported from		
Five main export countries		

2 Draw your own trade graphs to show Nigeria's trade pattern. Here are some recent figures:

Imports (value £8220 million)		Exports (value £9353 million)	
Machinery	29%	Crude oil	95%
Food	13%	Cocoa	1%
Motor vehicles	12%	Others	4%
Chemicals	8%		
Iron and steel	6%		
Small metal goods	5%		
Others	27%		
From:		**To:**	
United Kingdom	17%	U.S.A.	44%
West Germany	16%	Netherlands	12%
Japan	11%	West Germany	8%
U.S.A.	10%	France	8%
France	9%	U.K.	6%
Italy	6%	Others	22%
Others	31%		

3 What type of goods does Nigeria import and export?
4 With what kind of country does Nigeria mainly trade?
5 Look at fig 87. What conclusions can you make from it about the connection between the volume of trade and living standards?

Enterprise Earth

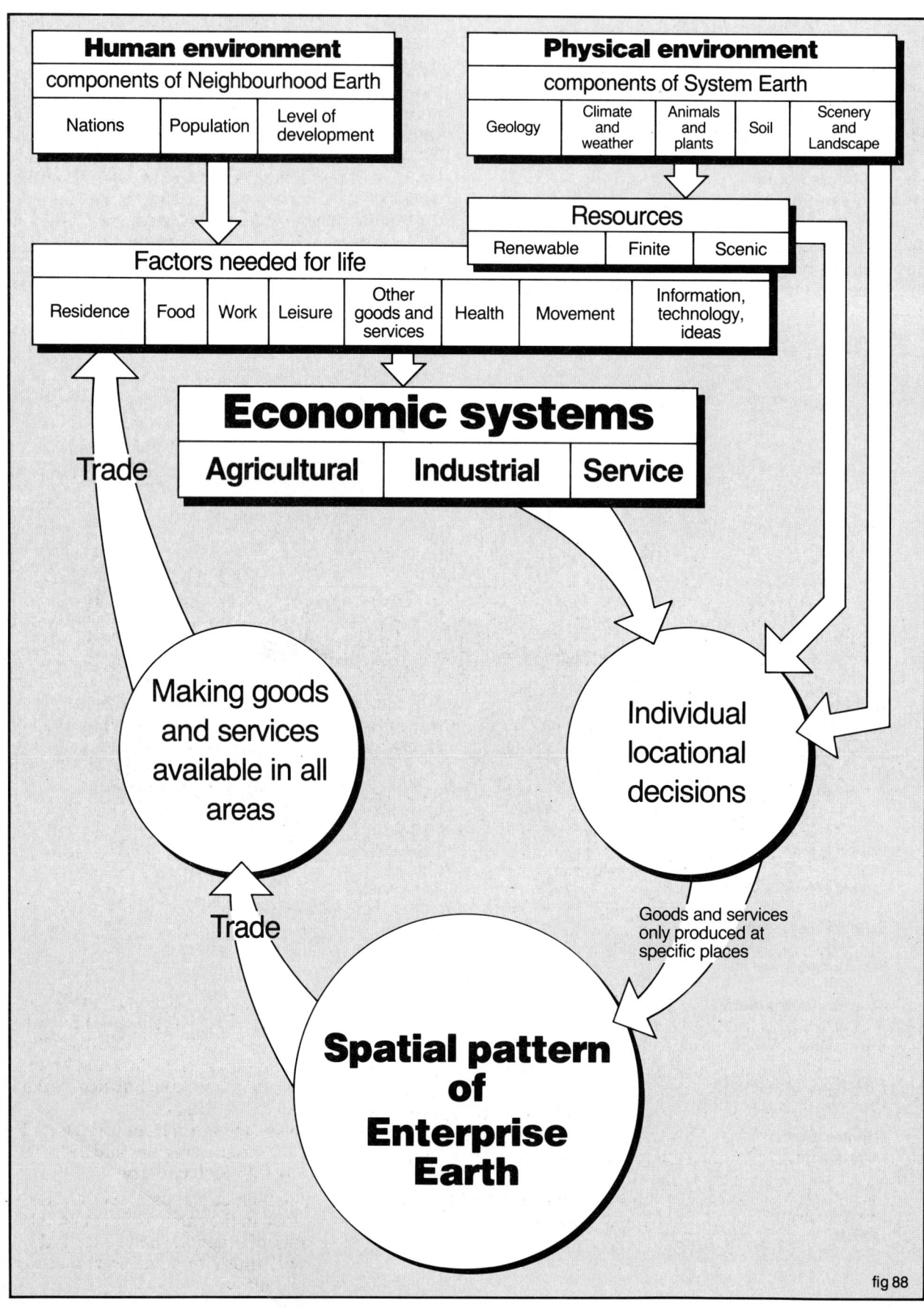

Human environment

components of Neighbourhood Earth

Nations	Population	Level of development

Physical environment

components of System Earth

Geology	Climate and weather	Animals and plants	Soil	Scenery and Landscape

Factors needed for life

Residence	Food	Work	Leisure	Other goods and services	Health	Movement	Information, technology, ideas

Resources

Renewable	Finite	Scenic

Economic systems

Agricultural	**Industrial**	**Service**

Trade

Making goods and services available in all areas

Individual locational decisions

Trade

Goods and services only produced at specific places

Spatial pattern of Enterprise Earth

fig 88

86

Your work so far has looked at case-studies of three kinds of activities: primary ones (like farming), secondary ones (like manufacturing) and tertiary services (like tourism).
- they all provide jobs for people
- they all are interlinked
- they each have a spatial pattern
- they all contribute to the economy of a country
- together they provide the factors needed for living
- they all may change over time
- they all may be set up as businesses or enterprises

The world pattern of these activities is very complicated. One way we have learned of dealing with such complications is to try to simplify them into a model. Such a model is shown in fig 88 and is called Enterprise Earth. It shows connections between the things needed for living, and activities supplying them.

The spatial patterns of activities result from the links between
- the physical environment: providing the resources for development
- the human environment: representing the different peoples and countries and their requirements for life

The economic systems of primary, secondary and tertiary activities work to satisfy the requirements for living. Every individual farm, factory, service or other enterprise is located by someone's decisions: all these decisions add up to a worldwide spatial pattern of activities.

Patterns of trade have arisen to make commodities and services available, not only where they are produced, but also around the world where they are needed.

In ideal circumstances, all the world's people could be supported by an effective and balanced use of all the world's resources.

photo 56: Combine harvester, India

Activity
Look at all the information on these two pages:
1 List the components of the 'human environment' and the 'physical environment'.
2 What is the difference between renewable and finite resources?
3 What factors are needed for life?
4 In a paragraph, explain what you understand by the phrase 'spatial patterns of enterprise'.
5 Explain the importance of trade in not less than 50 words.
6 Why is Enterprise Earth called 'a model'?

This is not an ideal world. In reality, the factors needed for life are not equally available to all the world's peoples and nations. There are very great **inequalities** in the living standards:
- in different nations of the world
- in different regions and districts within each country

Looking at the patterns of enterprise in the three different countries of Nigeria, Japan and India will illustrate some of these inequalities.

Enterprise Nigeria

Nigeria's coat-of-arms

The Y symbolises the junction of Nigeria's two great rivers, flowing across the black fertile soil of the country.
Can you name the rivers?

Nigeria is the most populated country in Africa, with nearly 100 million people. Only about a quarter live in large towns and cities. Few of its people enjoy a high standard of living. It is one of the world's countries where people do not fully share in the benefits of the earth's resources.

Fig 89 gives an idea of the scale and types of activities on which the Nigerian economy depends. The pattern of workers and the details of the value of goods and services produced by them shows:

- more than half the workers are engaged in farming but they produce only about a quarter of the total value of goods and services
- less than one-fifth of the workers produce nearly one-third of the wealth from manufacturing industry
- services employ about a quarter of the workers yet produce two-fifths of the value of national earnings

Overall, the economy produced £41 billion of goods and services in 1983. This may seem a great deal, but India's figure is twice as large and Japan's nearly 17 times greater.

Nigeria's trade pattern is similar to that of many developing countries. It mainly exports primary goods, often in an unrefined state. It is very fortunate that at least one of these is oil. Its imports are mainly of secondary manufactured goods. Nearly two-thirds are metal manufactures and chemicals.

Some measure of Nigeria's need to support its people is that it imports substantial quantities of food, even though over half its workers are in farming.

Nigeria is trying to improve the factors needed to support the lives of its people. To do this requires:

- an increase in food production
- the development of manufacturing, gradually, to save the cost of expensive imports
- building and providing a greater level of public services, such as transport, power supplies, housing, education, health care

Paying for all this means exporting to earn money. Having oil helps a great deal, but there is a problem about the changes in the world price of oil that happen quite often. What Nigeria earns, and can therefore spend on development, depends on this price; when it is low Nigeria goes into debt.

Nigeria needs to expand its businesses and activities more widely to make its earnings less risky, if it wishes to improve people's living standards and solve problems in the future.

Nigeria is divided into three broad regions. These are shown on the map on page 89.

- the wet, forested zone of the south. This region produces Nigeria's oil, coal, cocoa, timber and palm oil. It also contains the main areas of industry around Lagos, Port Harcourt and Ibadan
- a sparsely populated middle belt with few major export commodities produced here. The valleys of the Niger and Benue rivers are heavily infested with tse-tse fly which prevents dense agricultural settlement
- the drier savannas of the north with productive farming of crops like groundnuts and cotton. Grassland savannas free of the tse-tse fly have extensive cattle grazing. On the Jos Plateau tin ore is mined, mainly for export

It is the southern forested region which produces the bulk of the export earnings.

Activity

Look at fig 89 and answer the following:

1 Use your atlas to find the names of the towns numbered on the map and the latitude and longitude of the lines shown.

2 Describe the "human environment" of Nigeria by quoting the statistics shown.

3 Draw out and fill in this table:

	Farming	Industry	Services
Workers (%)			
Total earnings (%)			

4 List the three main regions of Nigeria.

5 Look back to the maps about Nigerian farming (page 14), minerals (page 38) and industry (page 57). List all the main products of the three regions.

6 In about 75 words, try to describe how this pattern shows 'spatial inequalities'.

7 What effect do you think these inequalities might have on the people in each region?

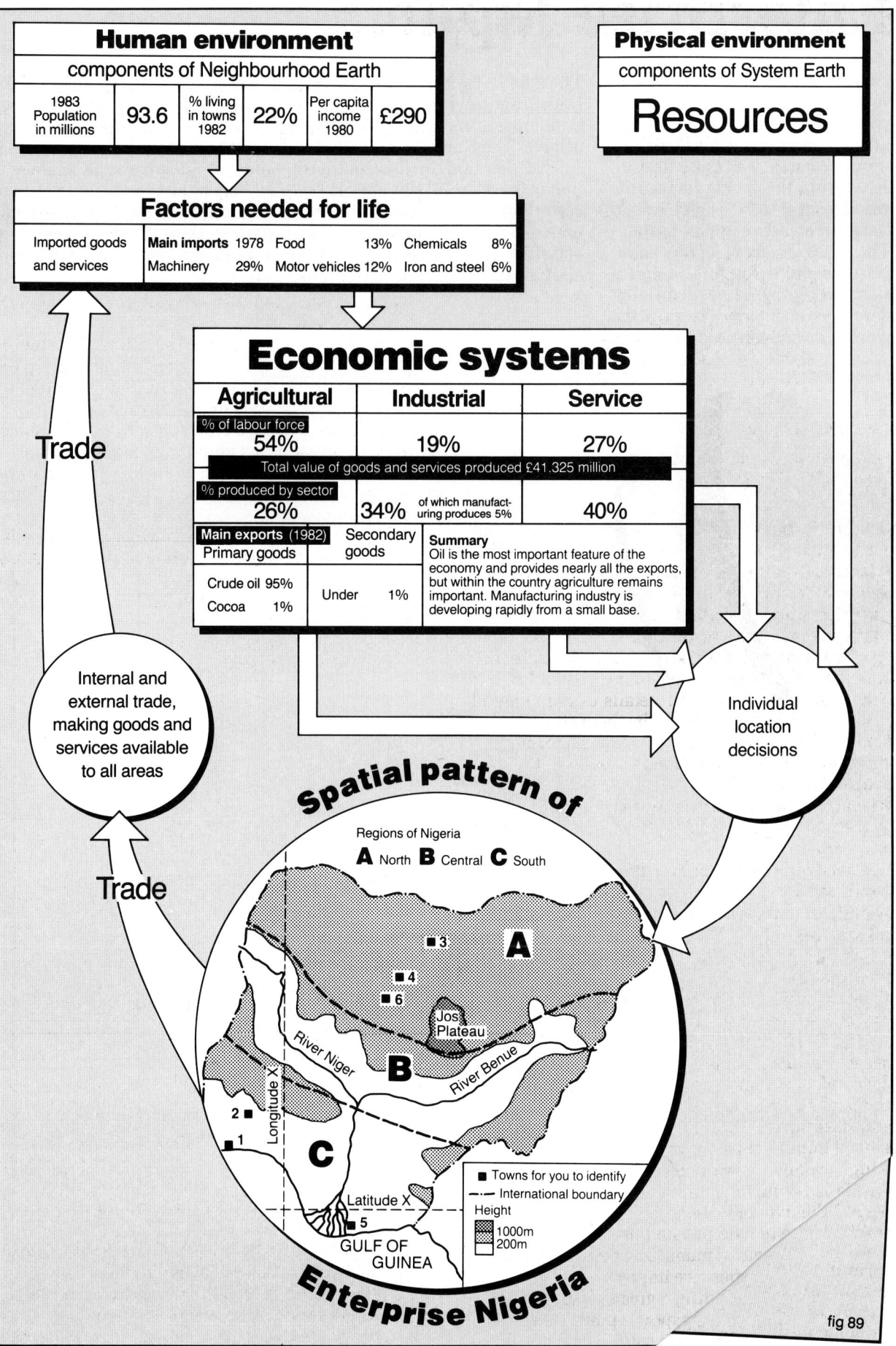

Human environment
components of Neighbourhood Earth

1983 Population in millions	93.6	% living in towns 1982	22%	Per capita income 1980	£290

Physical environment
components of System Earth

Resources

Factors needed for life

Imported goods and services	**Main imports** 1978	Food	13%	Chemicals	8%
	Machinery	29%	Motor vehicles 12%	Iron and steel	6%

Economic systems

Agricultural	Industrial	Service
% of labour force 54%	19%	27%

Total value of goods and services produced £41.325 million

% produced by sector 26%	34% of which manufacturing produces 5%	40%

Main exports (1982) Primary goods	Secondary goods	**Summary**
Crude oil 95% Cocoa 1%	Under 1%	Oil is the most important feature of the economy and provides nearly all the exports, but within the country agriculture remains important. Manufacturing industry is developing rapidly from a small base.

Trade

Internal and external trade, making goods and services available to all areas

Trade

Individual location decisions

Spatial pattern of

Regions of Nigeria
A North **B** Central **C** South

■3

■4

■6

Jos Plateau

■A

River Niger

B

River Benue

Longitude X

2■

■1

C

Latitude X

■5

GULF OF GUINEA

■ Towns for you to identify
-·-·- International boundary
Height
□ 1000m
▨ 200m

Enterprise Nigeria

fig 89

Enterprise Japan

Of Japan's 119.3 million people in 1983, only 24 per cent lived in rural areas. Most were city dwellers. The total value of goods and services produced was over £680 billion. As a result, the per capita income worked out at £3,471, which was 40 times greater than that of India.

The development of Japan's enterprise accounts for this. It has a rich, fast-growing, industrially-developed economy; it is one of the world's developed countries.

The map in fig 90 shows the strong grouping of large population concentrations called **conurbations.** They are all around the Inland Sea and in the southern part of the island of Honshu. These conurbations are massive built-up areas of people and economic activities. They result from the spatial clustering of so many linked activities of industry and services by the process that we have called **agglomeration.**

These agglomerations contain most of the advanced, high technology industries on which Japan's economic success is based. Together they create a **spiral of wealth-generating activities.**

Japanese Imperial coat-of-arms or 'Mon'
This has been the symbol of the Japanese Emperors for over 500 years. It is a stylised drawing of a chrysanthemum, itself a symbol of the sun. Japan is known as the 'Land of the rising sun'.

Japan's employment and trade patterns are very different from those of Nigeria and India.

- only 12 per cent of workers are employed in farming, compared to 39 per cent in industry and 49 per cent in services
- the major exports are secondary manufactured goods
- the main imports are primary goods and raw materials, to provide the requirements of the industrial base of the country

These features seem to be almost the exact reverse of Nigeria. Japan's economy is able to provide the factors needed for life far more successfully than is the case in Nigeria or India.

Activity

1 Add to your dictionary of geography these words: conurbation and agglomeration.

2 What do you think is meant by 'a spiral of wealth-generating activities'?

3 Draw a double page copy of this chart. Use the three Enterprise Country diagrams to complete it.

Enterprise features	Nigeria	India	Japan
Human environment % living in towns	22		
per capita income		£3471	
Economic system total value of goods and services			
% of workers in agriculture		71	
industry		13	
services		16	
Trade main primary exports			
main secondary exports			
main primary imports			
main secondary imports			
Summary			An industrial economy with a high rate of growth. Exports of motor cars, ships, telecommunications equipment, steel and electrical goods sell to a wide range of countries.

4 Try to write an essay of about 1-2 pages showing how Japan's enterprise system is different from that of developing countries like Nigeria and India. Use the following headings: wealth and income, economic activities, and trade.

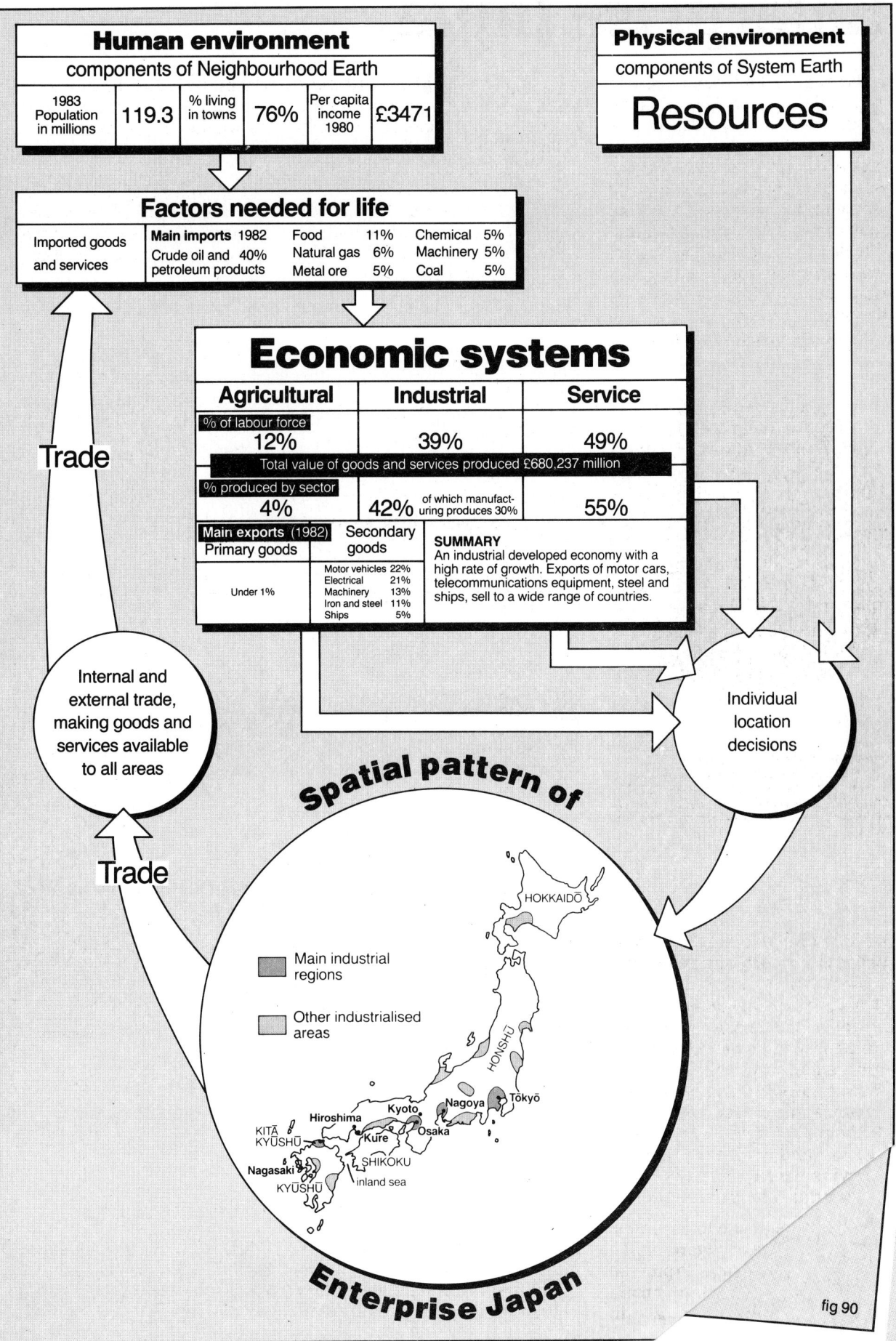

Human environment
components of Neighbourhood Earth

1983 Population in millions	119.3	% living in towns	76%	Per capita income 1980	£3471

Physical environment
components of System Earth
Resources

Factors needed for life

Imported goods and services	**Main imports** 1982				
	Crude oil and petroleum products	40%	Food	11%	Chemical 5%
			Natural gas	6%	Machinery 5%
			Metal ore	5%	Coal 5%

Economic systems

Agricultural	Industrial	Service
% of labour force 12%	39%	49%

Total value of goods and services produced £680,237 million

% produced by sector 4%	42% of which manufacturing produces 30%	55%

Main exports (1982) Primary goods	Secondary goods	SUMMARY
Under 1%	Motor vehicles 22% Electrical 21% Machinery 13% Iron and steel 11% Ships 5%	An industrial developed economy with a high rate of growth. Exports of motor cars, telecommunications equipment, steel and ships, sell to a wide range of countries.

Trade

Internal and external trade, making goods and services available to all areas

Trade

Individual location decisions

Spatial pattern of

HOKKAIDŌ

■ Main industrial regions

□ Other industrialised areas

HONSHŪ

Nagoya Tōkyō

Kyoto

Hiroshima Osaka

KITĀ KYŪSHŪ Kure

SHIKOKU

Nagasaki inland sea

KYŪSHŪ

Enterprise Japan

fig 90

91

Enterprise India

The economy of India produces over £100 billion worth of goods and services. This is twice that of Nigeria, and yet the per capita of India is only about one-third of Nigeria's. In a country four times as large, Indian enterprise has to provide the factors of life for a far greater number of people. Twice the national value of earnings has had to support seven times as many people. On average therefore, compared to Nigeria, each person benefits from a smaller share of the factors needed for life. This difference shows that there is not only the inequality between rich, advanced, industrial countries (like Japan) and developing countries (like India and Nigeria); there are inequalities between the developing countries as well.

The range of activities and enterprise in India reveals some unusual features:

● even though India is usually considered to have a major food problem, it is developing agriculture in many areas. Food surprisingly makes up one-quarter of its total exports. However, what is exported is not the essential staple foods but luxury items, like tea and coffee

● India has a greater industrial output than many people think. Although it employs only about an eighth of all workers, industry earns a quarter of the total value of goods and services. Just the three categories of textiles, clothing and machinery make up over a quarter of all exports. India is industrialising quickly and even makes aircraft and aerospace equipment

● although services only have one-seventh of workers, they produce nearly 40 per cent of all national earnings

To fuel its economy, India has to import large amounts of oil and oil products. The other major imports are, like Nigeria, manufactured goods.

photo 57: Farming, India

National flag of India
The saffron stripe symbolises the spirit of reconciliation and humility. The white stripe the path of 'light and truth'. The bottle green the dependence on and relationship with the soil and agriculture. The wheel in the centre is a Buddhist symbol.

Despite India's industrial expansion, there remain major problems. The Indian economy is not yet able to produce all the factors of life needed for all its people (see fig 91). Supporting the burden of a vast population poses major difficulties for Indian enterprise. This is shown by the excessive degrees of poverty:

● in many rural areas
● in the shanty areas of the main cities, like Calcutta where the influx of migrants where the rural areas swamps them poor services

Activity

1 Copy out the following paragraphs and fill in the blanks using information from fig 91.

'In 1983, India's population was over ____ million, of which __% lived in rural areas and only 24% in _____. The standard of living of the majority of people was very ____. Most workers were employed in _____ whereas 13% worked in _____ and __% in service activities.
All these workers produced goods and services to the value of £_____ million. Agriculture made up __% of this and industry and services together accounted for the remaining __%.
The main primary exports were ____, _____, _____, and iron ore. Manufactured or _____ exports included _____ at 15%, clothing at _% and machinery (5%).
India's main import was ____, making up __% of the total. Four other main imports were _____, _____, ____ and _____ and edible oils and fats.'

2 Write out the summary of economic systems as a conclusion to your paragraphs, from fig 91.

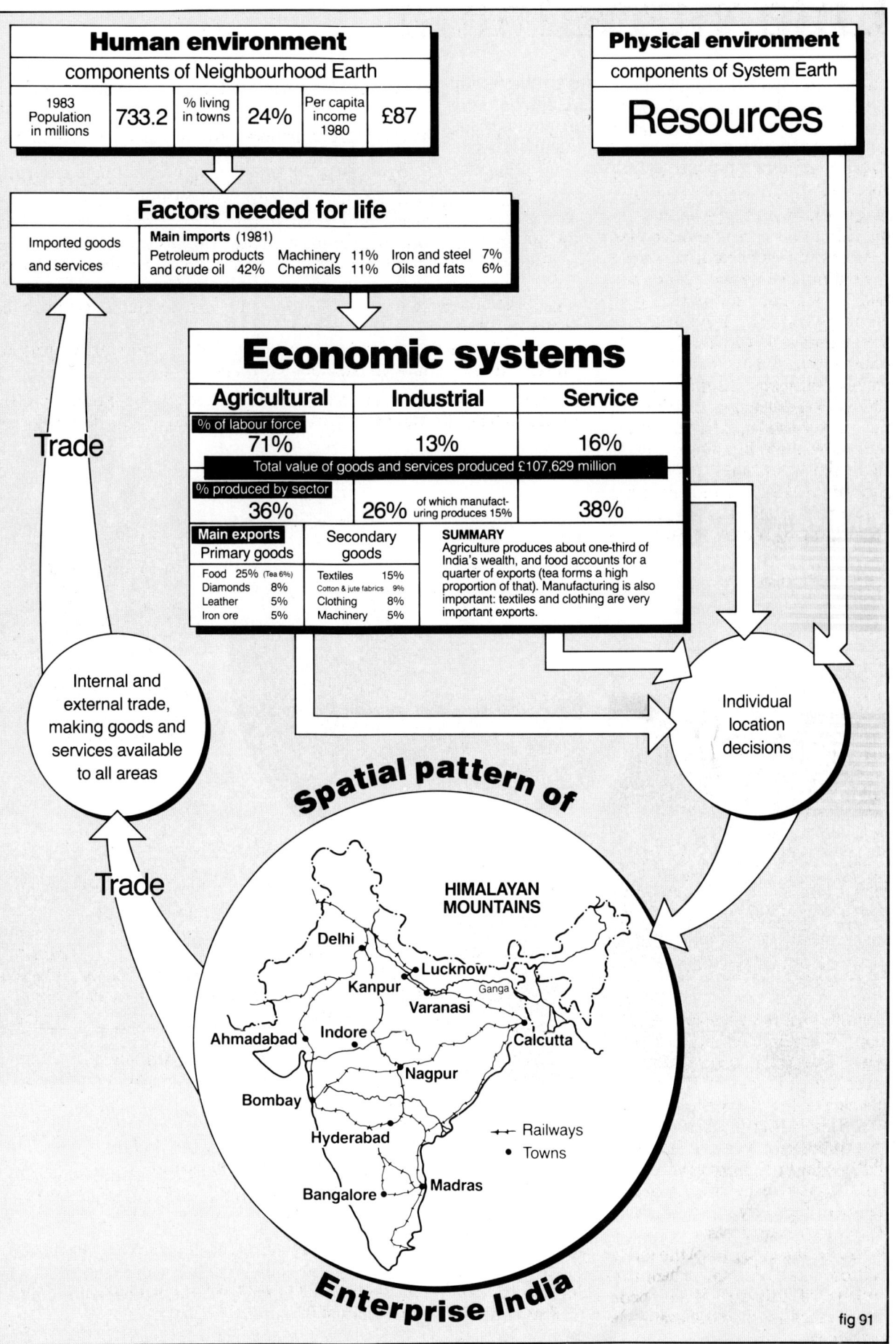

Human environment
components of Neighbourhood Earth

1983 Population in millions	733.2	% living in towns	24%	Per capita income 1980	£87

Physical environment
components of System Earth
Resources

Factors needed for life

Imported goods and services	**Main imports** (1981)

Main imports (1981)

| Petroleum products and crude oil | 42% | Machinery | 11% | Iron and steel | 7% |
| | | Chemicals | 11% | Oils and fats | 6% |

Economic systems

Agricultural	Industrial	Service
% of labour force 71%	13%	16%

Total value of goods and services produced £107,629 million

% produced by sector 36%	26% of which manufacturing produces 15%	38%

Main exports Primary goods	Secondary goods	**SUMMARY**
Food 25% (Tea 6%)	Textiles 15%	Agriculture produces about one-third of India's wealth, and food accounts for a quarter of exports (tea forms a high proportion of that). Manufacturing is also important: textiles and clothing are very important exports.
Diamonds 8%	Cotton & jute fabrics 9%	
Leather 5%	Clothing 8%	
Iron ore 5%	Machinery 5%	

Trade

Internal and external trade, making goods and services available to all areas

Trade

Individual location decisions

Spatial pattern of

HIMALAYAN MOUNTAINS

Delhi
Lucknow
Kanpur
Ganga
Varanasi
Ahmadabad
Indore
Calcutta
Nagpur
Bombay
Hyderabad
Bangalore
Madras

⊢⊣ Railways
• Towns

Enterprise India

fig 91

One World

There are many different enterprises in the world business system. These are all linked together and affect each other. However, the world now faces a number of problems because of an unequal distribution of environment, activities, and impacts.

Questions arise about:
- supporting all the world's people at an acceptable standard of living
- sharing the benefits of the Earth's resources
- sharing the wealth created by human enterprise
- preventing further environmental damage and conserving resources and the environment

photo 58: South Africa

photo 59: Nigeria

photo 60: India

photo 61: Japan

Activity

Arrange a debate at the United Nations where some of your class act as representatives of Nigeria, South Africa, India, Japan, Australia and the United Kingdom. Appoint a neutral person to act as President of the debate.

Each group of representatives should discuss amongst themselves what contributions they could make and what help they would require to cooperate in working as the countries of One World.

Elect a member from each group to present the groups' ideas. The President can then arrange a meeting of the representatives of these nations and the writing of a group report.

Key Word Index

Activity
This index lists **key words** used in this book. Find out more about them. Use the page references, and resources at home and in your school library, to help you. Add the information to your own dictionary of geography.